PEOPLE OF INDIA

DAMAN AND DIU

Volume XIX

PEOPLE OF INDIA

NATIONAL SERIES

VOL. I	PEOPLE OF INDIA	AN INTRODUCTION
VOL. II	PEOPLE OF INDIA	THE SCHEDULED CASTES
VOL. III	PEOPLE OF INDIA	THE SCHEDULED TRIBES
VOL. IV	PEOPLE OF INDIA	ALL COMMUNITIES
VOL. V	PEOPLE OF INDIA	ALL COMMUNITIES
VOL. VI	PEOPLE OF INDIA	ALL COMMUNITIES
VOL. VII	PEOPLE OF INDIA	IDENTITY, ECOLOGY, SOCIAL ORGANIZATION ECONOMY, DEVELOPMENT PROCESS AND LINKAGES: A QUANTITATIVE PROFILE
VOL. VIII	PEOPLE OF INDIA	COMMUNITIES, SEGMENTS, SYNONYMS, SURNAMES AND TITLES
VOL. IX	PEOPLE OF INDIA	LANGUAGES AND SCRIPTS
VOL. X	PEOPLE OF INDIA	THE BIOLOGICAL VARIATION IN INDIAN POPULATIONS
VOL. XI	PEOPLE OF INDIA	AN ANTHROPOLOGICAL ATLAS

STATES SERIES

VOL. XII	ANDAMAN AND NICOBAR ISLANDS
VOL. XIII	ANDHRA PRADESH
VOL. XIV	ARUNACHAL PRADESH
VOL.XV	ASSAM
VOL.XVI	BIHAR
VOL.XVII	CHANDIGARH
VOL.XVIII	DADRA AND NAGAR HAVELI
VOL.XIX	DAMAN AND DIU
VOL.XX	DELHI
VOL.XXI	GOA
VOL.XXII	GUJARAT
VOL.XXIII	HARYANA
VOL.XXIV	HIMACHAL PRADESH
VOL.XXV	JAMMU AND KASHMIR
VOL.XXVI	KARNATAKA
VOL.XXVII	KERALA
VOL.XXVIII	LAKSHADWEEP
VOL.XXIX	MADHYA PRADESH
VOL.XXX	MAHARASHTRA
VOL.XXXI	MANIPUR
VOL.XXXII	MEGHALAYA
VOL.XXXIII	MIZORAM
VOL.XXXIV	NAGALAND
VOL.XXXV	ORISSA
VOL.XXXVI	PONDICHERRY
VOL.XXXVII	PUNJAB
VOL.XXXVIII	RAJASTHAN
VOL.XXXIX	SIKKIM
VOL.XL	TAMIL NADU
VOL.XLI	TRIPURA
VOL.XLII	UTTAR PRADESH
VOL XLIII	WEST BENGAL

PEOPLE OF INDIA

DAMAN AND DIU

Volume XIX

General Editor

K. S. SINGH

Editors

B. R. Solanki

N. K. Sinha

Jaime F. Pereira

ANTHROPOLOGICAL SURVEY OF INDIA

POPULAR PRAKASHAN PVT. LTD.

BOMBAY

POPULAR PRAKASHAN PVT LTD
Bombay

People of India : *Daman and Diu*

First Published 1994

Typeset by PRINTOX, New Delhi
Printed in India at Gopsons Papers (Pvt.) Ltd., A 28, Sector IX NOIDA
Published by Ramdas Bhatkal for Popular Prakashan Pvt Ltd
35C, Pandit Madan Mohan Malaviya Marg, Tardeo
Bombay-400 034

ISBN 81 - 7154 - 761 - 3

(3533)

CONTENTS

List of Illustrations VI
A Note on the Series VII
Foreword XIII
Acknowledgement XVII
Introduction 01

The Communities:

Baria 20
Bhandari 25
Bhangi 31
Bhoiraj/Bhoi 37
Brahman 44
Christian 50
Dhobi 56
Dhodia 62
Dubla 68
Hadi 74
Kamli 80
Kharwa 85
Khoja 93
Koli 99
Koli Patel 109
Kumbhar 116
Machhi 121
Mahyavanshi 127
Mangela 134
Mitna 140
Momin 145
Sagar 150
Salat 155
Sangharia 162
Siddi 168
Vania 174
Vanja 181
Vankar 186

Appendix 192
Glossary 197
Select Bibliography 209
Map 212
Index 214

ILLUSTRATIONS

following page XVIII

1. Baria women, Daman
2. A Bhoi family, Diu
3. A Christian family, Daman
4. A Dhobi on his work, Diu
5. Dhodia men and women engaged in ploughing, Daman
6. A Dubla family, Daman
7. A Koli woman with her child, Diu
8. Kharwa men on their return from sea-hunt, Diu
9. A Khoja family, Diu
10. A Khoja man, Diu
11. A Kumbhar, Diu
12. A Machhi family, Daman
13. A Mangela community marriage, Daman
14. A Momin couple, Daman
15. A Mahyavanshi newly married couple, Daman
16. A Sagar family, Daman
17. Salat youths with their grandmother, Diu
18. A Sangharia and his turtle-shell craft, Diu
19. A Siddi woman with her child, Diu
20. A Siddi man, Diu
21. Vania youths, Diu
22. A Vanja family, Diu
23. A Vankar woman, Diu
24. Drying fish, Diu
25. Salt-making, Daman
26. Fishing boats, Diu
27. An underground temple, Diu

A NOTE ON THE SERIES

There exists an information gap on a very large number of communities in India, and the information that exists on them is scanty or needs to be updated. The Anthropological Survey of India (An.S.I.) launched a project on the People of India on 2nd October 1985. The objective of the project was to generate a brief, descriptive anthropological profile of all the communities of India, the impact on them of change and development processes and the links that bring them together. This was in accordance with the objectives of the An.S.I., established forty-seven years ago in December 1945. The An.S.I. has been pursuing bio-cultural research among different population groups from its eight regional centres. Its objectives have been redefined in the policy resolution adopted in 1985, which commits this organization to the survey of the human surface of India.

The identification of the communities and their listing have had a long history which started from the early period of our history with Manu. Regional lists of communities figured in Sanskrit works. Medieval chronicles contained a description of communities located in various parts of the country. Listings in the colonial period were undertaken on an extensive scale after 1806. The process gathered momentum in course of the censuses from 1881 to 1941. In our compilation of the lists of the communities of India under the People of India project, we drew upon ethnographic surveys, the lists of Scheduled Castes and Scheduled Tribes drawn up by the Government of India, the lists of backward classes prepared by Backward Classes Commissions set up by various State governments, and the list that exists in the Mandal Commission Report. We were able to put together about 6748 communities at the start. This list was taken to the field, tested and checked, and finally 4635 communities were identified and studied.

Unlike surveys in the colonial period, which covered British India and a few princely states, our project covers the whole country, bringing within its ambit such parts that had not been ethnographically surveyed earlier or where the survey had been done in a perfunctory way. Each State and Union Territory was treated as a unit of study. It was decided to start with the investigation of the least-known communities, and then move on to a field study of the lesser-known and better-known ones. Investigators for the survey were identified for each area on the basis of their experience and expertise. Teams of investigators of the Survey, as well as local scholars, were set up for each State and Union Territory to plan the surveys, seek the co-operation of local scholars, generate and evaluate findings, etc. Later, Editorial Boards consisting of local scholars — one or more of these were nominated as Co-Editor/s for each local volume — were set up for each State and Union Territory. We sought the co-operation of the State Governments in implementing the project, and this we received in ample measure, particularly from the Welfare and Backward Classes Departments of the State Governments, local officers of the Census of India, tribal research institutes, university departments of anthropology, other departments of local universities, etc. Local scholars participated enthusiastically in our project as well as in the discussion at seminars held by us.

The progress in the investigation and coverage of communities from 2nd October 1985 to 31st March 1992 was steady and impressive. We were able to identify, locate and study 4635 communities in all the States and Union Territories of India, out of the 6748 listed initially. As many as 600 scholars participated in this project, including 197 from 26 institutions. About 100 workshops and rounds of discussions were held in all the States and Union Territories, and in these about 3000 scholars participated. The investigators spent 26510 days in the field, which works out to 5.5 days per community studied in the various States and Union Territories of India. Our scholars interviewed a large number of people, out of whom we have recorded only the key informants, i.e. 24951. This works out to about five 'informed' informants per community. Of the informants, 4981 were women. Our instruction to the investigators was to study a community at two or three places, and in at least two or three cultural regions into which the larger States of India are divided. Interviews were conducted in connection with the study of the communities in 3581 villages, mostly multi-community villages, and in 1011 towns and cities spread over almost all the districts of India, i.e. 421 districts and 91 cultural regions. We were able, thus, to study on an average a community at about two places. It should be noted that most of the smaller communities could be studied at only one place since they are not located in more than one area.

A major achievement of this project was the preparation of cartographic maps showing the distribution of the communities and the locations where they were studied. About 4000 maps were prepared. Yet another achievement was the visual documentation of the People of India as part of the field operations. About 21,362 photographs were generated, most of them in black and white, and a substantial number in colour, by amateur photographers.

At an early stage of our project in March 1985, we decided to transfer the data to a computer. We were subsequently able to develop probably the first software in the country — and one of the first in the world — in ethnography, in close collaboration with the National Informatics Centre. From 28th May 1988 we started transferring the quantitative data collected in computer format to floppies. Simultaneously, the transfer of descriptive data (abstracts etc.) to the computer also started at almost all the regional centres. We succeeded in computerizing an enormous mass of data, and also in producing the first results of univariate analysis by March 1990.

The descriptive material, running into 120 manuscript volumes, and the quantitative data contained in 257 diskettes, were released on 1st October 1990 by Sri Chimanbhai Mehta, Minister of State for Human Resource Development, in the presence of a distinguished audience in Delhi, for use by scholars at the Nehru Memorial Museum and Library, and at eight Regional Centres of the An.S.I.

The phase of more elaborate analysis started in July 1991 in collaboration with the Centre for Ecological Sciences, Indian Institute of Science, Bangalore. This resulted in a voluminous output of analysed data, which has been presented in a comprehensive matrix consisting of the four categories of populations — the constitutional, religious, occupational and locational. These sets of data, together with a map, were released by Shri Arjun Singh, Minister of Human Resource Development, on 24th December 1991. The last Workshop on the People of India project was held at the Indian Institute of Social and Economic Change in Bangalore, where the preliminary results of the analysis presented by the An.S.I. were discussed by distinguished scholars.

It should be noted that the study of the communities has been conducted in 3581 villages and 1011 towns situated in 421 districts of the States and Union Territories of India. The information was collected from about 25000 of the 'learned' informants by our scholars, 500 of them, over the period 1985 to 1992. Therefore, the observations relate to this limited time frame and to the universe of the ethnographic project titled People of India. The percentages relate strictly to the responses made by the informants to the questionnaire contained in the scheduled guideline and computer format, and to the queries made by the investigators at the places of investigation. The responses have been supplemented with the observations of the investigators, the secondary material from the census, ethnographic records etc. The material has been checked and cross-checked by scholars, particularly local scholars, at many levels with other sources of information.

We are presenting the material published under the People of India project in two parts which are interrelated. The first consists of the ten-volume national series, five of which contain an abstract on all communities across the length and breadth of the country. The data generated in this respect has been strengthened by the addition of information from census and other secondary sources. These volumes include two on the Scheduled Castes and Scheduled Tribes, prepared as part of the celebration of Dr B.R. Ambedkar's Birth Centenary; three on all the communities of India, and two containing data on the languages and biological structures of Indian population. The remaining volumes contain description of the quantitative profile, communities and their segments, community-specific languages and the biological structure of Indian populations.

The second part comprises the State/Union Territory volumes, with detailed descriptive account of each community of India. The contributors to the national volumes on the SC, ST and all communities are listed in the last volume, Volume VI. The Glossary given in Volume VI is common to all the national volumes. At the end of each account, we have given references to the texts from which we have quoted, or references for further reading. This is only illustrative. An exhaustive bibliography appears at the end of the national volumes, in Volume VI.

A consortium of publishers has been set up to publish the material on States and Union Territories. Seven volumes each for the northern States, southern States and the Islands, the central and western States will be published respectively by M/s Manohar Publishers and Distributors (New Delhi), M/s Affiliated East-West Press Private Limited (Madras) and M/s Popular Prakashan Pvt. Ltd. (Bombay). The eleven volumes on the north-eastern and eastern States will be published by M/s Seagull Books Private Limited (Calcutta), which has already published the introductory national volume, which in its turn will be followed by the other national volumes to be published by the Oxford University Press.

I trust this series on the People of India, which is based on a comprehensive anthropological survey of the country, will be found useful by all sections of our people, including students, researchers, teachers, social activists, administrators and political leaders. I hope we have laid the groundwork for a comprehensive ethnography of the People of India which needs to be continually updated and built upon by successive generations of researchers and scholars.

K. S. Singh

FOREWORD

In all twentyfive communities were identified and studied for the first time in Daman and Diu. For the purpose of the ethnographic survey under the People of India project (POI) the entire territory was considered one ethnographic area. Out of these communities five are fisherfolk, five peasants, three tribes, two Muslim and three are scheduled castes. Daman and Diu were historically and culturally an extension of South Gujarat and Saurashtra respectively.

The historical account has it that in the territory a Koli chief ruled who had even repulsed the Portuguese in 1583 A.D. Earlier a Koli chief was said to have been defeated by a Rajput prince about 1262 A.D. who established the rule of his lineage at Asheri near Daman. The Koli is a dominant community of the region which broke up into three segments namely Rajput Koli, Khedut Koli and Kadiya Koli. Rajputisation is the dominant model for many communities seeking upward social mobility. The Portuguese rule of 450 years introduced many elements of change. Apart from the rise of a Christian community, this long period also witnessed the introduction of new practices such as dropping or banning of surname, worship of the Christian shrine Nossa Senhora dos Remidios (our Lady of Remedy) considered by the Machhi and Mangela one of the seven sisters of Goddess Laxmi who had lost her caste (the Chapel was erected in 1607 by the Portuguese), upgradation of status of Hadis as cooks and government servants etc. As in other territories, the Portuguese law did not permit consanguinity among the Christians except with the permission of the church. The Portuguese also introduced new crafts such as manufacture of bangles out of turtle shell. Some members of communities in search of occupation etc. visited other countries which were under Portuguese control. Thus a measure of mobility was introduced by the colonial regime. After the liberation, the communities have gone back to affixing their surnames as their titles and have revived their affinity with the members of their larger communities in Gujarat etc.

Most of the communities of Daman and Diu (89%) therefore perceive their identity at regional level in terms of their linkages with larger communities. They have their ethnographic accounts. Most of them consider themselves as migrants. Considering their ecology most of the communities are non-vegetarian who mostly take fish. Non-vegetarianism among the women is highest (75%) in the country. The communities mostly consume rice, tur, bajra, groundnut. Consumption of roots and tubers is lowest in the country. Those who take alcoholic drink again form one of the highest percentages in the country. Supply of milk and milk products from Gujarat make consumption of these items relatively high, as is the supply of betel, tobacco, bidi etc. Social division exists in all communities except the Momin who claim that they have no social division. Of special interest is the existence of vansha division (Suryavanshi/Chandravanshi) which are endogamous among the Machhi and Sagar. Such divisions as clans, lineages etc. exist to regulate marriage. Varna hierarchy is widely recognised and most of the communities (14) claim the status of Kshatriya, though others do not accept this claim. This only testifies to the existence of the model of Rajputisation or Kshatriyaisation, as mentioned above. Exogamy at village level exists in 7 communities and at surname level (5). Consanguinity exists mainly among the scheduled castes, scheduled tribes and Muslims. The father's sister (fui) and mother's brother (mamu) have a special role in life-cycle rituals. Both junior sororate and junior levirate are widely permitted. Incidence of polygyny has been reported from five communities, even though monogamy is the general rule (27). The rule of residence is patrilocal. Divorce is permissible among most of the communities (18). An interesting practice is the remarriage of widows first to the trees, the full observance of rituals in case of the marriage of an unmarried girl to a widower and in case of inter-community remarriage of widow. *Neel* (ghost marriage) which seems to be an important feature is the marriage of the unmarried deceased person to a cow because the belief generally is that unless the deceased person is "married off" even after death, other marriages in the family will not be auspicious. Most of the communities have both extended and nuclear families (22) except the Christian. The norms of avoidance are almost all pervasive among all communities including the Muslims. Many of the Hindu practices survive among Muslim and Christian communities such as pre-delivery ritual (25), notion of pollutin (27), death pollution etc.

An interesting feature of the social scenario is the rule of male ultimogeniture for paternal residence and residential land, while the rule of male equigeniture exists for other forms of property including cultivable land in most of the communities (26). While the women continue to play a major role in all fields, particularly economy, maintenance of family, their status is generally low (26). They have little role in decision making and in political sphere.

There is an important aspect of folk religion, the clan deity being worshipped once in a year during Gaurmata festival to reinforce clan solidarity. Shiva is perceived both as a pan-Hindu god and as a local deity. There are deities of the sea who are propitiated by village communities to ensure safe expedition, good catches and prosperity. There is a great deal of oral traditions that survive, even though there seems to be a distinct separation of gender roles except among the Christians. In ten communities the men have stopped singing while the women continue to sing (11). Similarly, only among ten communities both men and women dance.

The communities are dependent mostly on land (11) and water resources (6). As many as five communities have reported settled cultivation, and as many as nine communities have reported labour as their major occupation. There is a sizeable concentration of communities practising business (14) and trade (4). Members of twentyfive communities have reported employment in government services etc. One community Mitna is entirely dependent on salt making and another Sangharia on making of bangles out of turtle shell. The weavers at one time wove special sarees for the women of the fisherfolk. The Salat work in stone.

All communities have reported existence of a very strong traditional panchayat which regulates their social life. The punishment awarded by such panchayat for infringement of rules of solidarity is harsh indeed! The data on linkages of communities is impressive. Most of them are linked with one another through their traditional occupation. It seems that the tradition of sharing is much stronger in this area, and that rigidity of castes and untouchability, is relatively low. One of the reasons could be the high status given by the Portuguese to the such sections of the depressed castes by employing them as cooks, in police services etc.

Yet another feature seems to be all pervasive impact of the development process. The fishing communities have undoubtedly benefited from various measures taken by the government to mechanise fishing operations and to improve productivity. The extent of dropout is very high and should be a cause for concern.

Though a small territory, Daman and Diu has speakers of as many as five languages. Gujarati language is spoken by the largest number of communities (22) including the Dubla community who are a Scheduled Tribe. Marathi language is spoken by the Mangela community. The Momin are Urdu speakers. The Christian are multilingual in Portuguese, English and Gujarati. The Dhodia speak their own language - Dhodia. All the languages spoken in Daman and Diu belong to the Indo-Aryan language family. Gujarati and Devanagari scripts are commonly used in the Territory.

K.S. Singh

ACKNOWLEDGEMENT

We are grateful to the administration of Daman and Diu for taking keen interest and extending co-operation at all stages of research. Our sincere thanks are also due to Shri Jaime F Pereira of Daman and Dr. Baba Rama Solanki of Diu for going through the reports and making necessary corrections.

We acknowledge the contributions of the friends and informants from various communities of Daman and Diu such as P J Bamania, Accounts Officer, Diu, Shri Mulchand Bhai (Chief Officer, Municipality), Shri K H Shah (UDC in Administration of Diu), Shri Fakir Chand (Deputy Director, Planning and Statistics, Daman), Shri N K Patel (Statistical Assistant) and Md Ramjan Bhai Ali Abdul Rahman (cloth merchant, Daman). We are thankful to Shri Bindaji Shyamji (Gandhi Para, Diu) and Shri Bhikhabhai Shankar Damania (Bhamti, Daman) who worked as a field guide and helped in collecting data for the study. Shri B B Das, Regional Centre, Dehradun photographed the communities. Thanks are also due to Shri D S Hooda, cartographer from North West Regional Centre, Dehradun, for preparing the maps and to Mrs. Kum Kum Srivastava, Designer, for preparing the jacket design

1. Baria women, Daman

3. A Christian family, Daman

2 A Bhoi family, Diu

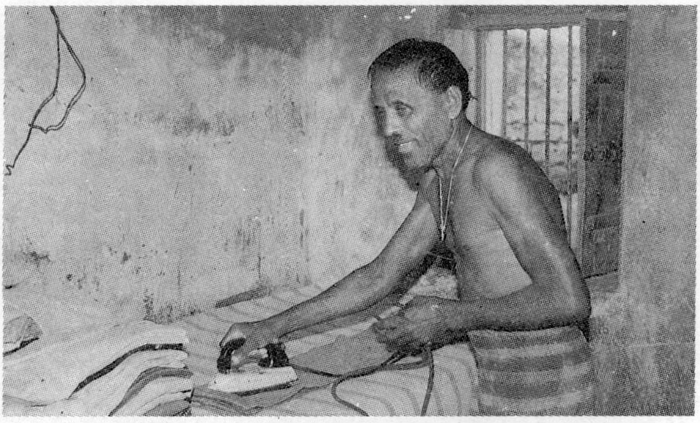

4. A Dhobi at work, Diu

5. Dhodia men and women
engaged in ploughing, Daman

6. A Dubla family, Daman

7 A Koli woman
with her child, Diu

8. Kharwa men on their return from sea-hunt, Diu

9. A Khoja family, Diu

10. A Khoja man, Diu

11. A Kumbhar, Diu

12. A Machhi family, Daman

13. A Mangela Community marriage, Daman

14. A Momin couple, Daman

15. A Mahyavanshi newly married couple, Daman

16. A Sagar family, Daman

17. Salat youths with their gradmother

18. A Sangharia and his turtle-shell craft, Diu

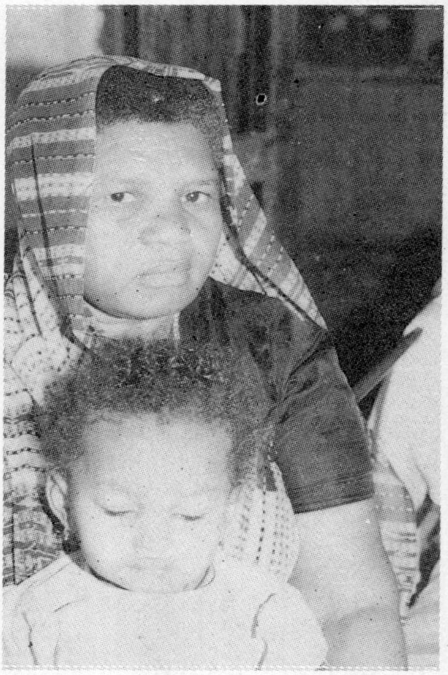

19. A Siddi woman
with her child, Diu

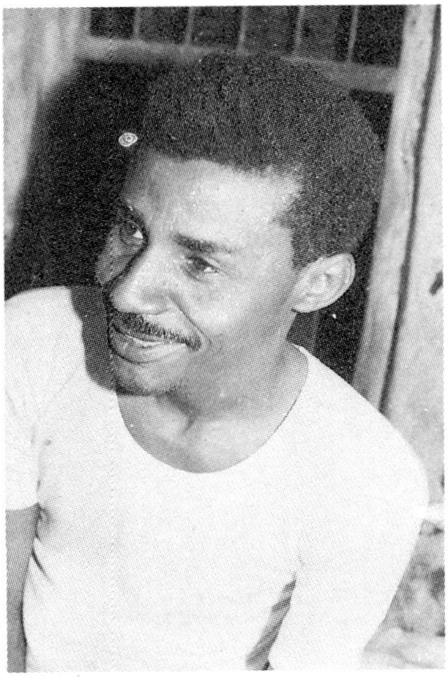

20. A Siddi man, Diu

21. Vania youths, Diu

22. A Vanja family, Diu

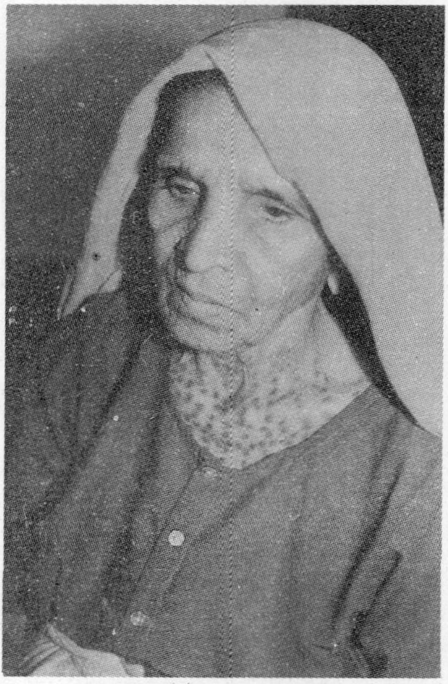

23. A Vankar woman, Diu

24. Drying fish, Diu

25. Salt making, Daman

26. Fishing boats, Diu

27. An underground temple, Diu

INTRODUCTION

Goa, Daman and Diu were the main Portuguese possessions in India which remained under the Portuguese rule for nearly 450 years. They were liberated on 19 December, 1961 during *Operation Vijay* and in the following year, i.e. in 1962 they were constituted into a separate Union Territory administered by a Lieut.-Governor and a popular Ministry. After Goa became a State, a Union Territory was formed on 30 May, 1987 consisting of two separate districts of Daman and Diu. Both districts have a different landscape at a distance of 792 kms. from each other. Daman is situated about 100 miles north of Bombay and eleven kms. west of Vapi railway station. Daman forms part of south Gujarat coastal strips surrounded on its three sides by Gujarat and on its west by Arabian Sea. It is bounded by Bhagwan or Kolak river (Rio coilegue) on the north, Valsad district of Gujarat on the east, Kalu river (Rio calern or Kalai) on the south and Gulf of Cambay on the west. Daman is divided into two blocks by Daman Ganga river (Rio Sandalcalo) known as Moti Daman (Damao Grande) and Nani Daman (Damao Pequene) and is connected by a bridge. *Gazetteer of Goa, Daman and Diu* (1979-Part II & III page-1) states that Daman lies on 20 degree 21' 55" and 20 degree 28' 35 " North Latitude and 70 degree 48' 18" and 72 degree 5' 16" East Longitude with the total area of 72 sq. kms. It has 21 villages and one town which is the district headquarters. Diu is a small island situated in the Gulf of Cambay 111 kms. east of Verawal Port adhering to the extreme southern Saurashtra Peninsula separated by a creek and connected by a bridge. The village Ghogla on the north in the mainland, a part of Diu, is separated from Diu by a narrow channel through a sweep. It has been now linked by a bridge, inaugurated by the then Deputy Prime Minister Devi Lal on 13 June, 1990 and is bounded by Amreli district in the north and by the Arabian sea from three sides. It lies between 70 degree 50' 17" and 71 degree 00' 20" East Longitude and 20 degree 40' 55" and 20 degree 40' 55" and 20 degree 44' 32" North

Latitude. The town of Diu is located at the east end of the island. The total area of the district of Diu off the coast of Saurashtra is 40 sq. kms. It is connected with the mainland by a bridge near Thad village which is also called Thad bridge. Simbher, a typical fishing village about 60 kms. east of Diu in the mainland, is bustling with activity during the fishing season which commences in October and lasts till March. Diu has five villages namely Ghogla, Vanakvada, Buchadvada, Fudam and Simbher and one town. Nagoa Beach, one of the places of tourist interest, is a horse-shoe beach and constitutes an ideal location for sea-bathing.

The landscape of Daman and Diu is an extension of the general scene in the coastal area of Gujarat and Saurashtra. The principal rivers in Daman are Bhagwan or Kolak, forming the southern boundary and the Daman Ganga rising about 40 miles east of Daman and dividing the town into two, i.e. Moti Daman and Nani Daman. All these rivers fall into the Arabian sea. The climate of Daman and Diu is moderate and healthy throughout the year. The average rainfall of Daman is 206 cms. and July is the rainiest of all the months when average rainfall is about 45% of the annual average. The average rainfall of Diu is 59 cms. out of which 90% occurs during the monsoon. Humdity is high in both the districts owing to the proximity of sea which is generally over 80%. The maximum summer temperature of Daman is 40 degree C while of Diu it is 30 degree C. The minimum winter temperature of Daman is 7 degree C while of Diu it is 11 Degree C. During the winter the maximum temperature ranges from 20 to 25 degree C. In May the termperature is at its highest while in January the temperature is at its lowest. The soil is moist and fertile in Daman. Of the total Daman area of 5713 hectares *(Gazetteer of Goa, Daman and Diu)*, 3636 hectares are covered by foodcrops, such as *chokha* (rice), wheat and *jowar* and pulses of *thur* (red gram) and *mag*(green gram). About 735 hectares are covered by the cash crops like coconut, vegetables and fruits such as *okra* or *makambra* (hyphaene indica).

There is no forest in both the districts except the small patch of degenerated thorny scrubs and palm trees scattered over the barren sandy coastal area. A tree plantation scheme was initiated by the Forest Department in 1974-75 for ecological balance. In fauna also the region has much less to offer. No wild animals are found in Daman and Diu. Both resident and winter migrant birds are found mainly in Diu. The main attraction of the island of Diu is that of migrating birds such as flamingoes, stork, *kunj* (Great Indian Bustard), and different types of egrets, herem, plovers, larks, minivets, skimmers. Similarly sub-birds, babblers, robins are also in this region. The people domesticate cattle like buffalo, sheep and goat. Poultry keeping is, however, very common among the people of Daman as well as of Diu. Cats and dogs, though not domesticated, are also found widely in the area.

The distinguished Portuguese sailor Vasco da Gama who left Lisbon and sailed with three ships in July 1497 could locate the Indian subcontinent and landed at Kappka Daveeon near Calicut on 17.5.1498 (Orlando Aibeiro,1956). In course of time Goa was occupied by the Portuguese in 1510. Daman, one of the three Portuguese possessions, is known to have formed a part of the country known as *lata* which was one of the seven divisions of the *aparanta* or Konkan *vishaya*, between second century B.C. and thirteenth century A.D. (*Gazetteer of Goa, Daman and Diu*, part 3, page-8). Antonio Francisco (1928:I:14) states that the first Portuguese who discovered Daman was Diogo-de-Melo who was sailing towards Ormuz in the year 1523. On his way he had the misfortune of being cought in a violent storm in the Indian Ocean and thought that his salvage was impossible. The boat was blown towards the coast of Damam (Daman). This is how Daman came to be known to the Portuguese. He further (1900:101) says that Damao (Daman) was invaded seven times firstly by Martin Attonso between 1528 and 1538 and was finally conquered by Dom Constantino -De-Braganja from the valiant Abyssinian Bofeta on 2.2.1559 by means of a treaty with Shah of Gujarat. *Imperial Gazetteer of India* (1908, Vol. XI-128) says that the town of Daman was ruined by the Portuguese in 1531 which was rebuilt by the natives and was retaken by the Portuguese in 1559 who made it one of their permanent establishments in India. The Koli Patel legend says that once Daman (a part of Ram Nagar State) was ruled by a Koli chief who was defeated by the King of Mewar. Supporting the above statement *Gazetteer of Goa, Daman and Diu* (part II-18) says that the Rajput ruler Ram Shah after losing his ancestral patrimony at Udaipur during the Muslim conquest came down to south and seems to have defeated the Koli chief Nathoat and established himself in the hilly tract at Asheri or Asserseta near Daman about 1262 A.D. Due to the Koli resistance the Portuguese could occupy Daman only between 1528 and 1559.

Diu, another possession of the Portuguese, has been well known since the Pauranic period. Diu has been derived from the Sanskrit word *dweep* meaning 'island' where the Pandavas during their fourteen years of exile passed a few days at a place known as Mani Nagar which was under the Yadavas led by Krishna Vasudeva during Mahabharata period. Sinha (1980) opines that according to the tradition Diu was ruled by the great king Jalandhar who was a *daitya* (demon) and was killed by Lord Vishnu with his *Sudarshan chakra* (disc). The temple of Jalandhar is still there. *Gazetteer of Goa, Daman and Diu* (Part 3, page 10) says that Diu was known as *Jalandhar kshetra* during *Satayug* and is famous for its Jalandhar temple. As *daitya* (demon) Jalandhar harassed the gods, Lord Vishnu killed him but was cursed by his wife Vrinda. The place where Lord Vishnu left *sudarshan chakra* after killing Jalandhar is known as Chakra Tirtha which is situated in Diu. Gazetteer (1979-11) further describes that Diu was ruled by the Mauryans during 322-320 B.C. and was the main trade centre on the Saurashtra coast. The State of Saurashtra including Diu was ruled by the Kshatrapas from the 1st century A.D. to A.D.415, by the Guptas from A.D.415 to A.D.467, by the Maitrakas from A.D.470 to A.D.788, by the Chavada dynasty of Gujarat and Saurashtra from A.D.789 to A.D.941 who kept their capital at Diu; by the Chalukyas who succeeded to the power in A.D.941 and the Chavdas ruled over Somnath Patan and Diu under the Chalukyas as local chieftains. In A.D.1020 Sultan Mahmud of Ghazni attacked the Chalukyas and came up to Diu and rocked them. On the return of Mahmud to Ghazni, his native place, Chavdas of Diu seem to have increased their power but in A.D.1064 the Chalukyas came back again in power and Diu was successively under the sway of Chauda and Vaghela Rajputs, who built a fort there and who were dislodged by Allauddin Khilji, Sultan of Delhi in A.D.1297. A Vaja Raja Brahmdas tried to capture it but the attack was repulsed and the Raja had to take shelter in Diu. Muzaffar Khan, the then governor of Gujarat, proclaimed himself Sultan of Gujarat in A.D.1407 and assumed the title of Shah. Diu was under the Shah of Gujarat and it was attacked several times by the Portuguese because of its strategic importance right from 1518 to 1535. When the Mughal emperor Humayun attacked the Shah, the latter entered into a treaty with the Portuguese for their help against Humayun on 5.10.1535 and Diu was rewarded to the Portuguese. Governor Nuno da Cunha constructed a fort in Diu and raised his arsenal. Diu was finally seized by the Governor Joao-de-Costro on 10th November 1546. Simber, a village, was conquered in 1722.

Both Daman and Diu were governed from Goa till their liberation on 19th December 1961.

Before the Portuguese period, from fourteenth to sixteenth century, Diu was one of the best ports and naval bases and both Daman and Diu were noted for their weaving and dyeing. Merchants from various places came for trading with India, specially Turkey, during the regime of Shah rulers. Gazetteer (1979) says that an Italian traveller Ludovikodi De Vastherma visited Diu in A.D.1504 and called Diu 'Bandar Atturk' and it is described as 'Bundar Afarmi' in the writings of Muslim scholars. Vastherma himself calls Diu 'Diu Bandar Farmaci' (Diu, Port of Turks). In the days of Malckayan, the sea-shore of Saurashtra was linked by iron chains to facilitate the movement of vessels from Diu. Hence Diu is also known as 'Sankalseat'. During the Portuguese period both Diu and Daman maintained mercantile relations with several parts of India and specially with Mozambique in the East Africa for the export of Gujarat-made cotton fabrics. They used to import opium from China and export it to Karachi. Both the places enjoyed a high position for their docks and ship-building yards.

The Union Territory comprises two districts as is evident from its name. The headquarters of the territory is at Daman for administrative purposes. The Collector of Daman is the Head of the Department in the Union Territory while the Governor of Goa is the Administrator of the Territory. The newly formed Union Territory has a Pradesh Council which consists of fifteen members with the Administrator as the Chairman and the two ex M.L.As. as councillors. It has also one parliamentary seat for which the first election was held on 7.11.87.

The Union Territory of Daman and Diu were part of Gujarat before the Portuguese conquered them. Traditionally they carry on the life pattern of Gujarat and Saurashtra cultural region. While Daman represents the general scene of South Gujarat cultural zone, Diu is an extension of Kathiawad cultural zone which influences language, dress patterns, food habits, customs and practices and other cultural elements. Administratively Daman is divided into six Panchayats, namely Marwad, Bhimpore, Dabel, Vashurd, Magarwada and Damanwada and one Municipal council of Daman, and Diu is divided into three Panchayats namely Ghogla, Buchadwada and Vanakvada and one Municipal Corporation at Diu town.

The ethnic mosaic of Daman and Diu comprises Hindus, viz. the Kharwa, Koli Patel, Koli, Brahman, Bania, Vanja, Sangharia, Salat,

Sagar, Barla, Kamli, Mitna, Mangela, Bhandari, Machhi, Kumbhar, Bhoi Raj, Dhobi, Vankar, Hadi, Bhangi and Mahyavanshi; the tribals, namely the Dhodia, Dubla and Siddi; the Muslims, viz. Momin and Khoja, and the Catholic Christians. Most of the Hindu communities consider themselves the descendants of Rajputs which referring to the *atak* (surname) *gotra* (clan) names. While the Kharwa, Koli, Koli Patel, Vanja, Mangela, Bhandari, Sagar and Salat claim to be the original inhabitants of the Union Territory, others perceive them as migrants from the various places of Gujarat and Saurashtra. *Tribal sub-plan for Daman-1971 to 1979*-(1987:3) says that tribals of Daman migrated to Daman generations before from the adjoining areas. Though they belong to original tribal groups, they have now adopted the life of the common people but still maintain the individuality of their tribe. The Parsi firstly landed in Diu during seventh century and then migrated to Sanjan. The *Agyari*, (holy fire temple) and *dakhma*, (tower of silence) are still found in Diu. They seem to have lived in Diu for a longer period. The statue of a Parsi near Port, and the presence of *dakhma* (tower of silence), place of the disposal of the dead and a settlement in the name of a Parsi at Diu justify their claim. Now, there is not a single Parsi in Diu. A few live in Daman but being big businessmen, they have settled in Bombay, Surat, Navsari, Baroda etc. The ethnic composition around the places of Gujarat is similar and represents the communities as found in Daman and Diu. The economic blockage of Territory during 1954-1961 caused the migration of some communities, specially the fishing communities, viz. the Kharwa, Machhi and Khoja from Daman and Diu to the neighbouring areas of Gujarat, Bombay, and other Portuguese colonies in East Africa.

Structurally, Daman and Diu do not represent a single settlement in which the various communities share a common and compact settlement site, but a nucleus consisting of 21 villages was established. This nucleus is on the seashore in the west of Daman and east and west of Diu, while the scattered settlements of the villages are in the range of three to seven kilometres on way to the towns. The nucleus settlement is inhabited by the Christian, Machhi, Koli Patel, Khoja, Momin, Brahman, Bania, Vanja, Salat and Sangharia; while the scattered settlements are inhabited by all other ethnic groups of Daman and Diu.

Road is an important medium of transport and plays an important role in communication. Both Daman and Diu have a good network of metalled roads spread throughout the territory linking all the villages and also the areas of Gujarat. Una is the nearest railway station from Diu while Vapi is the nearest railway station from Daman. Diu is connected with the mainland by a road bridge. Bus services are frequent which run from Daman and Diu to various places in Gujarat. People of the Vanakvada village and Diu cross the lagoon by boat and enter Ghogla of Diu and Gujarat, while the people of Kadaiya village in Daman cross the Kolak river by boat and enter Gujarat. These services require less time to approach various places in Gujarat. All the Panchayats of Daman and Diu have sub-post offices with the head post office in towns. Recently, the Doordarshan has established a relay transmission centre at Daman and Diu. Daman is linked by Air services to Bombay, Bhavnagar and Kesodh in Gujarat. Kesodh is the nearest airport from Diu.

Though ecological conditions influence the construction of house, it also depends upon the economic condition of the people. The houses and hutments of the people residing in Daman and Diu, especially the Koli, Machi, Mangela and Kharwa are erected on the seashore. While the poor men erect huts with thatch without plastering the floor, those economically sound build their *pucca* houses having stone walls in Diu and brick walls in Daman and Mangalor tiles on roof. The houses comprise two to three rooms, kitchen, outer verandah and toilet-bathroom. The people living in the villages build their houses with bamboo, mud and palm leaves and they have one to two rooms. The one-room house is used for dining, sleeping, cooking, bathing and storing of household materials. One room in the two-room house is used for kitchen, bathroom and dining while the other room is used for sleeping, and storing. Outer verandah is a special feature of all types of houses and it is used to receive visitors. There is no provision for toilet in the houses in the villages and the people visit the field or the seashore to ease themselvs. As regards the accessibility of sunlight, ventilation and drainage, few have these facilities. The drainage system operates in towns and in the modern houses constructed after liberation. The income of the people, especially the Koli, Kharwa, Koli Patel, Machhi, Khoja, Kamli, Momin and Bania, has risen owing to their increased involvement in fishing business and other trades.

Ornaments reflect the economic condition and taste of the people. Certain ornaments like bangle, *chunk* etc. are worn daily as a mark of social customs, whereas costly ornaments are kept for festive occasions. Ornaments of gold and silver are worn by both male and female.

Males generally wear *anguthi* (ring of gold or silver) and *modaliya* (chain of gold or silver) round the neck. A silver *kandoro* round the waist is found to be very common among the Koli, Kharwa, Machhi, Mangela and Koli Patel. *Modaliya* is common among the Vania, Koli, Koli Patel Machhi, Sangharia, Vanja, Khoja, Mangela, Kharwa and Momin. Men also wear *buti* (ear-tops). The Christian men do not wear any ornaments. Women have a varied taste in ornaments. Silver bangles of generally one *tola* (a unit of measure) each are invariably worn by the women of all the communities. They wear *nath* (nose-ring) and *kada*, made of silver, on the ankle. *Laving* is invariably worn in the ears by the women. Other ornaments used by the Hindu and Muslim women are bangles made of ivory, lac and turtle-shell, *kada, hady, vali, mala, kambi, jod, zanzar* (ankle-chain), *buti, chipiya* (hair-pin) etc. Most of the ornaments used by the people are supplied by the Soni, a sub-group of the Vania. The taboo regarding dress and ornaments is applicable mainly to the Hindu and Muslim widows as ornament is also a part of marital status. This is not applicable in case of the Christians.

The dress of the Hindu and Muslim communities of Daman and Diu is like that the communities of Gujarat which consists of *pyjama* (pant), shirt, made of cotton, and a cap on the head for the males. Boys wear shirts and shorts. The traditional dress of the Hindu female folk is *kapad* (blouse) without button but provided with strings on the back, *ghaghra* (red or orange petticoat) and *odhani* (covering the abdomen, breast and shoulders). The dress of the male among the tribals consists of *dhoti* (loin-cloth) up to the knee, half shirt and cap. The women use a dark blue saree and a form of *kachha* and narrow *cholo*. The dress of Koli and Kharwa of Diu resembles the traditional dress of Kathiyawad region. The dresses for the festive occasions, especially for the wedding, hugely vary from the regular dress. The dress for the groom is termed as *jhul* and for a girl it consists *ghaghra, cholee* (blouse) and red *chunree*. The changes were reported in the dresses which they borrowed from the interaction with the people of the urban areas of Gujarat and Maharashtra and the outside world as the fisher folk and sea-men visit foreign countries often. Pants and shirts made from strechlon, terryn and other synthetic fabrics are used by them. The Christian can be identified by their European costumes.

Food habits in Daman and Diu are governed by the ecological conditions. As Daman and Diu are situated on the seashore, communities are mainly dependent on the sea-catches. The Brahman, Salat,

Baniya and Sangharia are vegetarians. Rice, *bajra*, *jowar* and wheat form the staple of their food and this is supplemented by pulses of *tur* (red gram), *urad* (black gram) and *mag* (green gram). *Rotli* (bread of wheat) and tea is taken for breakfast, *rotla* (bread of *bajra*, *jowar* and rice) is taken at lunch with *sag* (includes fish as well as vegetable curry) and *chokha* (boiled rice), *sag* and curry are taken for dinner. There are special food preparations on the festive occasions. *Puri* (fried bread), *lapsee* (a pastelike preparation of wheat flour, ghee/oil and sugar), *potaya* (made form of wheat flour, sugar and toddy all fried in groundnut oil), *dudh-pag* (rice boiled in milk mixed with sugar), *pla* (Biriyani), *dhakanu* (made from wheat or gram flour, sugar and toddy) and also non-vegetarian dishes are prepared on festive occasions. The Christians prepare various dishes made from pork, mutton chicken, goat and fish. Alcoholic drinks are commonly used by the men while toddy is consumed by both the men and women. Only a few Christian women enjoy the alcoholic drinks.

A *khatla* (a crude wooden cot) is the main piece of furniture, supported by chair, in their houses. Other articles include *tapli* (basket), *ghanti* (grinder), *supudo* (winnowing fan), *sharauni* (broom), *mode* (rack). The economically sound people keep wooden furniture and utencils of stainless steel.

The crafts of pottery and basketry thrive among them. The craft of weaving a special *saree* for the Kharwa women is already a legend. The craft of making bangles from turtle-shell by the Sangharias still survives a unique craft of Diu not only in India but also in Asia as a whole. The Sangharias borrowed the art in course of their voyages to Mozambique during Portuguese regime.

The implements possessed by the communities are indigenous. Improved implements are not adopted by them except by a few who avail themselves of an electrically operated pump and tube-well. The largely used agricultural implements are *hal* (plough), *oadari* (yoke), *dantal* (plough rake), *datedu* (sickel) *rapdi* or *belly* (iron edge in plough) *pavdo* (shovel), *kodali* (hoe), *kuhadi* (axe), *kosh* (leather bucket) and *charan* used while winnowing. In all, the plough and the cart are the major agricultural implements in the village. The fishing implements are *jhar* (bet), *ojha* (Japanese style net), bottom set gill nets, *khunti* (hook), *jharee* (small net), *lodhiya* and *machava* (big boats) and *hodi* (small boats).

The non-materialistic elements of culture of the communities of Daman and Diu are represented by *satiyo/ satiya* (floor design) designed in front of the entrance of the house in the morning to involve prosperity; *chundar* (tattooing), the folk dances of *garba, gher* and *dandiya ras* (also common in Gujarat) are enjoyed during Ujjani, Ghourmata festival and Diwali while *koli* folk dance is enjoyed by the Koli Patels of Daman during harvesting. *Tur- thali* dance is enjoyed by the Dhodia and Dubla of Daman only. The Siddi enjoy *dhamal* folk dance during festive occasions.

The Christian folk songs are in the style of *mando* of Goa which are sung in Konkani and Portuguese languages to the accompaniment of the *batuque* (a percussion musical instrument).

The main festivals observed by the Hindus are Diwali, Holi, Navratra, Athem, Shivratri, Ujjani, Bhai Bij, Raksha Bandhan, Shravani Poonam. The tribals observe Diwaso, Holi, Athem and Diwali. The Momin, Siddi and Khoja celebrate Id-ul- Fitr, Id-ul-Zoha and Muharram, and the Christians celebrate Christmas, Good Friday, Monday and Thursday, the feasts of St. Francis Xavier and that of Immaculate Conception, New Year's Day and Carnival. Shivratri at Gangeshwar temple, and Poonam Mela at Kalka Mata temple are the main fairs in Diu while Shivratri is the main fair in Daman obsersved by the Hindu communities only. The tribals of Daman are idol worshippers and they prepare the idols in a crude way with the stone. They also believe in sacrificing cocks and goats in order to fulfil their vows.

Gujarati is the main language spoken in Daman and Diu by all the communities. Besides Gujarati, other dialects are also used by the various communities. These are Dhodi by the Dhodia, Dubli by the Dublas, Mangeli (an admixture of Marathi & Gujarati) by the Mangela, Urdu by the Momin, Khoja and Portuguese by the Christians. Though the Kharwa of Diu also speak Gujarati they pronounce the same consonants with a little variation. The Siddi of Diu speak the dialect within the community which is termed Siddi. Besides the said dialects, they are also conversant with Hindi and English. Gujarati, Roman Devnagari and Arabic are used as the script for the communities.

The total population of Daman, according to *Census of India 1981*, is 48,500 and of Diu 30,421. Of the total population of Diu, Hindus account for as much as 93.11 per cent, Muslims for six per cent, Christians for 0.76 per cent, 0.09 per cent Jains, 0.03 per cent Sikhs and 0.01 per cent professed various other religions. Out of the total population of Daman Christians account for 4.36 per cent, Hindus 84.14 per cent, Muslims 10.95 per cent, 0.23 per cent Jains, 0.08 per cent Sikhs and 0.24 per cent professed other religions. The economic blockade of the territory (1950-1960) under Portuguese occupation has positively affected the population and many families are believed to have moved to the neighbouring states and other Portuguese coloniesin East Africa between 1950 and 1960 and have immigrated to Daman and Diu between 1962 and 1971. The decennial population growth rate from 1960-71 is 73.02% for Daman and 67.45% for Diu (*Census of India*, Series 28-Part (X-A) & (X-B). The population of Daman including Diu in 1981 being 78,981 increased to 101,586 persons in 1991, showing 28.62 per cent growth rate during the decade 1981-91.

The religious beliefs and practices of the Hindu and tribal communities of Daman and Diu recognize the existence of two different sources of spiritual forces. Firstly, these centre on a belief in malevolent and benevolent spirits that inhabit certain localities and control many activities of the living. Secondly, their belief in the various deities related to naturism, animism, and in Hindu gods and goddesses based on mythology, finds reflection in the life-cycle rituals, religious festivals and during any auspicious work. The sea-ecology has played an important role in the life of the people who have a belief in a sea-deity and the fisherman pay their homage to the Sea God on Shravani Poonam.

In all there are four religions, viz. Hinduism, Islam, Christianity and Animism, and these are professed by the communities of Daman and Diu. Though the Khojas profess Islam, they are the followers of Imam Hajrat Ali and their present prophet is Agha Khan, the 49th descendant of Imam Hazrat Ali. The distinct feature of the religious beliefs among the fishermen of Daman, especially of the Mangela and Machhi, is that they have also faith in Nossa Senhora dos Remidios (Our Lady of Remedy) one of the Christian shrine which the fishermen consider as one of the seven sisters of Goddess Laxmi who lost her caste. They visit the said shrine, in Nani Daman, once a year at the end of June to show their deep gratitude for the safe fishing expeditions and good catches and make offerings of bread, eggs and vegetables. Mothers place their new born babies on the steps of the altar of the church for blessings. Antonio Francisco (1900, p.219) has discussed the same. The chapel of Our Lady of Remedy, whom they consider the mother of sea ' was constructed by the Portuguese Rey de Mello Sanpaio, Captain Governor of Daman in 1607 after they had conquered Daman and it was subsequently converted into a church. Apart from these major religions, people are the followers of other sects, viz. Sanatan Dharma, Swaydhya Parivar, Jalan Ram and Kabir Panth. Though the temples of various deities have been built from time to time by the communities but there is no pilgrim centre in the territory. However, they visit Somnath, Dwaraka, Amba Mata, Shiva temple at Palsana, Mahalakshmi temple near Dahanu for their pilgrimage which are located in Gujarat and Maharashtra. Birpore, Chardad village in Varoda and Tattva Gyan Vidyapeeth at Thane in Maharashtra are the centres of religious importance for the Koli, Koli Patel, Machhi, Mangela, Sagar, Baria, and the Mahya Vanshi. Kalinki Mata temple in Buchodwada village of Diu has been important for not only the Hindu communities of Diu but also for the people of the neighbouring districts of Gujarat who pay homage once a year during *Poonam Mela.*

The temples of Shri Ram (Nani Daman), Satyanarayan (Nani Daman), Kathiria (Nani Daman), Somnath (Dabel), Vishvakarma (Nani Daman), Yogeshwar Bhagwan (Moti Daman), Hanuman (Moti Daman) and Shri Lakshmi Narayan (Varkund) are the places of worship for the Hindus.

The churches of Bom Jesus (Moti Daman), Our Lady of Sea (Nani Daman) and Chapel of Our Lady of Rosary are meant for the Christians.

The Muslims visit the mosques of Jama-e-Masjid (Dholar), Jumma Masjid (Marwad), Nurani Masjid (Nani Daman), Bhabhi Masjid (Jampor) and Varkund Masjid (Nani Daman).

The temples of Chandika Mata (Diu), Bhutnath (Ghogla), Ganeshwar (Fudam), Hatkeshwar (Diu & Ghogla), Harsidh Mata (Diu), Jagdish (Diu), Jain Derasar (Diu), Kalangi Mata (Buchadwada). Ramdevji (Buchadwada), Somnath (Diu) Kalika Mata (Diu), Hanumanji (Diu) and Randal Mata (Diu) are for the Hindus.

The churches of St Francis of Assisi (Diu), St. Paul (Diu), Our Lady of Mercy (Vanakbara) and Our Lady of Remedios (Fudam) are meant for the Christians.

The mosques of Jama-e-Masjid (Diu) and Karwan Masjid (Diu) and Khoja-Khana (Vanakbara) are visited by the Muslims.

The economy of Daman and Diu has been studied under sub-heads such as fishing, agriculture, various trades, services, and allied activities. The sea ecology has provided fishing and allied activities to the communities of Daman and Diu for both the economy of subsistence and commercial purposes. The Kharwa, Koli, Machhi and Mangela are the communities which follow the occupation of fishing and work as seamen in cargoships. Traditionally, they adopt the indigenous method and do their fishing with the help of small and big nets and use boats for deep sea hunting. They do not carry their catches from the boat to their homes but deliver them out right to the various agencies, viz. Castlelock Company of Bombay and Konkard Company of Goa with whom they enter into a contract for the year. The sea-catches from Daman and Diu are exported to Iran, Canada, Japan and other European countries. The agriculture complex of the communities, viz. the Koli Patel, Kamli, Dhodia, Dubla, Koli, Sagar, Bhandari consists of nature of production and technique involved in it, the relations that are developed between the people of the territory among themselves or with outsiders for the purpose of production of rice, *jowar, bajra,* pulses of *tur, urad* and *mag,* vegetables, and lastly distribution and exchange. The salty water of sea in Diu is hardly calculated to promote better cropping while in Daman the prospect of agriculture is better because the soil is moist and fertile in comparison to that of Diu. The occupations of turtle-shell craft, pottery, basketry, toddy- tapping, salt production, jewellery making, labourers' jobs and services in various private and government agencies keep the communities of Daman and Diu profitably busy.

The development process has brought about a great change among the people after liberation. The Directorate of Fisheries, wanting to improve the fish production, introduced the scheme for the mechanization of the fishing craft, i.e. in and out board engines manufactured by Kirloskar, Tapelo, Yama and Rustan which have been provided on a loan-cum-subsidy basis. Various co-operative societies have been formed to help the poor fishermen. In the field of agriculture various measures have been taken up to enhance the agricultural production. The Mundakar Act provided the right of land ownership after the land survey was done and a special legislation, namely Daman (Abolition of Proprietorship of Villages) Regulation, 1962, was introduced. Land Ceiling Act provided the land to the landless and the Minimum Wage Policy provided better wages for agricultural and industrial labourers. The loan-cum-subsidy scheme allowed the cultivator to avail himself of the modern irrigation facilities and better seeds and chemical fertilizers to improve his production. Tribals were not provided with special facilities during the Portuguese rule and were rather exploited. Even after liberation not much effort to improve their condition was visible. It was only in 1967-78 that classification of the backward class people into SC and ST was notified to bring them within the purview of constitutional safeguards.

Social institution is the means through which a society maintains social order and reduces social disorder. The law or rule exists in a society only if there are constituted legal tribunals vested with the power to enforce their judgment by means of organized sanction. From early youth, people listen to this myth and lore, although they receive negligible education of a formal nature. They learn as they grow up, first in the family and later in the larger circle of the village, to acquaint themselves with the social values and ethics that govern the life of the people. The level and the mechanism of social control of the various communities are regulated by their *gnyat panch/samaj* (traditional caste councils) which regulate their daily activities within the village, at regional level and at inter-regional level. The chief function of these traditional councils is to interlink the members of the community, to punish the miscreants, to prevent breach of customary law and to adjucate on civil and other social squabbles which may upset the equilibrium of the communities. They also take decisions on economic and religious matters. Excommunication and cash fine are the forms of punishment imposed by these traditional councils in case of a breach of traditional norms and rules. These councils still hold the people of Daman and Diu under sway and nobody ever can give a mandate in the periodical elections against the decisions of the council's chief.

With the introduction of adult franchise and Panchayati Raj system, a modern political system has taken shape. The adult franchise has generated divisions among the people and is not regarded as conducive to caste unity. The periodical elections for Statutory Panchayat, Pradesh Council and Parliament have divided the people into parties. One of the major changes in the political set-up of Daman and Diu is introduction of the Panchayat Act which centres on the welfare and implementation of the developmental activities.

In every society an individual belongs to a number of groups, overlapping in membership and differentiated by functions. All the communities of Daman and Diu enjoy a monopoly over an occupation and this makes people united as well as divided into certain categories. Unity is there in the sense that they co-operate and help each other in the various walks of life and in adversities. The Brahmans are considered high in Diu but they are placed high only ritually and in fact, economically, the Kharwa, Vania and Koli dominate the society. In Daman Koli Patel and Machhi dominate. The Hadi, Bhangi, Mahyavanshi and the tribals, viz. the Dhodia and Dubla are considered inferior. The Momin, Khoja and Christian are placed in the middle.

Among the Hindus and Muslims, there still exist extended families. The extended family may be split by its members into a nuclear one and it can also 'update' any one of its members giving him due shares, and a member can also leave voluntarily. Unmarried women and other members of the family who possess their own properties nevertheless have a right to live in the family and the family, as an obligation, has to feed them. The head of the family is called *karta* who is competent to regulate the mode of administration and to make all acts and contracts. The right of inheritance is governed by the code of Usages and Custom of 1854 (*Gazetteer of Goa, Daman and Diu, 1979*) for non-Christians as amended in 1922 and the provision of the Portuguese Civil Code of 1887 is applicable to the non-Christians to the extent that they are not in conflict with the Code of 1922. According to the provision of the Code, the eldest in the family is empowered to administer all properties, rites, and valuables that the extended family possessed. The income from the self acquired property can be administered on alienation separately as private property. However, nowadays extended families are spilitting under the impact of social and economic changes.

When a person, living in the extended family, dies without leaving descendants and ascendants, the extended family succeeds to all the properties of the deceased. A widow succeeds her husband in preference to all other relatives that live separately including the sons. Any person is free to make a will in accordance with the General Law (Civil Code of 1887). The Christians follow the rule of equigeniture while the Muslims follow the Islamic Law.

Marriage of a boy and a girl belonging to the same *kul* (clan) usually does not take place but such marriages are considered valid and lawful. The rules of exogamy applies to certain prohibited degrees which vary according to the customs followed by the various communities. Child marriage was the traditional norm which has been replaced by adult marriage owing to the spread of education and changes in the social environment. Negotiations for marriage commence with the girl's party in higher castes while among the Scheduled Castes and Tribes, the boy's relatives make the approach. Both dowry and brideprice are practised among the various communities of Daman and Diu both in cash and in kind. Muslims have the practice of *mehar* (mehr) while the Christians do not have such a practice; *natra* (remarriage) is allowed among all the communities excepting the Brahmans, Salat, Sangharia, Baria and Bania. Divorce is also allowed to both men and women except among the Brahman, Vania, Sangharia and Baria as they consider marriage a sacrament. Marriage is negotiated among all the communities except the Christians where they practise self-arranged marriages.

The life-cycle rituals among the Muslims and Christians of Daman and Diu are governed by their respective laws. The first rite in the life of the Hindus starts from *panchamasi/rakhadi* which takes place at the beginning of the fifth month of pregnancy performed at the husband's house and the second is *simant* or *khola-bharo* which is performed in the seventh month of pregnancy which corresponds with the Vedic Samskara of *Vishnuvali* for safe delivery. The expectant mother visits her parents' house for the first confinement. *Chhathi* is the first post-birth ritual performed on the sixth day after birth under the superstition that the goddess of Fate comes to the child and writes his fate. *Barse/nampari* (naming) is performed by the *fui* (father's sister) on the seventh day after procuring *rashinam* (zodiac name) from the priest which is followed by *bal-utree/chaula/badha-utranuani* (tonsure) performed in the third or fifth month after birth. *Botan*, corresponding to the Vedic rite of *annaprashan*, is performed in the sixth or eighth month after birth only among the Brahman, Vania, Salat, Sangharia and Koli Patel casts. In the eighth year of birth, *yajnopavit* (investiture with the sacred thread is performed among the Brahman, Salat and Vania communities by the family priest. Boys and girls both get their ear pierced by the goldsmith—a practice prevalent only among the Dhodia of Daman. *Sagai/Vevisar* (betrothal) takes place one-to-three years prior to marriage which is solemnized at the bride's residence. Marriage is a matter of three days and rituals are performed at both the places. The important rituals connected with marriage are *ghana* (rice powdering), rubbing of *pithee* on the bodies of both the groom and the bride, erection of *mandva* (marriage booth) *and deva* or *graha shanthi* (worship of clan deity) on first day. The *jan* (marriage procession) arrives at the bride's village on the third day where marriage is solemnized. The principal rituals connected with marriage are *jaimal, hartoda* (exchange of garland), *hast-milap* (joining of hands), *agniparikrama /saptapadi, chauri-ferwa* (making five or seven rounds of the celestial fire lighted in *mandva*, and *kanyadan* (handing over the bride). These rituals are performed on the third day at night in the above order. *Ana* (return of the bride) is performed after fifteen days to three months but this period varies from community to community. Feast, in the marriage, is given by the bride's party. Marriage is consummated at the groom's residence.

They cremate their dead with the exception of those below one year and whose death is caused by smallpox and snake-bite are buried. The eldest son acts as the chief mourner. The funeral rites generally begin on the third day after death. The chief mourner visits the cremation ground, pours milk and water over the cold embers, collects the ashes and bones and disposes them off in sea with flowers which is called *phool-padhraw*. Funeral rites are performed on the tenth, eleventh, twelfth and thirteenth days after death. The chief mourner and the male members of the family shave their heads and moustaches on eleventh day and take bath to free themselves from pollution. *Kriya/Shraddha* is performed on the eleventh and twelfth days when *got* men shave their heads and rice is offered to the departed soul and ancestors. The thirteenth day *shraddha* is performed when the articles designated for the use of the departed soul are presented to the family priest. The fishermen also perform certain magico-religious rites to pacify the departed soul. They are *madhejawawan*, *darah*, *tutke*, and *neel* (ghost marriage) which have been discussed in descriptions of the community concerned. When a death occurs in sea, while on fishing, and the body is not found, all the funeral rites are performed in absentia, as usual. This is done when all the fishermen and their relatives return from their fishing expedition. An effigy of the deceased, made from banana plant, the eyes from oyster and the teeth from pomegranate seeds, is carried as per the date fixed by the *gynat samaj* Patel, to the cremation ground and finally cremated. This rite is of multiple significance. Firstly, as it is for taking over of the interest of the certain supernatural power, it provides relief to the soul of the dead and finally after such rites, the departed soul remains friendly to the members of the fishing expedtion.

In the pre-liberation days, there were no industries worth naming in the Territory. It is only in the 1970s that Industrial State of Daman and Diu was established, and the Govt. of India declared the Territory an industrially backward area so that special incentives could be offered to entrepreneurs for setting up industries. As a result till 1987, there were 40 registered industrial units operating. Besides, there are about 340 small scale industrial units, viz. hosiery goods, liquor, engineering goods, salt making, bangle making, groundnut oil etc. The average number of workers employed in small scale industries was 2000 as per the Department of Planning and Statistics, Daman (1987). Daman and Diu is now connected with STD through microwave link with other parts of the country. With the increase in industrial activities particularly in last decades, the UT has witnessed a boost in the trade of fishing leading to economic growth. Until March 1986 the fish catch had increased to 19000 tons. In all 10000 engines and mechanized boats were allotted to the fishermen. On the other hand, the financial assistance of Rs. 8,29,000 as loan and Rs. 24,31,000 as subsidy has changed the state of economy. There have been sub-plans to uplift the weaker sections, especially the tribals.

The attitude towards the developmental programmes is generally favourable. The communities of Daman and Diu are aware of the provisions of education, health and medical facilities, drinking water, electricity, IRDP and Integrated Child Development Scheme. Boys study up to primary level in as many as 19 communities (67.86%), up to secondary level 7 communities (25%), up to college level in 12 communities (42.86%), and up to postgraduate level in 7 communities (25%). Girls study up to primary level in 18 communities (64.29%), Secondary level in 16 communities (57.14%), college level in two communities (7.14%), and post-graduate level in one community (3.57%). In all three govt. hospitals and 20 family welfare schemes are functioning in UT. Nearly 22 communities (78.57%) make use of modern medicare. All communities avail themselves of the facilities of drinking water sources through mainly piped water and dug wells. Not a single village is left without electricity according to the Basic Statistics by the Department of Planning and Statistics, Daman (1988).

The ethnographic information on the territory is scanty. There are some publications such as *Imperial Gazetteer of India* (1908), Gazetteer of Daman and Diu by Gune (1974), Census of India (1971, 1981 and 1991), and the stray works done by Antonio Francisco (1904), Rubberio Orlando (1965), Chib (1977), N. K. Sinha (1977), S. S. Dessai (1976), Antonio-de-Menzes (1987), Ramesh V. Ravel (1990) and Brij Mohan Pandey (1989). The major work in the form of a village study in the Union Territory was done by N.K. Sinha and J. Paul on behalf of the Anthropological Survey of India in 1976-78. The present study is the first descriptive ethnography of all the communities of Daman and Diu in terms of a modern anthropoligical survey. The data collected in 24 villages of Daman and Diu, is based on observation and interviews, especially with the 'key' informants who include men as well as women.

No separate list of communities was available for Daman and Diu after its separation from Goa in 1987. In all 28 communities were identified by us in the course of field work in 1985-86. Antonio Franciso (1904) discussed 54 communities. Thus 26 communities were reported missing by us. The reason might have been migration (during the blockade from 1954 to 1961) and change of identity through merger. No data on Physical Anthropology have been generated except in the case of one study of sickle-cell trait carried out by Negi (1968) among the Koli and others but which was not reported in Diu. No survey on the other bio-anthropological traits has been carried out among the communities of Daman and Diu until now.

N.K. Sinha

BARIA

The Baria, also known as Bari, are an agricultural community of Daman. The term 'Baria' has been derived from the word '*bari*' which denotes excommunication. According to their legend they claim to be one of the exogamous sub-divisions of the Koli of Saurashtra. They were *gnyat bar* (excommunicated) from the Machhi Kolis due to deviating from the traditional norms during the attack of Mahmud Ghazni. Enthoven (1920, Vol. I, page 65) and Sherring (1879, Vol. II, page 316) have also called them as one of the sub-groups of the Kolis. Antonio Francisco (1974-128) has described the Baria as an independent community. They also identify themselves as an independent community. They migrated from Saurashtra and settled on the coastal areas of Gujarat, Maharashtra and Daman. They are mainly distributed in Dholar Panchayat of Daman. They are also distributed in other 22 villages of Daman, Valsad district of Gujarat and Thana district of Maharashtra. Population figure is not available.

Traditionally, they are vegetarian but the menfolk have started taking non vegetarian dishes while the female folk remain vegetarian. Their staple food includes rice, *jowar*, pulses of *tur* (red gram) and *mag* (green gram). They take plenty of vegetables as per availability. They also take fish and meat of goat. They take alcoholic drinks and toddy available in the market and consider these drinks as digestive in accordance with the climate and water around the sea. *Puri* (fried bread), *lapsee* (porridge), *dudhpag* (rice boiled in milk mixing sugar) and *potya* (wheat flour fried in oil and mixing with toddy and jaggery) are their special food preparations enjoyed on the festive occasions.

The Baria of Daman are divided into four exogamous sub-divisions based on *kul* (clan) namely Khot, Chinchini, Motegeriya and Tonvargiya. The basis of differentiation of the *kul* is on social level through which they trace their descent. These *kuls* do not have any stratification. The chief function of *kul* is to regulate the marriage alliances. They suffix 'Baria' to their names to maintain their integrity. They perceive their position inferior to the Brahman, Bhandari and Sagar and superior to the Koli Patel, Machhi, Mangela, Kamli, Mitna, Dhodia, Dubla, Mahyavanshi, Christian and Momin Muslim in regional social hierarchy. They are well aware of the *varna* system and recognize their position as Vaishya. They practise community endogamy. Marriage is prohibited within the same *kul*. They practise adult marriage and the age for a boy ranges from 20 to 25 years and for girl from 16 to 21 years. A difference of two to three years is maintained between a boy and girl. Marriage is settled by negotiation only. Monogamy is the only way of acquiring mate. *Kanku* (vermilion mark on forehead) and *kali-kanthi* (marriage pendant) are marriage symbols for women. *Dej* (dowry) has taken the place of bride price and one of the reasons is the rise in female population. The bride price was fixed at Rs. 500/- by the *samaj*. The regional council of the Baria made some changes in 1979 and fixed dowry in kind in place of bride-price. The bride's father has to give two *tola* of golden and 50 *tola* of silver ornaments in marriage. They practise patrilocal rule of residence. Divorce is not permissible. *Natra* is local term for remarriage which takes place between a widow and a widower. *Diyarbatu* (junior levirate) and *saree-batu* (junior sororate) are allowed. Parents and brother of the widow take the responsibility of getting the *natra* done. A feast is given to the *samaj* (traditional council) and *kanku* (red mark on forehead) to the woman by the oldest female member of her village. If either of spouses is bachelor, the regular form of marriage is resorted to in full. The significant change in their institution of marriage is changing from bride price to dowry.

The Baria prefer the family living, eating and working jointly in a house. They have families of extended and nuclear types. Men and women are equal partners in every day economic activities. Respect is duely paid to the widowed mother by the successor after the father's death. Avoidance is maintained between a mother-in-law and a son-in-law, father-in-law and daughter-in-law, with husband's elder brother and younger brother's wife. They have joking relationship with elder brother's wife, husband's younger brother, with wife's elder and younger sisters and wife's elder and younger brothers. Female members are supposed to cover their head in front of the elderly relatives. Conflict and confrontations in the family arise after son's marriage and father's death in property matters which result into breaking of extended family to nuclear family. Sister's husband attends the role of *anvario* (accompanier) and mother's brother brings *maushala* (customary gift of marriage dresss) in his/her marriage. Eldest son succeeds the authority. A widow mother also acts as the head of the family till sons are immature. They practise the rule of male ultimogeniture for residential land and male equigeniture for other properties. The interfamily linkages are sought during life cycle rituals, economic activities, religious functions and during the election of *samaj* Patel. A Baria woman has low status in the society. They have role in agricultural activities during transplantation, harvesting and sowing, collection of fuel, bringing potable water, ritual observances and in religious sphere. They also contribute to family income by doing government services. They are forbidden to interfere in political matters. *Fui* (father's sister) plays an important role during *barse* (naming) and *chaula* (tonsure) ceremonies.

Srimant/KholoBharva is the prebirth ritual performed in the seventh month of pregnancy. *Chhathi* is performed on the sixth day after birth followed by *chaula* (tonsure) on seventh or ninth day after birth. *Kijra/barse* (naming) ceremony is performed after five weeks of birth by the *fui* (father's sister). The pollution period extends upto 40th day. *Adarni/sagai* (betrothal) takes place one month prior to *lagan* (marriage) at the bride's residence. Marriage is the matter of three to five days and rituals are performed at both the houses but is solemnized at bride's residence. The principal ceremonies related with marriage are *jaimal, kanyadan, hast-milap, mangal fera* with the recitation of marriage verses by the Brahman. The groom and the bride feed each other with sweets and *ashirvad* (blessing) are given by the participants. The consummation of marriage takes place at groom's residence. The Baria cremate their deads. Ashes and bones are collected on the third day and disposed off in the sea. Pollution period runs for three days, but the mourning period extendes upto the tenth day. *Shradhas* (memorial rites) are performed on tenth, eleventh and twelfth days.

Land is the major economic resource for the Baria which is under the control of individual proprietors and they are mainly a land-owning community. Agriculture is the traditional as well as present primary occupation for them. Fiṣhing, *khajura* (toddy) selling, service in government offices, wood merchant and transport business are the secondary as well as subsidiary occupation for them. Agricultural activities among them are based on the production of crops on subsistence level. The agricultural implements possessed by them are indigenous. However, a few of them avail the facilities of electrically handled pump and tubewells for irrigation. They produce paddy, gram, pulses and vegetables. Vegetables are directly sold in the daily regulated market. Local market is fully regulated and the link with market exists directly and the transaction is made both in cash and kind. The secondary occupation of fishing seems to be traditional being the sub-group of Machhi Koli before they were excommunicated.

Social control of the Baria is exercised by their *samaj*, the traditional caste council, at three levels, namely *gnyat panch* at village level, Baria *samaj sat gram panch* at regional level comprising of Daman and Umbergaon, Nargo, Danhi, Maroli, Dungri, Faliya, Kalgaon villages of Valsad in Gujarat and Bari Baria Samaj Sangh at inter-regional level comprising of Daman, Gujarat and Maharashtra. The *gnyat panch* is constituted of nine *karobharis* (members) headed by Patel who is elected by voice vote. The Baria *samaj sat gam panch* is headed by Pramukh and assisted by *uppramukh* and Patels of all the *gnyat panch*. The *Bari Baria Samaj Sangh*, a post-independence organisation is constituted of an Adhyaksha (Chairman), three *upadhyaksha* (deputy chairman), a *sarchitnish* (secretary), two *chitnish* (assistant secretarises) and one *khajanchi* (accountant). Social problems pertaining to breach of traditional rules are dealt by the *gnyat panch*, failing to decide, it is dealt with by the *sat gam panch*. The *sabha* (meeting) of the *Bari Baria Samaj Sangh* is called once in every year on alternate villages to decide some problems and reformation of certain evil customs. An offender is punished by excommunication and cash fine of Rs.1000/-. The members of the bigger organization have to pay rupees two as membership fee per year while a life member has to pay Rs.1000/-. Plan implementation and welfare development activities are the role of modern statutory panchayat.

They profess Hinduism and follow the Sanatan Dharma, a sect initiated by Sri Pandurang Shastree at Madhav Bag Pathshala at Bombay in 1967. Their favourite object of worship, *Isht Devta*, is Lord Shiva who is also the village deity. Name of *kul* deity is not traceable and they are referred as *gotrej*. Somnath and Bhuleshwar temples in Gujarat are considered their major sacred centres. Their main festivals includes Ujjani, Holi and Shivratri. They are active disciples of Swadhyay Pariwar in the socio-religious movement started by Sri Pandu Shashtree at Madhav Bag Pathshala, Bombay in 1967. They are attached with it's institution the Tattva Gyan Vidyapeeth at Thana in Maharashtra with the aim and objective of self immunisation, social service for the upliftment of the poor through the religious preachings of the Geeta. Their sacred specialists are the Brahmans who officiate at the life cycle rituals. The Baria do not own any specific elements of culture. *Satiyo* (floor design), folk songs and *garba* dance are common to all the Hindu communities of Daman except the Machhi, Mangla and the Kamli who have *Koli* dance. Only women participate in folk dance.

Through their occupation of agriculture and fishing they have traditional linkages with the Koli Patel, Kamli, Machhi and Dubla. Services of the Brahman is sought during the lifecycle rituals and religious practices. They accept water, *kachha* and *pucca* food from the Brahman, Koli Patel, Kamli, Bhandari and Sagar. They share the crematorium with the Sagar. They share well and water resources with all the communities except the Mahyavanshi. They have their own temple. They participate with the said communities in marriage and with all during Shivratree fair at Palsana in Gujarat. Receiving and rendering of service is maintained with the Sagar and Koli Patel. They engage the Dublas and Dhodia as agricultural labourer. They have businessmen, teachers, engineers and doctors. Their political leadership has emerged at village panchayat.

They have a positive attitude regarding the development programmes. The literacy level has gone up. Boys study upto college level and drop out from study as they have to earn to support their family. Girls study upto secondary level and drop out due to social reason and also to earn to support their family. They avail of all the civic facilities introduced by the various government agencies. The source of irrigation is rain water and a few of them have tubewell. They use chemical fertiliser and organic manure. The media of mass communication for them are radio, television, news paper, cinema, etc.

N.K. Sinha

REFERENCES

Enthoven, R.E., *The Tribes and Castes of Bombay*, vol. I, 1920, Bombay, The Government Central Press, Reprint, vol.I, P.65, 1975, Cosmo Publications, Delhi..

Francisco, Antonio, *Noticas-e-Documenta Para, A Historia De Damao*, Bastoria, (Goa), vol.II, page 128, 1904.

Sherring, M.A., *The Hindu Castes and Tribes*, vol. II, 1879, Calcutta, Thakar, Spinks and Co, Reprint; vol. II, page 316, 1974, Cosmo Publications, Delhi.

BHANDARI

The Bhandari are also known as the Bhandari Patel. Enthoven (1920, vol. I page 97) states that the term Bhandari denotes '*bhandar*' (treasury) and they worked as treasury guards. During Rajput supremacy in North India an army of Rajput defeated an uprising in Deccan and were called Bhandari meaning the quellers of rebellion. He (1920:98) further refers to the Rober Xavier Murphy's statement in 1830 that the Bhandari helped Bhimaraja to take possession of Bomaby in 1295 and that a Bhandari Chief, Shetya of Chawl, took the possession after dispossessing the successor but was later dispossessed by Muslims. During Portuguese invasion they assisted the invaders against the Muslims and established several petty kingdoms on western coast with their help. Sherring (1879:185) has also discussed the process. Marathas and Britishers employed them as foot soldiers and honorary guards. The Bhandari of Daman believe today that the term Bhandari originated from 'bhander' meaning 'treasury' they formally worked as the treasury guards of the then Dharampur state prior to the Portuguese occupied the region. According to their *Bhandar Gnyate Basti* (caste history) they trace their origin from the Shesh Vansh Grasia. They had been inhabitants of Daman before Portuguese established their rule and this has been supported by Antonio Francisco (1904-128). The Bhandaris of Maharasshtra and Gujarat are the migrants from Daman and the coastal region of Valsad and Surat districts of Gujarat, and Thane district of Maharashtra. Census figures are not available.

They are vegetarian, and their staple food includes rice, wheat and jowar. They take fish and egg occasionally. Pulses of *mug* (green graam) and *tur* (redgram) and vegetables are the suppliments to their staple food. Alcoholic drinks and *tady* (toddy) are enjoyed by the community regularly while the female folk take *tady* (toddy). *Lapsi* (preparation of wheat, ghee and sugar) and *puri* (fried bread) are the speical food enjoyed on the festive occasions. Non-vegetarian dishes are the part of change during the Portuguese.

The Bhandari of Daman are divided into three endogamous divisions viz; Khalgura, Kirpal and Shinde and out of these, the first one is considered lower in hierarchy. Enthoven (1922-99) has discussed eight endogamous divisions. The exogamous divisions based on *kul* are Jadhav, Kadam, Chavan. More Surve, Bhosla, Rane etc. Some of them suffix Patel which indicates the position of authority. The chief function of *kul* (clan) is to trace the descent, to regulate marriage and to participate in the life cycle rituals. They place their position after Brahmins in social hierarchy. They are well aware of the *varna* system and perceive their position as Kahatriya in the *varna* order. They resort to community and sub-division endogamy and *kul* and village exogamy. Marriage is not permitted with the five ascending generations from the father's side. They allow marriage between the sister's husband's sister's childern. Pre-puberty marriage was the traditional norm which has taken the place of adult marriage due to higher education. Marriage is settled by negotiation with the initative taken by boy's father. The form of marriage is monogamy which is a part of change from polygyny. *Kali kanthi* (marriage pendant of black pearl) and *kanku* (red marks on forehead) are the symbols of married women. Earlier they had practice of bride-price, now they go for dowry ranges from Rs. 5000/- to Rs. 10,000/- from girl's father. *Chhutta-chheda* (divorce) is granted to both by the *gnyat* Patel (caste chief). Quarrelsome nature and adultery are the reasons for divorce. Divorce fee of Rs. 101/- is paid to the traditional council by both the parties and a drink party is given. The post divorce maintenance is the liability of mother. *Natra* (remarriage) is permitted between widow, widower and divorcees. Widow-marriage among the Bhandari is performed in the presence of traditional council. Before this the widow is freed from the spirit of her deceased husband by the *bhagat*. The new husband presents her with a new dress. A drink party is given to the *gnyat panch* and *tika* (red mark) is marked on the forehead to the lady by the oldest woman of the female side. Unmarried women are not permitted to observe the remarriage ceremony. Matrimonial relation with the Bhandaris of Gujarat and Maharashtra, adult marriage, divorce in court and monogamy are the changes that took place in the institution of marriage recently.

The common forms of *kutumb* (family) are of extended and nuclear types. They have prescribed kinship usages viz; joking and avoidance relationship. Important role is played by mother's brother and sister's husband during the marriage. Conflict and confrontation arise after father's death and son's marriage in financial matters. Right of inheritence is granted as per the Portuguese Property Act. In absence of son, brother's son is adopted. Eldest son succeeds the *karta* (authority) in the family. Inter-family linkages are sought during the life cycle rituals, political and religious activities. Nuclear family is the changed form recently. A Bhandari woman keeps the low status in the society. Right of inheritance is not granted to women. Their roles are defined in social, religious and economic activities. They are forbidden to interfere in political matters except only to cast their votes during the periodical elections with the consultation of their menfolk. *Fui* (father's sister) plays an important role during naming and head-shaving ceremonies.

Srimant is the prebirth ritual performed in the seventh month of pregnancy and the expectant mother leaves for her parents house for the first delivery. *Chhathi* is the first post-birth ritual performed on the sixth day followed by the pollution bath to bathe the infant and mother on eleventh day and the 'well' worship is performed. Mother with the infant visits seven families of the community to get them acquainted with her motherhood. *Barse* (naming) is performed on twelfth day by *fui*. *Chaula* (tonsure) is performed after 40 days. Pollution period is extended upto 40 days and the mother is restricted to enter the kitchen and to visit the religious places. *Gharena-Ganthwanu* (betrothal) takes place one month prior to *lagan* (marriage) at bridegroom's residence. Marriage is the matter of three days which starts with the erection of *mandava* (marriage booth) and installation of *devak* or *gotrej* (*kul* deity) which is worshipped at both the houses with the sacrifice of cock and the blood is homaged to the deity on the first day. The maternal uncle brings *maushala* (marriage dress and ornaments) on the second day. *Pithee* is rubbed on the bodies of the both the bride and the groom for three days at their respective houses. The *jan* (marriage party) arrives at the bride's village and are given *janwas* (separate lodging). The groom arrives at the bride's house and is received by the bride's mother near *toran* after garlanding a white sacred thread. The bride's brother presents the gift to the groom there. The principal ceremonies connected with marriage are *hast-milap*, *jaimal*, *mangal-fera*, *sapt padi*, *kanyadan*, garlanding of *mangalsutra* and worship of *gotrej*. *Mangalfera* is the main rituals. *Bhattji* (Brahman priest) officiates at the marriage ceremonies. Marriage dinner is given by the bride's parent and the *jan* returns back on the next day. *Ana* (return of the bride) takes place after three to five days which was earlier with an interval of one year next day after Magh *poonam*.

The Bhandari cremate their dead with the exception of children below eight years and death causing of small pox are buried. The rites connnected with death are performed by the eldest son, the chief mourner, who disposes off ashes and bones into the sea in the vicinity third day after cremation. *Darha* is performed on eleventh day to pacify the departed soul and *shraddha* on twelfth day when articles, designated for the use of the departed soul, and *sidha* are presented to the Brahman and a caste dinner is given. The pollution period runs till eleventh day when the *kul's* male members including the chief mourner shave their moustaches and heads.

Toddy tapping is the traditional as well as the primary occupation for them. They own palm trees of their own and sell toddy, after tapping, to the toddy shop. Dubla women also sell toddy in the market after purchasing it from the Bhandaris. Agriculture, services and wine shops are the subsidiary occupation for them. Majority of the Bhandaris are employed in the different government offices. Some of them are landless day labourers, who work in the field of the Koli Patel getting remunerations in cash as well as in kind.

The social control of the Bhandaris is fully regulated by their *samaj* at village level and Samast Bhandari Gnyat Mandal at regional level comprises Daman, Gujarat and Maharashtra. The *samaj* consists of five *sabhyas* who are elected by voice vote. The Bhandaris of Daman were included in the regional council in 1947 which is headed by Pramukh and assisted by *upapramukh, mantri* (secretary), *khajanchi* (accountant) and fifteen *sabhyas* (members). One member is represented by four to five villages. Social problems pertaining to deviation from the traditional norms, marriage, adultery, inter-family disputes are dealt with by the *samaj*. The regional council's meeting is called once in a year to discuss the religious and social matters. The traditional village panchayat comprising of all communities settles the intercommunity disputes. *Gnyat-bar* (excommunication) and cash fine of Rs. 101/- are the form of punishment and an offender is expiated after the payment of fine. Plan implementation and welfare and development activities are the role of modern statutory panchayat.

The Bhandari are Hindu. They worship all Hindu deities and observe all the Hindu fasts and festivals. They also believe in ancestor worship. Amba Mata is their community deity. The *kul* deity is called *gotrej* and these deities are worshipped during birth and marriage ceremonies with the sacrifice of cock. The village deities are Holi Mata and Lakshmi Mata. The married couple is supposed to pay homage after marriage. Their favourite god is Lord Vishnu. They also have belief on Jalaram, the great devotee of Lord Krishna. The temples of village deities are located at the *padarma* (boundary) of village. Their major shrines includes Mahalakshmi temple at Danu in Maharashtra, Ranchor Rai (Lord Krishna) temple at Dakor in Gujarat and Dwarka. Their main festivals are Diwali, Holi, *Bolley* (Rakshabandhan) and Janmashtami associated with social and religious significance. The Brahmans play the role of sacred specialists and help them in performing life cycle rituals, worship and paying homages. They do not represent any specific element of art and culture except *satiya* (floor design) and *chundar* (tattooing) which are commmon to all the Hindu communities of Daman. They use *bhongulee* (trumpet), a percussion instrument, during festive occasions. The folk songs connected with birth and marriage are sung by women only. Women only participate in dance.

Through their occupation of toddy tapping, their traditional linkages with all the communities are maintained. Brahman is invited during the life cycle rituals and on religious festivals. They accept *kacha* and *pucca* food from the Brahman, Koli Patel and Barla. *Dharma behan* (putative kinship) is maintained with the Machhis. They share well and water resources with other communities. They share the crematorium with the Machhi, Koli Patel and Mangela etc. Cultivator labour relationship is maintained with the Koli Patel and Kamli. They took part in the political movement for the liberation of Goa, Daman and Diu in 1958. The periodical elections have given the route of the modern linkages with the other communities. The community have members holding white collar jobs and engineers. The political leadership has emerged at village panchayat where a member is Sarpanch in statutory panchayat.

The literacy level among the boys and girls has gone up after liberation where boys study upto college and girls upto the secondary levels. They avail all the civic facilities introduced by the various government agencies, viz. drinking water, electricity, public distribution system, family welfare, health and medical care, banking facilities, post office, chemical fertilizer and organic manure. The midday-meal-scheme for the children and ICDS schemes are availed of. They are linked with the mass communication network through radio, television, newspaper, cinema etc.

N.K. Sinha

REFERENCES

Enthoven, R.E., *The Tribes and Castes of Bombay*, vol. I, 1920, Bombay, The Government Central Press, Reprint; vol.I, p.94, 1975, Cosmo Publications, Delhi.

Francisco, Antonio, *Notice-E-Documentas-Para, A Historia De Damao*, Bastoria (Goa), Vol. II, page 128, 1904.

Sherring, M.A., *The Hindu Castes and Tribes*, vol.II, 1879, Calcutta, Thakar Spink & Co. Reprint; vol. II, p. 185, 1974.Cosmo Publications, Delhi.

BHANGI

The Bhangi, are also known as the Harijan. They are a Scheduled Caste. According to their legend, they trace their origin to the Pauranic times. Once during that time, a cow died and a sage carried the dead cow and disposed it off in water. For this act of offence against the social norm of higher caste, the sage was outcast by the assembly of sages and was isolated by being given the status of untouchable. Enthoven's (1920: Vol. I - 105) statement supports the version of the community. Crooke (1974) notes that the Sanskrit word 'Bhangi' means 'hemp' in allusion to the drunken habits of tribe who are the representatives of Chandala of Manu and who are said to have descended by a Shudra from a Brahman woman. They have been residing in the region since immemorial times. They percieve their distribution in Diu and in the different districts of Gujarat. Census figure is not available separately as they are clubbed with the Hadi.

The Bhangi are non-vegetarian who don't take pork and beef. The cereals and pulses used are common to all. Being economically weak, they consume fruits occasionally. The consumption of *daru* (liquor) is common among them. They are fond of smoking *bidi* and chewing betel.

Got is the basis of their social division which is exogamous. The *gots* Bodwaha, Rathod, Pathia, Parmar, Makwana, Sawang, Bargria, Solanki and Washe. They suffix these to their names as their *atak* (surname). There is no stratification among the various *gots* and the basis of differentiation is social. The chief function of *got* is to trace descent and to regulate marriage alliances. They are well aware of the *varna* system and recognize their place as Shudra. They perceive their position at the lowest in the regional social hierarchy.

They resort to community endogamy and *got* exogamy. They allow marriage alliances with the mother's brother's daughter and father's sister's daughter. Junior sororate is permitted. A marriage cannot be solemnized without the prior permission of the *gnyat* Patel (traditional council chief). One has to procure the certificate from the Marriage

Registration Office at Diu and then only the Patel gives approval. They practise adult marriage which has taken the place of child marriage. The marriage age for a boy ranges from 20 to 25 years while for a girl from 18 to 21 years. Marriage is settled by negotiation only initiated by boy's father with the help of his wife's brother. They practise monogamy only. Pre-marital sex is neither allowed nor tolerated. A married woman uses *kanku* (vermilion mark on forehead) and *katchkorh-bangdi* bangles of turtle shell) as marriage symbol. *Dej*, (bride-price) is given in cash which is fixed for Rs. 201/- by the Patel. They practise patrilocal rule of residence. Divorce is considered a social offence and they do not encourage it. *Ghodghode* is the local term for remarriage which occurs only in case of the death of either of spouse. This is not a regular form of marriage where no rituals are performed. He or she has to take prior approval from the Patel. A bond is prepared and is signed by the man and woman in the presence of the Patel. A feast is given to the gnyat Patels. In case of widower marrying an unmarried girl, the regular form of marriage is resorted to in full.

The common form of family among the Bhangi is of the extended type. They have prescribed kinship usages, i.e. joking and avoidance relationship. Joking relationship is maintained with elder brother's wife, husband's younger brother, with wife's younger and elder sisters, with wife's elder and younger brothers and wife's younger sister's husband. Avoidance relationship exists with mother-in-law, with younger brother's wife and husband's elder brother. Conflict and confrontation in the family arise after father's death or after son's marrriage in property and financial matters. The Bhangi practise the rule of male ultimogeniture for the residential land and male equigeniture for movable properties. After the death of father half of the property goes to widow and rest is equally distributed among the sons only. She can have her will to anybody during her life-span. Eldest son succeeds the authority after father's death. Inter-family linkages become the natural phenomenon for the Bhangis during the life-cycle rituals, on religious festivals, economic activities and during the election of community's Patel. Women, in the family, have roles in collection of fuel, bringing potable water, social functions and ritual performances. They have low status. They help their male members in economic activities. They also contribute to family income by doing sweeper's job in municipality. *Fui* (father's sister) has specific role during *nampari* (naming) and *balmaudi* (tonsure) ceremonies. The folk songs during various social and religious rituals are sung by women only. They do not find any place in political matter.

The life cycle rituals right from pregnency to death of the Bhangis are common to all other Hindu communities of Diu as discussed in the Introduction.

They are landless. The present primary source of income is through the service as sweepers in the municipality. Both men and women sweep the road and government institutions and bury the dead animals although the traditional occupation is carrying of night soil and dead animal. They also do labourer's job. Payment varies according to the nature of jobs. The Bhangi working in municipality get their remuneration monthly while the labourers work on daily wages. They sell the products of bamboo work directly on cash transaction in daily regulated market in Diu and weekly *hat* (mart) in the villages of Diu. They also do private services as the night soil carriers and sweepers and receive the remuneration in cash. The cloth, rapped on the dead body, is given to a Bhangi before cremation as a part of customary right. Service in police department and other offices is a recent development so far their occupation is concerned.

Social control is regulated by the traditional council at the village level. They are bound together by strong group awarness and have their *gnyat panch* (caste council) at village level only which is fairly effective in dealing with social disputes. The body constitutes of five elderly members of the community who elect a Patel (chief) by voice vote for a period of five years. The Patel is elected from the community on the basis of the high intra-community social standings. The age factor is also an important criterion. Patel is elected from each *got* on alternate tenure as per community decision. The council functions at *baithale* (a fixed place). Social problems pertaining to adultery, remarriage and breach of traditional awareness are dealt by the *panch*. The Patel inflicts cash fine to an offender as a punishment. Punishment is given in the form of excommunication also and an offender is expiated again after giving a community feast. Seduction of an unmarried girl is also severely punished unless the boy is an eligible Bhangi and in such case a marriage is insisted upon. Plan implementation and welfare development activities are the role of modern statutory panchayat. Though the statutory panchayat was introduced after liberation but it does not have any interference with the traditional council of course. The periodical elections for panchayat and assembly have some linkages with the traditional council when the Patel is approached by the political parties. Since obedience to the custom of the community is insured, disputes are settled and reforms can be introduced by the *gnyat panch*.

The Bhangi believe in Hinduism. Their religious belief and practices recognize the existence of two supernatural powers, viz. *got* and village deities chiefly of Hindu myth and belief in spirits that inhabit certain localities. Their favourite deities of worship are Lord Shiva, *tulsi* (basil) and Ram Dev Pir. Lord Shiva is their village deity while the *got* deities are Chawda, Golie and Kodia. The *got* deities have specific role during birth and marriage, and are worshipped during these occasions. They have temple of Lord Shiva, the village deity, which is maintained by the *panch* and the deities are looked after by the community itself. They do also have belief on Kalika Mata, the temple at Buchadwada, where they fulfill their vows. The Bhangi consider Somnath and Dwarka, (both in Gujarat), as their major shrines for pilgrimages where they visit during Shravan month. Images of other Hindu deities, viz. Hanuman, Durga and Lakshmi are placed in their houses for worship. They sacrifice goat at Kalika Mata temple occasionally to clear their vows. *Bhuas*, the magico-religious specialists, perform their act by enduring spirits by violently shaking their bodies. The act of evil spirits are pacified by him through some recitation. *Darha*, a death ritual, is a magico-religious practice to pacify the spirit. Their major festivals are Gokulashtami, Shivratri and Ganesh Chaturthi. Poonam Mela, near the Kalika Mata temple, in Brehandwada on full moon of the Chaitra month and Shravani Poonam in Nogoa village are their major fairs which are attended by the other Hindus also. They also celebrate the other Hindu festivals, viz. Holi, Navratri and Diwali with full vision. The change in the religious behaviour took place after enforcement of Protection of Civil Right Act, 1955 in Diu after 1961 where Bhangis were allowed to enter in the Lord Shiva temple in Nagoa and Kalika Mata temple at Buchadwada.

They are specialists in the craft of basketry. The products of the craft are *tapli* (basket) for keeping fish and vegetables, *supoddo* (winowing fan) and *shawarni* (broom). They procure bamboos from the forest areas of Diu and adjoining areas of Gujarat. They sell their products in the daily markets of Diu and at rural bi-weekly *hat* (markets) in the different villages of Diu on cash transaction. The folk songs related to birth, marrriage and Shravani Poonam are common to all. *Chundar* (tattooing), with different marks, which are used by them are also common to all. They use *dhol* (drum) and wind instruments during birth and marriage. *Gheria* dance is the folk dance which is performed by women only.

They accept water, *kacha* and *pucca* food, and *sidha* from all the communities. Being ritually placed lowest in social hierarchy others do not accept anything from them. Though the enactment of Protection of Civil Right Act has oriented them to visit Kalika Mata temple but they have their own temple in their settlement. They share crematorium with the Hadi. They have their own water sources for drinking. A Brahman officiates at their marriage rituals but does not eat anything. He does'nt even accept *sidha* from them. They get cash as their remuneration. They have a school upto primary level in their settlement run by the government. In changing situation the feeling of untouchability has lessened and they are invited by the youngsters of other communities during marriage but they do not interdine. The relation is maintained only up to the exchange of gifts. The periodical elections of panchayat and assembly have provided with the chance of interaction of the Bhangis with other communities and the political parties through *gnyat* Patel. Participation in the multiethnic religious fairs and festivals and visit of sacred centres like Somnath, Prachi and Dilwada are some of the changes that have place recently.

The Bhangi have a positive attitude towards the development programmes of the Union Government which have enhanced their social and economic status. Socially, the level of the feeling of untouchability has lessened after the rule regarding the atrocities on the so called untouchables under Protection of Civil Right Act, 1955 has been introduced. They are well benefited from the adopted policy for the development during the Sixth Five Year plan for S.C., i.e. education, housing, employment (reservation policy), financial aids under IRDP for the self-employment. They also avail of the facilities of health and medicare, supply of drinking water, electricity, nutrition programme, provision for ration and development of GIDC to have more job opportunites. The administration is constitutionally committed to improve the quality of life of the Bhangis. Each beneficiary family of the Bhangi has been provided with a copy of the Vikas Patrika (identity card) and duplicate copy of the same is maintained in the office of the BDO at Diu for record. It is envisaged to undertake an evaluation on the spot visits which would reveal the actual position in respect of the individual family. They are exposed to mass communication by radio, cinema etc.

N.K.Sinha

REFERENCES

Crooke, W., *The Tribes and Castes of the North-Western India*, Cosmo Publications, Delhi, Vol. I, page 259, 1974.

Enthoven, R.E., *The Tribes and Castes of Bombay*, vol. I, 1920, Bombay, The Government Central Press, Reprint; vol.I, p. 104, 1975, Cosmo Publications, Delhi.

BHOIRAJ/BHOI

The Bhoi, also known as Bhoiraj, claim to be one of the fifty sub-castes of the Bhoi distributed throughout India. Enthoven (1920, page 182) has divided the Bhoi into five territorial groups, viz. Maratha, Khandesh, Karnataka, Kanarha and Gujarati. The Bhoiraj of Diu include themselves within the Gujarati Bhoi. The community believes that the term 'Bhoi' has been derived from the Sanskrit word '*bhumi*' and that their traditional occupation was to carry *palki* (palanquin). The story regarding their origin has been described by different scholars. Enthoven (1920, page 181) says that the term Bhoi, besides being the name of a caste, is also used to denote a litter bearer and has consequently been appropriated by the members of other castes persuing the same occupation. This statement has been supported by Sherring (1879, pages 119, 199 & 284), Thurston (1919, page 267), Bahadur (1981, page 2) and Russel and Lal (1916, Vol. I & III, pages 350 & 291). Gunvat Roy Acharya (page 43 Vol. I) described, in his book "Vishal Dev", the Bhoi as the water carrier on the shoulder. The Bhoiraj claim to be Rajputs from Lucknow of the United Provinces who migrated to Gujarat. Supporting their claim the *Jati Puran* of Bhoiraj of Diu has described about the Ramchandra Dev son of Dunoi Vidya Dhar, the Bhoi king, who ruled one of the feudatory states of Orissa during 17th century and reinstalled the Jagannath Temple at Puri. The Gazetteers of the Orissa and feudatory states (Volume XXII : Part I, page 164) has noted that about the middle of the 17th century, one Singha Vidya Dhar, a section of the then Khurda (Puri) Raj family, is said to have conquered the country and founded the state of Puri. They migrated from Jafrabad (Gujarat) to Ghogla first and then to Diu sometime during the 15th century. They percieve their distribution in the Ghogla village and Diu. Somehow, they are also distributed in Bhavnagar and Junagadh districts of Gujarat. During the last century of the Portuguese rules, some Bhoiraj shifted to the other colonies in Africa and Portugal, viz. Mojambic, Kenya, Dare-E-Salam and Lisbon to work as dock-worker.

Gujarati is a language as well as script used by them. Besides Gujarati they also speak Portuguese, English and Hindi.

They are non-vegetarian and their staple food includes *machhee* (fish), *bhat* (rice), *rotla* (bread prepared of *bajra*), *sag* (vegetables) and pulses of *mag* and *tur*. Fruits are taken daily in the evening available in the market. Alcoholic drinks and *neera* (toddy) are commonly used by them available in the market which are considered as digestive. The special foods viz. *puri*, *vatana* (peanut) and *bateta* (potato) curry, *farsan* (*pakorah*), *lapsee* (paste like preparation of milk wheat sugar fried in ghee), and *potaya* (prepared of wheat flour, sugar, toddy after frying in groundnut oil) are taken on the festive occassions like Dulhendi and Ujjani.

Goter or *got* (clan) is the basis of social sub-division among the Bhoiraj. There are sixteen *gots* among them namely Chudasama, Solanki, Chauhan Bamania, Jethva, Kumbathi, Bhokaria, Chawda, Waghela, Thakarsi etc. which are suffixed to their names. There is no stratification among these subgroups. The functions of the subgroups are to regulate marriage and to invite the members of the group during the life-cycle rituals. They perceive their position inferior to the Brahman, Vania, Salat, Sanghariya, Kharwa. They are well aware of *varna* system and recognize their place as Vaishya. The Bhoiraj resort to community endogamy and *goter* exogamy. The bride and the bridegroom should not have blood relation for four *pedhee* (ascending generations) from the mother's side. A marriage can not take place without the permission of *gnyat* Patel. They practise adult marriage and age of consent for a boy is 20 years while for a girl this is 16 years. The marriage is settled by negotiation only. They strictly follow monogamy. A married women puts *chandla* (red vermilion mark on forehead) and wears bangles of turtle shell. Brideprice or dowry is not permitted. A girl after marriage goes to stay with her-in-laws. *Chutta* (divorce) is not permitted. *Natra* or *punalagna* is the local term for the remarriage which takes place between a widow and a widower. They are not reluctant for the community endogamy in case of remarriage and allow *natra* with the Vania, Kharva, Koli and Vanja.

Kutumb is the local term for family. Their institution of family constitutes extended and nuclear. Avoidance, in terms of talking, with husband's elder brother and elderly male and female members of her husband is maintained. Joking relationship is maintained with elder brother's wife and wife's younger sister and brother. Mother's brother plays an important role during marriage. Conflict and confrontation arise after son's mariage and father's death in property and financial matters. In absence of son, the brother's son is adopted through the official procedure in the court. After the death of father half of the property goes to mother and the rest is divided among the sons. Mother has full right to give her part to anybody during her life time. But registration of property is done in the name of the eldest son. Eldest son succeeds the authority in the family. Inter-family linkage becomes the natural phenomenon for them in life- cycle rituals, election of *gnyat* Patel, religious festivals and assistance in the economic activities. The joint and extended families have lost their significance due to the arising conflict within the family members on financial ground. Right of inheritance is given also to the daughters now.

Women have roles in economic, social and religious spheres. In political matter, women are forbidden to interfere except to cast their votes in the periodical elections. They are assigned to household works only. They have low status. They are not permitted to work outside. They have specific role in life-cycle rituals specially during naming and head-shaving ceremony of a child where *fui* (father's sister) performs it. Women are considered lower than men in the community.

Life-cycle rituals are common to all other Hindu communities of Diu which have been already discussed in the Introduction. There are certain terminological differences of the rituals. *Vevisar* (betrothal) is called *sagpan*. *Uthamna* is a death rite performed on the third day after death when the mourner chew the leaf of *neem* and *supari* (hard nut) near well of the village temple to mark the state of mourning. In changing situation the Bhoiraj of Diu are going for the matrimonial relation to the adjoining districts of Gujarat and up to Bombay. Marriage rituals have been reduced from five to three days. One of the marriage rituals, the *mayura*, is out of practice now. *Mangalsutra*, has been introduced as a symbol for the married woman.

The Bhoiraj are a landless community. They are engaged in government services, small trades like hawkers and betel shops and day labourers. As stated earlier, their traditional occupation was carrying palanquins and litters before their migration from Lucknow to Gujarat where they shifted to the occupation of fishing, growing water-chestnuts, shopkeepers and labourers. The reason for the migration of the Bhoiraj from Gujarat to Diu was not traceable but to author's mind, Bhoiraj of Gujarat might have been recruited by the Koli of Diu as labourer in fishing trade during the 15th century (the expected period of their migration). While discussing about the Bhois of Gujarat, Enthoven (1920, Vol. I, page 181) says that 'Bhois' have doubtlessly been recruited in the past from Koli. In course of time, they developed their efficiency in other jobs. They are still working as dock porter is very much related to their efficiency of traditionnal occupation of palanquins and litter carriers. A labour gets his remuneration in cash which varies on the nature of job.

Their *gnyat panch* (traditional council) exercises social control at village and regional levels. Composition of the Bhoiraj *gnyat panch* includes one *gnyat* Patel and eleven *panches* including one accountant. Patel (chief) is elected by voice vote by the *panches* who are elected by the members of the community on the high social standing. The council functions at a fix place called *baithale*. Social disputes pertaining to marriage, adultery, and disputes within the family are referred to it for settlement. Other functions include the maintenance of temple, organising the religious gathering and regulations of the norms and values of the community and registration of marriage in the *sagpan* (betrothal) register. The *panch* collects registration fee from the bridegroom's father during the time of *sagpan* as the contribution to the *panch* to spend in the maintenance of temple and assistance to the aggrieved person of the community. *Panch* imposes punishment in the form of excommunication only. Seduction of an unmarried girl is also severly punished unless the boy is an eligible Bhoiraj and in such cases a marriage is insisted upon. The council at regional level is called Bargam Samast Bhoi Samaj and consists of twelve places namely Diu, Una, Jafrabad, Verawal, Mangrol, Prabhash Pataon, Bhavnagar, Jamnagar, Surat, Bharoch, Porbandar of Gujarat and Bombay. The regional council consists of two committees, i.e. *samanya samiti* (Executive Committee) and *salahkar samiti* (Advisory Committee) headed by Pramukh (the chief). Both the committees are having twelve *sabhyas* (members). The Pramukh is elected by the *gnyat* Patels of the different places and his tenure changes after every three years. The *gnyat* Patels are elected as Pramukh on rotation. The sitting of the regional council is called after every four years at the twelve places alternatively. The total expenditure is borne by the *gnyat* Patel of the village where *sabha* (meeting) is called. The function of the regional council is to resolve the social and religious problems and make reforms. The regional caste council was reorganised in 1970 which was earlier disorganised after

1940 meeting at Porbandar.

They profess Hinduism. They worship all the leading Hindu gods and goddesses and observe the principal Hindu festivals. Harshidh Mata is their village deity. Every *got* (clan) has a separate deity. Some of them are :

Got	*Deity*
1. Chudasama	: Khodia Mata
2. Solanki	: Matra Mata
3. Chawhan	: Chamunda Mata
4. Bamania	: Chavda Mata
5. Jethwa	: Brahami Mata
6. Bhokaria	: Nakeshwari Mata

They have the temple of Harshidh Mata. The *got* deities are worhipped during birth and marriage and before doing any important work like construction of house. They have faith in Kalinki Mata which is one of main deities worshipped by all other Hindu communities of Diu. This temple was constructed in the Samvat 1776 on third of Kartik-Sudh. The statue of the Goddess was carried from Bardo, a place in Diu district, to this place by Parimal Bhoi, the Bhoiraj, and the temple was constructed by the Vanias. This was done after the Kalinki Mata dreamed of the reinstallation of her statue at a proper place from the place where it submerged. Every year on Chaitra Shukla-Ashtami, a religious fair is organized where all the Hindu communities pay homage. As per tradition, the members from the Bhoiraj of Chudasama *got* are the first to pay homage to the Mata on the auspicious day with coconut. They consider Somnath, Birpur, Bhubneshwari and Gupta Prayag (all in Gujarat) as major sacred centres. The scared specialist helps them in religious offerings and homages during their visit to the aforesaid centres. Ujjani, another religious fair, is common to all the Hindu communities where community deities are worshipped in the month of Jyestha on different dates by different communities. The Bhoiraj celebrate Ujjani at the temple of Harshidh Mata, the caste deity, on every Jyeshtha Shukla Paksha Duitiya. Diwali, Makar Sankranti, Mahashivaratri, Holi, Janamashtami and Navratra etc. are the major festivals celebrated by them. They have only the nonmaterialistic cultural elements in the form of wall paintings during the festive occasions. They have special folk songs which are sung during the time of the worship of Harshidh Mata, the community deity.

They maintain traditional linkages with the Koli, Sangharias and Brahmans at economic, social and religious levels. Economically, they have linkages with the Koli who engage them as labourer. The Brahmans, being ritually placed in high position, are invited by them to perform the rituals during marriage, birth and death and are paid remuneration in both cash and kind. They accept water, *pucca* and *kacha* food from the Brahman, Vania, Salat, Sangharia, Kharwa, Vanja and Koli. They maintain relations with the Sangharias in religious sphere when both visit the Kalinki Mata for worship. The bangles of ivory and turtle-shell are purchased from the Sangharia. They have their own temples and crematorium since long. They participate in the public function at local as well as at district level. The principal fair in the district, held at Kalinki Mata temple in Buchadwada in the month of Chaitra on Poonam and on Ashadhi Panchami, is also attended by them which is followed by another fair held at Gangeshvar temple at Fudam on the day of Mahashivaratri. They allow inter-community widow remarriage with the Vanias, Kolis, Kharwa. The periodical elections for statutory panchayat, Assembly and Parliament seats have given the chance for interaction of the Bhoirajs with the other communities and political leaders of Diu district through their *gnyat* panch. They have teacher, doctors, and members holding white collar jobs.

They have a positive attitude regarding the development programmes in the field of education, health, family welfare, drinking water, electricity, employment under IRDP Banking facilities have provided them loan to undertake self employment in fishing, betel-shop, and tailoring. Expansion of the GIDC has given the chance for the employment and establishment of the educational institutions upto Higher Secondary and diploma in ITI level facilities. Some of the Bhoiraj get employment in Government service and schools. Further they desire to be constitutionally classified as a backward class as done by Bakshi Panch in Gujarat which will give the prospect of more facilities to uproot their economical condition. They avail of the facilities of nutrition programmes for the children under Balwadi, for the mental and physical growth. Literacy level has been quite low specially among the girls due to economic conditions and orthodox feeling. They do not like to send their girls for education and labour jobs. They are exposed to mass communication by cinema, radio, television, roads, post-offices, newspapers.

N.K. Sinha

REFERENCES

Bahadur, K.P., *Castes, Tribes and Culture of India*, Ess Ess Publisher, Delhi, Vol. VII (Western Maharashtra & Gujarat) Page 84, 1981.

Enthoven, R.E., *The Tribes and Castes of Bombay*, vol. I, 1920, Bombay, The Government Central Press, Reprint; vol.I,pp.181-193, 1975, Cosmo Publication, Delhi.

C. A.P., *The Gazetteers of Orissa and the Fudetorty States, Part-I*, Vol.XXII, P 164, 1910.

Russell, R.V. and Hira Lal, *Tribes & Castes of Central Provinces*. vol. I, 1920 and vol. III, 1922, Bombay, The Government Central Press, Reprint; vol. I & III, pp. 181 & 103, 1975, Cosmp Publications, Delhi.

Sherring, M.A., *Hindu Tribes and Castes*, vol. II, 1979, Calcutta, Thakar Spink & Co. Reprint; Vol.II, pp. 119, 199 & 294, 1974, Cosmo Publications, Delhi,

Thurston, E., *Castes & Tribes of Southern India*, Cosmo Publications, Madras, Vol. I, pp. 267, 1909.

BRAHMAN

The Brahman also call themselves Gujarati Brahman, i.e. the Brahman who originally belonged to Gujarat. The term Brahman relates to the term 'Brahm' meaning the Supreme, having the knowledge of universe. They trace their origin to the Vedic period when society was divided into four classes — the *varnas*, and the Brahman enjoyed the highest position as the priest. Though Enthoven (1920 Vol. I) has divided the Gujarati Brahman into 93 sub-divisions they are, as a matter of fact, divided into six engodamous territorial groups namely Nagar, Audich, Thalawadi, Khandoria, Saraswat and Unewal, who migrated from North India to Gujarat and finally to Diu long back. They explain that these subgroups were formed by people who were unwilling to mix with the local Brahmans, whom they considered inferior to them, both in matter of diet and blood. Out of the total population of the Brahman, thirty five families migrated to Diu from Rajkot, Jamnagar, Bhavnagar, Junagarh, Kesodh, Verawal, Una, Amreli, Kutch, Bhuj and Mojambique (Africa) after liberation. Some of the families from Diu migrated to Mozambique during the middle of Portuguese regime where they occupied themselves in teaching and trade, and after making sufficient money returned to Diu to spend the evening of their lives. They are distributed in Diu town and in different parts of Gujarat. Gujarati is their language as well as script. They are also conversant with Hindi, English and Portuguese.

The Brahman are strict vegetarians with a high level of vegetable consumption in their diet. Their staple food includes *bajra*, rice, wheat, pulses of *urad* and *tur* with jaggery. Groundnut oil is their cooking medium. They consume plenty of locally available fruits. Only men enjoy the alcoholic drinks available in the local market. They take tea, milk and buttermilk regularly. *Puri* (fried bread), *dudhpag* (rice boiled in milk mixed with sugar), *srikhand* (a sweet dish from curd) and *lapsee* (porridge of wheat flour fried in ghee and mixed with sugar) are their special food used on festive occasions. Taking of liquor is a recent change.

They are divided into ten exogamous *gotras*, the subgroups, which are said to be related with the name of rishis namely Upamanyu, Kaushik, Vatsa, Bandel, Bhargava, Shandilya, Gurg, Gautam, Vashistha and Parashar. These subgroups are common to earlier discussed endogamous divisions. They suffix Pandia, Joshi, Trivedi, Dave, Samarth and Bhatt to their names. The basis of differentiation is social. The chief function of *gotra* is to trace descent, to regulate marriage alliances and to help in the life cycle rituals. They perceive their position high in social hierarchy as well as in *varna* status and are so placed by others too. They resort to community and sub-division endogamy and *gotra* exogamy. Marriage is prohibited within *sapinda*, within seven ascending generations of father's side and five ascending generations of mother's side. Traditionally they had practice of child marriage when girls used to be married before attaining puberty. The practice of adult marriage is a recent change. Marriage is settled by negotiation and they practise monogamy. *Bangdi* (bangles of turtle shell and of ivory) and *mangalsutra* are their marriage symbols. They have practice of *dej* (dowry) in kind which is fixed during the negotiation. Divorce and remarriage are not permitted. They practise patrilocal rule of residence.

The institution of *kutumb* (family) consists of nuclear and extended types. Joking and avoidance relationships exist in a family. They maintain avoidance relationships with mother-in-law, son-in-law, daughter-in-law, father-in-law, younger brother's wife and husband's elder brother. Joking relationship exists with elder brother's wife, husband's younger brother, wife's elder and younger sisters and wife's elder and younger brothers. It is obligatory to play the role of *harvan* (accompanier) by sister's husband and bringing *maushala* (marriage dress) by the maternal uncle in marriage. Conflict and confrontation arise after father's death in property matters. All sons get equal share in father's property but the eldest son succeeds the authority in a family. Interfamily linkages can be envisaged during the life-cycle rituals and during the political activities. Women enjoy low status in society. Their roles are restricted to religious, social, ritual and household fields. They are forbidden to interfere in political matter. They also contribute to family income by doing services in different government organisations. *Fui* (father's sister) has an important role to play during *nampari* (naming) and *mundan* (head shaving) ceremonies.

They observe the Vedic *sanskaras* on appropriate occasions. The first delivery takes place at her parent's village. *Srimant* is the pre-birth ritual observed in the seventh month of pregnancy to guard the embryo from injury. After paying homage to the family deity with coconut, the emblem of fertility, the expectant mother leaves for her parent next day after *srimant*. An expectant mother has to observe certain restrictions for protection from evil eyes and miscarriages. *Chhathi* is performed on the sixth day after birth and *suraj* (the Sun God) and the *gotra* deities are worshipped. The purificatory bath takes place on tenth day but they observe birth pollution for 45 days. *Nampari* is performed on twelfth day after birth by *fui* after procuring the astronomical name from the family priest. *Janampatri* (horoscope) is prepared on the same day by the priest. *Mundan* is performed in the third or fifth year by the barber and *fui* collects the hair in a green cloth and disposes off in the sea. In the eighth year after birth *yajno-pavit* (investiture with the sacred thread) is performed to the male child by the family priest who invests the boy with sacred thread made of cotton implying that the boy has entered the stage of *brahmchari* (bachelor). *Sagai* (betrothal) takes place one to two months prior to *vivah* (marriage) at the bridegroom's residence. Marriage is the matter of three days which are performed at both the places and solemnized at the bride's residence. The three-day's rituals start with the installation of *manek-stambh* (sacred pole for the Ganpati) stained with turmeric and near it is placed a *kalash* (earthen pot) with water. *Mandava* (marriage booth) is erected thereafter. *Pithee* (paste of barely flour turmeric mixing with ground nut oil) is rubbed on the bodies of both the bride and groom for three days at their respective houses. *Maushale* (ceremonial marriage gift) is presented to both at their houses by their maternal uncles on the second day. *Dev-santak* (family deity worship) is performed in the night. The *jan* (marriage procession) starts for the bride's village on the third day where they are given *janawas* (separate lodging) on their arrival. The bride-groom, with the *jan*, arrives at bride's house where *ponkhavan* (reception) is performed near the *toran* (entrance to the marriage booth) by the bride's mother. *Har toda* (exchange of garland) is performed at *otah* (inner verandah) and the groom is led to *chauri* (square of sacrificial fire) in the *mandava* and is seated there. The bride also comes to the *chauri*, escorted by her mother's brother and is seated on the left side of the groom. *Kanyadan* is performed thereafter when groom is presented with a golden ring by the bride's father. The priest recites the appropriate verses and their robes are knotted together. *Hast milap* is performed when the priest holds the right hand of the bride and place it on the right hand of groom covered by a piece of cloth and recites the verses. *Saptpadi* is the principal ritual performed thereafter when both the bride and the groom move seven times round the *chauri* amidst the verses recited by the priest. The family deity is worshipped by both in the family oratory and the groom returns to *janawas*. *Chaturthi-karma* is performed next day in *chauri* when both feeds each other *kansar* (rice boiled in milk mixing jaggery). *Dej* (dowry) in kind is paid to the groom's father and the groom is presented with gifts by the bride's relatives. The groom with his bride returns back to his village in the evening and pays homage to his family deity. Consummation of marriage takes place in the *suhag-ghar*, at the groom's residence. *Ana* (return of bride) takes place after 29 days or three months. They cremate their dead and the rites connected with death are performed by the eldest son, the chief mourner. A *kalash* full of water and a lamp is kept in the house for the use of the deceased during the mourning period which extends up to ten days. Ashes and bones are collected after cremation and disposed off in Triveni Sangam near Somnath or Hirang Saraswati or other river. They observe pollution for ten days. *Pinddan* (offering of holy rice ball to seven ancestors) is performed, and family members shave their heads and moustaches and *gotra* members are fed on eleventh day. The second *pinddan* (offering of holy flour rice ball) to the departed soul on twelfth day and a community dinner is given. *Kriya* is performed on thirteenth day. The favourite articles of the deceased are donated to the priest who officiates the death rites.

The Brahman are a landless community. Traditionally they are priest and attend to the job of religious rites and rituals. Teaching is their secondary occupation. It has already been discussed earlier that the Brahman of Diu worked as teachers in Mozambique during the Portuguese regime. At present priesthood is their primary occupation. A few of them are employed in government service and engaged in petty business. Their services are required to attend to the life cycle rituals of all other Hindu communities.

They have their traditional council at two levels namely Sri Chaurashi Gnyat Brahman Samaj, Diu, at village level which was formed about 100 years back headed by a President and *Bahar Gam Gnyati Brahman Samaj* at regional level, headed by President, which includes Diu and ten districts of Gujarat viz. Rajkot, Jamnagar, Bhavnagar, Junagadh, Karodh, Verawal, Amreli, Kutch and Bhuj. The President of the village council is assisted by a vice-president, treasurer, secretary and three *sabhya* (members of executive committee). The Presidents are elected by voice vote. The election of the office bearers takes place after every three years. Social problem pertaining to breach of traditional rule and inter-family disputes are dealt by the councils. Inter-caste marriage is considered the biggest social offence and in such cases a man or woman is excommunicated. Other activities include the progress of the community, interaction with other communities and to educate the poor. The meeting of regional council is called once in a year at any of the above mentioned places to deal with the social problems. Plan implementation and development activities are the role of modern statutory panchayat.

The Brahman of Diu follow Vaishnavism. Their religious beliefs and practices recognize the existence of the supernatural power but they worship trees, plants, and animals. Worship of *pipal, tulsi* (basil), *vada* (banyan) and *val* (creeper), and devotion for cow is a predominant feature. Vishnu visits the earth in human or in animal form by a succession of *avtara* (incarnation). Lord Vishnu and Shiva are their village deities. They also worship other Hindu gods and goddesses and observe fasts and festivals. Somvedri Mata, Modeshwari Mata, Amba Mata are the *gotra* deities who are worshipped daily in the morning, in the evening and during life cycle rituals. Guru Poornima is their main festival associated with the worship of Shukracharya (mythical sage), and Pratpanda are the other festivals. They also celebrate other Hindu festivals viz. Ramnavmi, Janmashtami, Divali etc. with full vision. Mahi is celebrated on Shukla Paksha Dvitiya of Magh month which is associated with the worship of sea-god, an adaptation to sea ecology. The married female members of the family worship the sea-god for the prosperity and safety of the male members living outside. They consider Dwarka, Somnath and Birpur as their major sacred centers. They are the sacred specialists who help the other Hindu communities in paying homages and performing life cycle rituals. They do not have any material culture of their own. *Satiyo* (floor design), folk songs of marriage and festivals, and *garba* folk dance are enjoyed by the women only.

They accept *pucca* food only from the Sangharia. Being superior in hierarchy with in the community, Nagar Brahman do not accept *kachha* food from the other Brahmans of Diu. They accept *sidha* from the other Hindu communities except the Hadi, Vankar and Bhangi as their remuneration for performing the religious duties. They have their own crematorium. They share the drinking water sources with others. Traditional linkages are maintained with all the Hindu communities in religious spheres only. *Dharam Bhai* (putative relation) is maintained with the Vanja. The community has businessmen and teachers. Political leadership has emerged at village panchayat.

The attitude towards the development programmes is most positive. They avail of the facilities of education, and boys study upto the college and drop out as they have to earn to support their family and the girls study upto school final only and drop out from study due to social reason. They favour family planning programme but prefer to have three children and use modern methods where tubectomy is preferred. They avail of the facilities of drinking water through piped water and make use of electricity and both the traditional and modern medicare. Mid-day-meal for children under nutrition scheme and ICDS, ration distribution system are availed of. Firewood, cow dung cake, kerosene oil and L.P.G. are their fuel resources. The area has a good network of pucca roads for transportation from Diu to the other parts of Gujarat.

N.K. Sinha

REFERENCES

Enthoven, R.E., *The Tribes and Castes of Bombay*, vol. I, 1920, Bombay, The Government Central Press, Reprint; vol. I, p. 213, 1975, Cosmo Publications, Delhi.

Sinha , N.K., *Study of Ethnography and Change in Diu Village*, Unpublished report submitted to Anthropological Survey of India, 1980.

CHRISTIAN

The Christian are also known Roman Catholic or Catholic. They perceive their origin from the Hindus who were converted to Christianity after the capture of Goa in the 15th century by the Portuguese who considered Christianization a state of enterprise and entered upon a policy of conversion to Latin Church. Sahay (1980, page 17) reports that St. Fransis Xavier in 1541 with his mission attempted largescale conversion of the lower classes the in coastal areas of Western India. He got the support of the Portuguese authority. The doctrine of Padroado (jus patrobature established by the Papal Buel in 1514) placed the authority to convert local population effectively in the hands of the Portuguese Crown in areas where Portugal claimed political rights. After the conquest of Daman by Dom Constautino de Braganca in 1559 (Antonio Fransisco, 1900 - 101), some of the Christians were brought to Daman from Goa for the services in the Military establishments and other government offices. They do not admit the fact of recent conversion, and rather claim to be the descendants of the Christians in the jurisdiction of the Bishops of Latin rite with the subsequent addition of conversion from low Hindu castes. Chib's (1977:91) discription has supported the above statement. Thus the Christians of Daman are the descendants of the converted Christians of Goa. They perceive their distribution in Daman, Diu, Dadra and Nagar Haveli and also in Bombay and Goa. Their total population is recorded to be 2,094 (Census of India 1971), i.e., 5.41% of the total population of Daman. Portuguese is the language spoken within the community and the script is Roman. They also speak English and Gujarati with others. The knowledge of a colloquial Gujarati has helped the younger generations to learn Gujarati in school. The female folk can be easily identified by their dress. They wear long frocks or midi irrespective of their age and marital status.

They are regular non-vegetarian and eat egg, fish, meat of goat, fowls, beef and pork. Their staple food includes rice, wheat, bun, sliced bread and pulses of *tur*. They also consume locally available seasonal vegetables. Alcoholic drink is a part of their life which is enjoyed by both men and women regularly which they purchase from the local market. They smoke cigarette and chew betel. Groundnut and coconut oils are used for cooking purposes. The favourite dishes are *espetada-de-leitoo* (pig suchting barbeque), *sarpetal* (made of pork), *cabidel* (made of pork), *bafado* (pork preparation), *barrada* (pork or fish preparation), *dampaca* (chicken preparation), *alho pimenta* (fish preparation), *seco-seco* (fish preparation) and *ambat* (fish preparation). Cake, *biriyani*, rolls are special food preparations made use of on the festive occasions. Sweets made on festive occasions are *pao-de-lo, bebinca, doce-de-grao, bolo-de-sura, broa, pudim* etc.

The Christian do not have any hierarchical social divisions as among the Christians of Goa. They enjoyed high social position during the Portuguese regime being placed high in administration. Presently, they perceive their position as inferior to the Brahman, Vania, Koli Patel, Kamli, Bhandari, Sagar and Bari, and superior to the Machhi, Mangela, Mitna, Dhodia, Dubla, Momin and Mahyavanshi. They marry within the Christian. Marriage with the brother's or sister's children is not encouraged but can take place only after seeking permission from the Bishop. Cross-cousin marriages are thus allowed. They practise adult marriage at the age of 22 to 27 years for boys and from 18 to 25 years for girls. Marriage is settled by mutual selection on the basis of *namore* (love) and negotiation. Marriage by courtship is also permitted. Monogamy is the common form. Nuptial ring is the symbol for married people. They do not have any system of dowry or brideprice and a bride generally brings to her new house a bed, a cupboard a dressing table and a few dresses. A girl, after marriage, goes to live with her husband's new house which he establishes before marriage. They believe in living independently. They do not encourage divorce and the matrimony is broken only after the death of either of spouse and their religion says that God has joined together and let no man put as under. If a man or a woman desires, he or she can seek divorce by the judicial approval under the civil law. Remarriages are allowed between a widow and a widower and between the divorcees.

They believe in living independently in nuclear family and a son establishes a new household after marriage. They do not have the concept of avoidance relationships. Joking relationship exists with elder brother's wife, husband's younger brother and wife's brother and sister. Right of inheritance is granted as per the Portuguese General Law

(Civil Code of 1887) where mother gets half of the property and remaining half is equally distributed among the children. Eldest son succeeds the authority after father's death till sons are not married. Sister's husband plays the role of 'bestman' in marriage. The 'bestman' may be the groom's best friend. Inter-family linkages are sought during the life cycle rituals, political and religious activities. Man and woman are equal partner in day to day life. They have equal status in the society. They have roles in bringing potable water, social functions, ritual observances, political and religious spheres. They also manage and control the family expenditure. They contribute to family income by doing services in different government organisations. They get equal share in paternal property.

The Christian throughout the Union Territory have basically the same habits and customs, almost all of them being Indians converted to the Catholic religion by Portuguese Missionaries. However, there are some different geographical and ethnic background. They do not have any pre-birth rituals except that the mother is taken to her parents during seventh month for delivery. Doctor or nurse attends the job of delivery in hospital. They do not observe pollution period and the mother and the baby are given bath immediately after delivery. The sixth day after the birth of the child is celebrated by boiling six kinds of pulses plus wheat (the pulses are- *val* and *valli*, black eyed beans, *tur*, green peas and *kabuli channa*). This is distributed among the neighbours, relatives and friends in small dishes garnished with their slices of tender coconut. Post-natal restriction on mother exists and the mother remains in confinement for forty days for treatment and special diet is given. She does not go for her usual routine until after ninety days. *Baptism* is the first post - birth ritual performed in the church on seventh day when the baby is also named by the Father of the Church. This marks the initiation of the child into Christiandom. It is a sacrament that cleans from the original sin and gives the soul the new life of sanctifying grace by which the child becomes the child of God. A feast is given in the house. Sometimes it is performed after the completion of three years. Baptism is followed by Holy Communion, Confirmation, Penance, Annointy of the sick. The sacrament of the Holy Order is performed by only who desires to become priest. Marriage is performed according to the rules of Catholic Church. After the marriage alliance is settled, a day is fixed for the parents of the both, their relatives and friends to meet at the house of the bride for the formal betrothal.

A written promise on a paper, by the bride's father, to give his daughter in marrying to the boy selected and a similar promise by the groom's father to accept her, are made and are mutually exchanged in the presence of those assembled who are treated to a dinner and the day for the wedding is fixed. On the wedding day the bride and the groom, well-dressed, accompanied by their relatives and friends, go to her parish church and attend the mass (prayer). The groom is accompanied by his 'bestman' his sister's husband. Marriage service is read by the Father, followed by the exchange of nuptial ring and the Father proclaims the both husband and wife. Offerings are made to the church. A bottle of wine and bread are presented to the priest who puts in the holy pot and then gives it to the couple to have the first wedding drink. The groom with his bride returns to his house with the party where guests are given dinner. They bury their dead. The corpse is placed in a coffin. The parish priest attends the funeral and offer prayers in the house for the peace of the departed soul. They body is then taken to the church in the parish and buried in the cemetry, where similar prayers are offered. During the period one can not participate in any festive occasions, can not enjoy liquor and meat and tie black ribbon on their upper arm to mark the mourning period for thirty days. On eleventh, fifteenth, seventeenth and twenty first day they attend mass. Special prayers are offered on the 30th day and on the first death anniversary and the priest of parish offer prayers both in the church and in the cemetry at the grave side. For three days after the death of a family member, relatives and meighbours bring food and share it with the bereaved family. A mass is said on the first anniversary for the peace of the departed soul.

The Christian are a landless community. Service in various government offices and private concern is their present primary as well as traditional occupation. They were well placed in administration during the Portuguese regime. Their condition, in service, deteriorated after liberation as they did not fulfil essential academic qualifications required by the government. Carpentry, masonary, running wine shop, and dealing in general merchantise are their other means of livelihood.

Social control is regulated by *Comprary* (church committee) and *Lagionary* of *Mary* headed by a Father (priest) in each parish who is assisted by the members. Problems pertaining to the management of the church, social and religious functions, raising of funds and supply of books to poor students are looked after by the *Comprary*. The main duty of the members of the *Lagionary of Mary* is to visit Catholic families to look after their welfare problems. To plan and implement welfare and development activities are the role of modern statutory panchayat.

As it has been discussed earlier that they are converts from Hindu. The proselytization was carried out by Portuguese Viceroy in 16th century at the initiative of St. Francis Xavior. The Church of N.S. Dos-Remedious (Our Lady of Remedies) is an important shrine to them and which is considered equivalent to the deity. It was originally built as Chapel at the expenses of Ruy DC Mello Sanpario, the then Captain Governor of Daman, in 1607 and subsequently enlarged and converted into a church. Ordinary masses are attended in the church on every Sunday while the Ceremonial mass comes once in a year in June. Churches in different parishes are the sacred centres for them. Visiting Rt. Paper's Cathedral in Rome and seeing the mumy of St. Francis Xavior (placed in the church at Panajim) are their main pilgrimage. While the parish priest officiates at the Baptism, Confession and Holy Communion, the marriage, mass and funeral rites, the Bishop officiates at the Confirmation and the sacrament of Order rites. The sacrament of Holy order is performed by only those who intends to become Bishop or Father. Chrismas, Good Friday and New Year Day are their festivals. They also observe the ordinary festivals of the church i.e. the day of the patron saint of each being celebrated with great pomp. Carnival, i.e. *Car* means flash and *Wal* mean feast, is the main fair celebrated only by the Christians of Goa, Daman, Diu, Dadra and Nagar Haveli in India. Their art is represented by the oral traditions. Their folk songs are in the style of *mando* of Goa with the exception that it is sung by both men and women in their dialect of the Portuguese language. They sing the songs at the sound of *batuque*, a percussion musical instrument. Both participate in dance together during the festive occasions.

Traditionally they are linked with all the communities through their services in police and administration. They accept water, *kacha* and *pucca* food from all the communities. They are invited by the Hindus and Muslims during their marriages and they also invite their friends from other communities during marriages. They do not have any feeling of untouchability, the reason being that the Mahayavanshis were employed as cooks and domestic servants in their houses since Portuguese period. They share well and other drinking water sources with others. They have members holdings white collar jobs, businessmen, teachers annd members in police service.

Though the attitude of the Christian towards formal education is favourable, their literacy level has not been encouraging due to economically weak conditions. Boys study upto secondary level and drop out as they have to contribute to their family income. Girls also study upto secondary level but can not continue as they are economically weak and have to earn to support their family. They make full use of modern medicare. Their attitude towards family planning is positive but they prefer to have three children with the help of modern family planning methods. They avail of the facilities of drinking water through piped water, ration distribution system, child and mother care under ICDS, and primary health centres. They make use of electricity. kerosene and L.P.G. are their fuel resources. The area has a good network of roads, which provide means of communication with rest of the country. They plan their expenses according to their earning and do not depend on money lenders or shopkeepers in need.

N.K. Sinha

REFERENCES

Chib, S.S., *This Beautiful India*, "*Union Territories of India*", Light and Life Publications, Delhi, 1977.

Census of India, Registrar General, Panjim, Goa, page 27, 1971.

Francisco, Antonio, *Noticas-E-Documentas-Para-A-Historica De Damao*. Bastoria, (Goa), Page 101, 1900.

Sahay, K.N., *Christianity and Culture Change in India*, Inter-India Publications, New Delhi, page 17, 1986.

DHOBI

The Dhobi, a community of washermen, also call themselves Rajput Dhobi. Though they claim to have a link with the Rajput there is no authentic information to verify their statement. They are divided into four endogamous territorial divisions namely Modasia (from Modasa), Saurathia (from Saurashtra) Bundela (from Bundel) and Bhawsar (from Bhawnagar) which are based on the place of their migration. They migrated from Gujarat sometimes in 1700 and settled in Ghogla village of Diu. The first to settle in Ghogla was Lala Rathod Modasia. In course of time Saurathia and Bhawsara came and settled in Diu town and Ghogla. They are distributed in Ghogla and Diu town. Somehow, they are also distributed in Una, Delwara, Kodinar, Junagarh, Jetpur, Rajkot, Bhavnagar and so on. They speak, write and learn in Gujarati within as well as outside the community. they are also conversant with Hindi. They do not have any constitutional status as in case of Dhobi of Gujarat who have been included in Bakshi Panch a status for the backward classes.

They are non-vegetarian and take meat of goat, fowls and fish. Their staple food includes *bajra*, rice, wheat and pulses of *urad* (black gram), *chana* (gram) and *moong* (green gram). The ecology has provided them fish which is the major content of their food. They also consume local vegetables as per availability. Groundnut oil is their cooking medium. Men are very much fond of enjoying liquor which they purchase from the local market. They also take milk, butter milk, smoke *bidi* and cigarette and chew betel and *tambacu* (tobacco). Seasonal fruits are taken occasionally. *Pla* (fried rice), *lapsee* (porridge), *potaya* and *dudhpag* are the special food preparations used on the festive occasions.

Among the four endogamous divisions viz. Modasia, Saurathia, Bundela and Bhawsar, the Modasia occupy the highest position claiming to be the descendants of Rajput. These divisions are divided into a number of exogamous sub-divisions based on *goter* namely

Modasia, Vaghela, Wada, Chudasama, Solanki, Chauhan, Rathod, Tethwa, Parmar, Vaja etc. and are suffixed to their names as *atak* (surname). The chief functions of the *goter* is to trace their descent, to regulate marriage and to participate in the life cycle rituals. They consider the Brahman, Salat, Sanghania, Bania, Kharwa, Vanja and Koli superior to them. They are well aware of the *varna* system and recognize their position as Kshatriya. Other perceive them low. The basis of differentiation among *goter* is social. They resort to community and division endogamy and *goter* exogamy. A marriage can not take place within the three ascending generations from mother's side when it is traced between the two contacting parties. The three endogamous groups; viz. Modasia, Saurathia and Bhavsaria, have marriage distance that Modasia negotiate in Una, Delwara, Ghogla, Kodinar (all in Gujarat) and Diu; Saurathia in Junagarh, Jetpur, Rajkot, Gondal (all in Gujarat) and Diu; and Bhavsaria in Junagadh, Bhavnagar (in Gujarat) and Diu. They practise adult marriage and the age for a boy is 21 years while for girl is 18 years at marriage. Marriage is settled by negotiation initiated by the boy's father. They practise monogamy. *Devarbatu* (junior levirate) and junior sororate are permitted. *Kanku* (vermilion mark on forehead), *bangdi* (bangles of turtle shell) and *kentho* (vermilion mark on hair parting) are the marriage symbols. *Dej* (dowry) has taken the place of *pally* (brideprice). Rule of residence is patrilocal. *Natra* (remarriage) is allowed for both the widow and widower. *Natra* is solemnized in a very simple way in the presence of he *gnyati* Patel (traditional council chief). They sit on wooden *patli* (stool) opposite to each other and sprinkle rice grain on each other. Brahman's presence is also sought who officiates and helps in paying homage to Lord Ganpati. When widower marrys an unmarried girl, the regular form of marriage is performed. In case a boy wishes to marry a widow, the rituals are performed under a *shami* tree. They do not encourage *far gati* (divorce).

Mixed extended *kutumb* (family) is common among them. They have prescribed kinship usages, viz. avoidance and joking relationships. Avoidance is maintained with mother-in-law, daughter-in-law, father-in-law, younger brother's wife and husband's elder brother. Joking is maintained with elderbrother's wife, husband's younger brother, wife's elder and younger sister, wife's elder brother and wife's younger brother. Sister's husband plays the role of *anwar* (accompanier) and maternal uncle brings *maushala* (marriage gift) in marriage. Conflict and confrontation arise after son's marriage and after father's death in financial matters. After father's death half of the property goes to the widow mother and half is equally distributed among the sons. In absence of male child, the daughter's son is adopted. The widow mother can have her will to any of her sons, the part of her property. The eldest son succeeds the authority. Inter-family interactions are sought during the life cycle rituals and during the economic and political activities. Though women share the burden of day to day life but they enjoy low status. Their roles are restricted to religious rituals, economic spheres and household jobs. They are forbidden to interfere in political matters except to cast their votes during the periodical elections of Assembly and panchayat after the consultation with their male members. *Fui* (father's sister) plays an important role during *nampari* (naming) and *balmaudi* (tonsure) ceremonies. The folk songs on the festive occasions, are sung by the women only. They also contribute to family income by doing teaching jobs.

Khoro-bharho, the pre-birth ritual is performed in the seventh month of pregnancy for the safe delivery and to ward off evil eyes. The expectant mother leaves for her parents next day after the ritual. *Chhathi* is performed on the sixth day after birth when the *goter* deity is worshipped in the evening and the *got* dinner is given in the night. *Nampari* (naming) ceremony is performed on the same day in the evening by the *fui* after procuring the astronomical name from the Brahman. They observe birth pollution for 40 days and post-natal restrictions are maintained. *Bal maudi* (tonsure) ceremony is performed by the barber with the help of *fui* for the male child after the completion of one or three years after birth. *Sagai* (betrothal) takes place fifteen to twenty days prior to *lagan* (marriage). The rituals connected with marriage are performed at both the houses of the bride and the groom but is solemnized at the bride's residence. A Brahman officiates the marriage ceremony. The three-day marriage ceremony starts with the installation of *manekstambh* (pole for Ganpati) at both the houses and erection of *mandva* (marriage booth) at bride's house. *Pithee* (paste of turmeric and groundnut oil) is rubbed on the bodies of both of the bride and the groom for three days at their respective houses. The maternal uncle of the both brings *maushala* (marriage dresses and ornament) on the second day as a part of the customary obligation. The groom with the *jan* (marriage procession) arrives in the bride's village on third day where they are given *janiwas* (separate lodging). The *jan*, with the groom, arrives at the bride's residence in the evening where *ponkhavan* (reception of groom) is performed by the bride's mother. *Barmal* is performed at *otah* (inner verandah) and the groom is led to *chauri* (square of sacrificial fire) into *mandava* escorted by *harwan* and is seeated there. The bride is also led to *mandava* escorted by her maternal uncle and is seated opposite to the groom on a *patli* (wooden plank) where *hast milap* is performed. *Chauri ferwa* is performed thereafter when the bride and the groom circumambulate round the *chauri* four times and the bride sits to the left of the groom. *Kansar khao* (feeding of the couple to each other) is performed and the priest proclaims the both as husband and wife. The couple pays visit to the *goter* deity in a room. *Chauri fera* is the principal ceremony connected with marriage. The *jan* returns back in the night. The couple visits the *goter* and village deities of the bride next day after marriage and then only the groom returns to his village with his bride escorted by *harwan*. The consummation of marriage takes place at the groom's residence on the fourth day of marriage in the night. *Ana* (return of the bride) takes place fifteen days after marriage and the bride groom takes back the bride from her village next day after the first Holi. The Dhobi cremate their dead and the rites connected with death are performed by the eldest son, the chief mourner. The female members accompany the funeral procession upto the *gondra* (village boundary) and return back. *Phool-padhraon* is performed after the cremation where ashes and bones are collected and disposed off in the sea with flowers. The community members visit the house of the deceased to condole and are served with salty tea to mark the state of mourning for three days. They observe death pollution for ten days. The *goter* members including the chief mourner shave their heads and moustaches. *Goter* dinner is given in the night. *Kriya* is performed on the twelfth day. *Madhe-jamawan* (feeding to the departed soul) is performed by the *bhu* (magico religious specialist) in the night. Memorial rites are performed after two months, after six months and after the completion of one year.

Water is their major economic resource. They are a landless community. Cloth washing is their traditional as well as present primary occupation. Services in different government organisations and schools and small trade, viz. liquor shops, grocers etc. are the other means of livelihoood. Women and grown up children assist them. Service of a Dhobi is required for washing garments. They are directly linked with the market and the transaction is made in cash. A Dhobi is employed on the occasion of birth or death. These events cause impurity and hence the clothes of all the family members must be washed when the impurity ceases. The Dhobi, with the trade of timber wood, get the log from Indore, Jabalpur and Nagpur. Shifting from primary to secondary occupation is the part of change that took place in their economic activities after liberation.

Social control is governed by the traditional caste councils at two levels namely the *gnyat panch* at village level and Bahargam Gnyati Dhobi Samaj at region level which comprises the villages of Diu and Gujarat with its headquarter at Rajkot in Gujarat. The *gnyati panch* is headed by a Patel who is elected by voice vote and assisted by a *khajanchi* (accountant) and a *kotwal* (messenger) who are nominated by the Patel. Social problems pertaining to inter-community marriage, adultery and breach of traditional norms are dealt with by the *gnyat panch*. The regional council is headed by a Pramukh and assisted by a *mehta* (accountant) and a *mukodam* (messenger). The meeting of the regional council is called once in a year at Rajkot to deal with the social problems and reformation of the traditional norms. The regional council remained discontinued from 1952 to 1961 and was reorganized in 1970 after liberation. Cash fine and excommunications are the forms of punishment. An offender is expiated after paying the fine, which ranges from Rs. 100/- to Rs. 500/- imposed by the *gnyat panch*. Plan implementation and welfare and development activities are the role of modern statutory panchayat. They maintain a register for their traditional constitution and for the registration of birth and marriage is called *gnyat-nu-bandhan*.

The Dhobi are Hindus by religion. They do not have any specific community deity. They pay visit to the temples of Lord Shiva, Ramdeo, and Amba Mata in the village. Their *goter* deities are Chamunda Mata and Kholia Mata who are worshipped during the life cycle rituals. They also believe in spirits and seek the help of *bhua* of their own community to ward off evil eyes and malevolent spirits. They consider Somnath and Birpur in Gujarat as their major sacred centres. Their sacred specialist is Brahman who helps them in religious offerings. Poonam Mela at Kalinki Mata temple in Buchodwada and Shivratri Mela at Gangeshwar temple in Fudam are their major fairs which are also common to other Hindu communities. They also celebrate the other Hindu festivals viz., Navratra, Diwali, Holi and Rakshabandhan with full vision. Mahibij is celebrated on Shukla Paksha, Dwitiya of Magh month which is associated with the worship of sea-deity, an adaptation with the sea ecology.

There is no specific elements to represent their art and culture. *Satiyo* (floor design), folk-songs and folk dances are common with all other Hindu communities. They use wind and percussion musical instruments during festive occasions. Only women participate in dance.

Their occupation has been the main factor in their traditional as well as modern linkages with all other communities of Diu. They accept water, *pucca* and *kacha* food from all the communities except the Muslims, Hadi, Vankar, Siddi and Bhangi. They share well and other water sources with other communities. The Brahman, Salat, Sangharia and Vania do not allow them to touch their water vessels. A Dhobi is considered by them next to the Scheduled Castes and Siddi due to his task of washing the clothes of women after child birth and his consequent association with puerperal blood, which is particularly disgusted. They have their own crematorium. Brahman officiates at their life-cycle rituals and religious performances. One of the Dhobis, B.D. Modasia, fought for the Assembly seat from Diu constituency in 1972 and 1977. Their political leadership has emerged at village where they have representation in statutory village panchayat.

The Dhobi have a positive attitude towards the government development programmes. Boys study upto post-graduate level. Girls study upto secondary level and drop out from studies due to social reasons and as they have to earn to support their family. They make use of both the traditional and modern medicare. Their attitude towards family planning is favourable, but they prefer to have three children. They use modern methods for this other than sterilization. They avail of the facilities of drinking water through tube well and piped water, nutrition programme for the children through midday meal scheme, self employment, ration distribution system. They make use of electricity. Attitude to saving is favourable and they do not depend on money lenders. Firewood, cow- dung cakes and kerosene oil are the fuel sources. There is well net work of metalled road where they reside and which has linked them to other parts of Gujarat for transportation. They are exposed to mass communication.

N.K. Sinha

DHODIA

The community is called Dhodi or Dhodia by themselves. Others call them Dhodia. The community do not have any legend of their origin except that they are the descendants of the Rajput prince of Kathiawad. They migrated to Daman from Dwarka in Kathiawad. Antonio Francisco (1904:128) has discussed their habitation. Shah (1964:19) explains that the term Dhodia might have derived from '*dhur*' or 'soil' because the tribe is essentially agricultural and has to work on soil or the term seems to be derived from the Dhulia, a town in west Khandesh, from where they might have migrated. Supporting the above statements Roy and Rizvi (1985:48) note that the Dhodia trace their origin from Lord Krishna. They further say that the progeny of Dan Singh and Roop singh, the Rajput princes of Saurashtra and Lini and Chhan, the Naika sister's were latter referred to as Dhodia. They perceive their distribution in the villages viz. Kachigam, Dunetha, Dalwada, Zari, Patlara, Kadaiya, Moti Daman, Machhiwada and Magarwada of Daman. The total population of Dhodia according to Census of India 1971 (part-x - A9xB, series - 28, page-11 - 113) is 903. Dhodi is the spoken dialect within the community while Gujarati and Hindi are also used. Gujarati is the script for them. They are a Scheduled Tribe.

They are non-vegetarian who take the meat of goat, rabbit, fish and eggs, fowls and crabs occasionally. *Chokha* (rice), *jowar* and wheat form the major contents of their food. They also consume pulses of *tur* (red gram) and *mag* (green gram). The consumption of locally available vegetables is high. Fruits viz. *kela* (banana), *jamrukh* (guava), *keri* (mango) and barries are taken occasionally. *Daru* (alcoholic drinks) and toddy are commonly used by the men folk daily, as a digestive and for enjoyment, available in the market. They also take beverages like tea, milk and butter-milk. *Dhokra* (stuffed fried chapati), *lapses* (paste like preparation of wheat flour with ghee and sugar), *pla* (viryani), *sira* (porridge), *dud-h pak* (rice boiled in milk) and *farsan* (pakoda) are made use of on the festive occasion.

They are divided into nine exogamous divisions based on *kul* (clan) viz. Banjaria, Baria, Parsi Mehta, Dori Fudosi, Velghrahi, Mulgarahiya, Athi, Bamania and Bilarkhaw, Attara. Some of the clan names show the existance of totemism among them, e.g. Mul Garahiya (name of goat) Bilarkhaw (named after cat) etc. Enthoven (1920 : 330) has discussed forty two exogamous sub-divisions of Dhodia living in Gujarat and Maharashtra. Roy and Rizvi (1985 : 55) has discussed 183 exogamous divisions of Dhodia of Gujarat based on *jut* (clan). The basis of differentiation of *kul* is at social level. The chief function of these divisions are to regulate their marriage, to trace their descent and to participate in the life cycle rotuals. There is no hierarchy among these sub-divisions. They have started suffixing Dhodi and Patel to their names to maintain their identification. They place themselves superior to the Mangela, Dubla, Mahyavanshi, Christian and Muslim in the social hierarchy. They claim their position as Kshatriya. Others place them in the Vaishya order. They practise community endogamy and *kul* (clan) and village exogamy. Marriage is forbidden with in the four ascending generations from both the father's and the mother's sides. A girl is married after she attains puberty. Marriage is settled by negotiation and the form of marriage is monogamy. Premarital relations is forbidden. If it occurs with a boy and a girl within the community and of different *kuls* (clan), the girl is married to him after imposing fine on the boy by the *gnyat panch*. *Kali ganthi* (marriage pendant) is the marriage symbol. They have practice of *dej* (brideprice) in cash which has been fixed at Rs. 160/- by their *gnyat panch* (traditional council). Residence is patrilocal. *Far gati/Chhutta-chhedi* (divorce) is granted to both men and women by the Patel (chief of the *gnyat panch*). Who so ever approaches for divorce he/she has to pay fine imposed, ranging from two to five thousand, by the *gnyat* Patel. In case of women seeking divorce, she has to refund the brideprice with the fine. It is ascertained from the man and woman that they are not willing to live together. The amount of the fine remains with the *gnyat panch*. The usual grounds for divorce are quarrelsome nature, adultery, witchcraft and sterility to either of the spouce. Post - divorce maintenance is borne by her brother/ parents. *Natra* (re-marriage) is allowed between widow and widower and the divorcees. It also takes place through *devar nata* (junior levirate) and the regular form of marriage is resorted to in full while in other form a social sanction is needed from the *gnyat panch*. Rise in marriage age, self arranged marriage and matrimonial relation with the Dhodia of

Gujarat are the changes taking place after liberation.

Kutumb is the local term for family. Extended and nuclear families are common among them. It is a part of the kinship obligation of the brother to take care of his sister (speciality after divorce and in widowhoood) and widow mother. *Bhawad* (sister's husband) and mother's brother plays the role of *anvaro* (accompanier) and brings *maushala* (customary gifts of marriage dress) in marriage. Avoidance relationship is maintained between a woman and her *jethu* (husband's elder brother), *vevai* (father-in-law), *vevan* (mother-in-law). A *vaho* (daughter-in-law) must keep her head covered before the kins with whom she is to observe avoidance. Joking relationship is maintained between *devar* (husband's younger brother), *bhabhi* (elder brother's wife) with *hono* (wife's brother), with *hani* (wife's sisters) and with *nanai* (wife's brother wife). Conflict and confrontation start after son's marriage and father's death in property matters. The rule of male ultimogeniture for the residential land and male equigeniture for other properties are practised. Eldest son succeeds the authority in the family after father's death. Inter-family linkages can be envisaged during life cycle rituals, economic activities and during the election of *gnyat* Patel (traditional council chief). The significant change is the institution of family is the formation of nuclear family. A Dhodia woman has low status in the society. They have roles in agricultural operation, collection of fuel, bringing potable water and participation in ritual and religious spheres. They contribute to the family income after doing labour job in agriculture and in service. They do not have any role in political activities except to cast their votes in the periodical elections with the consultation of their male members. *Fui* (father's sister) plays an important role during *panchre* (fifth day ceremony after birth), *barse* (naming) and *mundan/chola* (tonsure) ceremonies. Changes have taken place in the ceremonies of death. Their life cycle rituals are common to all the Hindu communities of Daman except a few specific rituals which have been discussed in the Introduction.

Land is their major economic resource which is under control of the individual proprietors. They are a landowning community. The traditional and present primary occupation of the Dhodia is agriculture and its allied activities. Agricultural labourers and service in government offices are their other means of livelihood. Traditionally they held the land as tenants of the Koli Patel, Vania and Kamli Patel who used to pay revenue after collecting it from the Dhodia. The tenants had to pay 1000 *eskude* (Portuguese currency) as the annual rent to the landlord. Apart from that, half of the total produce went to the land owner. The Progressive Goa, Daman and Diu Mundarkar Act in 1976 protected the right of tenants and the Dhodia became the owners of land. The agriculture implements possessed by them are indigenous. The crop callendar is divided into three parts viz. *siara* (winter) *unadu* (summer) and *chaumasa* (rainy season). Chokha (rice), *jawar*, wheat, *ragi*, pulses like *tur* (red gram) *mag* (green gram) and vegetable are grown during the aforesaid crop calendar. They are mostly dependent on rain. A few of them avail the facilities of electrically handled pump. Vegetables are directly sold in the market of Daman. The Dhodia working as agricultural labour, get their remuneration in cash and kind both. The introduction of Porogressive Mundaver Act, supply of chemical fertilizer and good quality of seeds from the government agencies, development of Industrial complex facilities of the job reservation are the changes that have taken place in their economic life after liberation.

Though the introduction of statutory panchayat has reduced the authority of tribal council, the *gnyat panchayat* (traditional council) still exercises social control. The community have two tier system of council, viz. *faliya panch* (hamlet council) and *gnyat panch* (village council). The traditional council regulates their day to day activities of *faliya* (hamlet) under village. The *faliya panch* comprises a Patel (chief) and have it's jurisdiction with in *faliya* (hamlet), the *gnyat panch* consist of *falia* Patels as the *panchas* headed by the Patel and assisted by a *avaldar* (messenger) and are elected by voice vote. The *faliya* Patel takes care of the social problems within the *faliya*, while *gnyat panch* deals with the problem, not solved by the *faliya panch* specially the inter-caste marriage, premarital sex, adultery, divorce, betrothal and remarriage. *Gnyatbar* (excommunication) and *dand* (cashfine) ranges from rupees two to five thousand, are the forms of punishment imposed by the *panch*. An offender expiates after providing the community dinner. Planning and implemention of welfare and development activities are the role of modern statutory panchayat.

They profess tribal religion. They believe in supernatural as well as the spiritual power. They accord Brahmadev a pre-eminent position among all community deities. *Dev* is their family deity. They make offerings to the deities on Sundays. They worship their dead ancestors and prepare images of wood called Khatra Dev. Their other deities are Samra Dev (deity of cholera), Kakawalia (deity of smallpox), Sitla Mata (deity of misels), Petfori Mata (deity of evil eye) and Kansari Mata (deity of corn). They also believe in *bhut* (ghost) to whom a small quantity of food and drinks are offered on every feast. The *bhua* (magico- religious specialist) is responsible for protecting from the malevolent spirits, to mediate between them and the deities and to cure from the prolonged diseases. He is one of the most respected person in the village through whom the forces of evil spirits and sorceries are countered. They also worship the Hindu deities like Hanuman and Mahadev. Their main festival is Divaso (June - July) associated with *dingla dingli lagan* (mock marriage) carried out by the young unmarried girls. The observance of this festival provides acquaintance with the marriage rituals. The date of the festivals is fixed by the *gnyat Patel*. They also celebrate the other festivals viz. Vag baras (October-November) Diwali (October- Novermber), Holi (February - March) and Dussehra (October). Their main sacred centre is the temple of Samradev located at Rudvel village in the Chikhali Taluka in Gujarat whom they pay homage between Kartik (October) and Falgun (March).

They have musical instruments and *chundar* (tattooing) mark. *Tur* (double headed drum) and *thali* (brass plate) are their traditional musical instruments used during marriage and on other festive occasions. *Chundar* is used by the female folk which are made on arms, hand with red and black pigments. *Gher*, the main folk dance, is enjoyed by men and women along with the relatives and separately (with strangers) during the Divaso and marriage. The different types of *tune* and stepping for the dance are called *chal*.

The community have different objects of totem, viz. donkey, cock, fowl and cattle which are associated with social custom and belief. The sickle, which is used for agricultural operation, has also the cultural significance for them that it protects from the evil eyes and the witchcraft.

The traditional linkages of the Dhodias of Daman are in terms of the cultivator-lanmdlord relationship with the neighbouring communities specially with the Koli Patel and the Kamil. They take the services of the Dubla as *hali* (agricultural labourer). They consider themselves as good as Hindus and accept water, *kacha* and *pucca* food from the Koli Patel, Brahman, Kamli, Mitna, Bari, Sagar, Machhi and Mangela. They accept only *pucca* food from the Dubla. They consider the Mahyavanshi as unclean and lower in rank from whom they do not accept any food. They do not dine also with the Christians and Muslims. They have their own

of Gujarat. They perceive their position superior to the Mahyavanshi and Muslim in the social hierarchy. They resort to community and sub-group endogamy. Their rules of exogamy is applied to the extent that no marriage can take place between the four ascending generations from both father's and mother's side. They practise adult marriage. *Kari ghanthi* (marriage pendant) is their marriage symbol for woman. Marriage is settled by negotiation and self arranged and the form of marriage is monogamy. *Dhej* (bride-price) is fixed for Rs. 45/- by the *gnyat panch* (traditional council). Patrilocal and neolocal are the rules of residence after marriage. *Far gati* (divorce) is granted to both by the traditional council. While granting divorce a certificate is prepared in duplicate, signed by the husband and wife and witnessed by the *gnyat panches* (members) of both the sides. The divorce fee ranges from Rs. 1000/- to Rs. 1500/- which remains in the account of the *gnyat panch*. The bride-price is returned back. The usual grounds for the divorce are adultery, cruel treatment, neglect of household jobs, barenness, witch craft. The post divorce maintenance is borne by her parents and brothers. *Natra* (remarriage) takes place through *devar- batu* (junior levirate) and *saree- lagna* (junior sororate). Child marriage to adult marriage, matrimonial relations with the Dublas of Gujarat, self-arranged marriage and rise in divorce due to the industrial development at Sarnath in Daman and at Vapi in Gujarat are some of the changes that have taken place after liberation.

Kutumb is the local term for family. Their families are of extended and nuclear types. Men and women are equal partners in day to day life. The relations between husband and wife remains cordial. Avoidance relationship is maintained between a women and her husband's elder brother, wife's elder brother/sister, *Aja* (husband's mother) or parent-in-laws and all those who belong to the upper generations of her husband. A woman goes out side her house covering her head whenever she happens to meet her avoidance relatives. Joking relationship is maintained between *devar* (husband's younger brother) and *bhabhi* (elder brother's wife), with *dai* (husband's sister), and with *chali* (wife's younger sister) and *chala* (wife's younger brother). Kinship obligation towards brother, sister (specially after divorce and in widowhood) and widow mother is a part of the function of the family. Sister's husband has prescribed role of *anvario* (accompanier) and *mama* (mother's brother) to send the *maushala* (marriage gifts) during the marriage. The rule of male ultimogeniture for residential land and male equiginature for the other properties are practicised by them. Eldest son succeeds the *karta* (authority) in the family. Inter family linkages can be envisaged during the life cycle ceremonies, economic activities and during the election of *gnyat* Patel (traditional council chief). The significant change in the institution of family is the formation of nuclear family. Dubla women have low status in the society. They have role in agriculture operation, collection of fuel, bringing potable water and participation in social and religious rituals. They do not have any role in political activities except to cast their vote in the periodical elections. They contribute to family income by doing labour jobs in nearby industries, fishing and agriculture. *Fui* (father's sister) play an important role during *chhathi* (sixth day ritual after birth), *nampari* (naming) and *mundan* (tonsure) ceremonies. Sister plays the role of *karvali* (companion) during her sister's marriage. Elder brother's wife also has some role during marriage ceremony. The life cycle rituals are common as among the other Hindu communities of Daman except a few rituals which has been discussed in the Introduction.

Land is the major economic resource for the Dublas which is under the control of individual proprietors. The community have both land owning and landless classes. Agricultural labour is their primary as well as traditional occupation. Fishing labour is their other means of livelihood. The landless Dublas were provided with residential land by the Koli Patel, Kamli Patel, Vania and Dhodia, whom they served. A few of Dublas who own lands, do agriculture at subsistance level. They produce *chokha* (rice), *jawar* and *val* (a type of nut) and vegetables. They depend on their subsidiary occupation to run their livelihood. The agricultural labourers receive their remuneration in cash and kind. During the peak agricultural season, women are also engaged and they get cash plus one time food. Traditionally a few of Dublas held land as tenants of the Koli- Patel and Kamli Patel, and 50% of the produce went to the landlord. The agricultural labour worked as *hali* (labour on contract for the year), who got fifty paise and four *seers* (a unit of measurement) of *chokha* (rice), morning tea and tobacoo from his *dhani* (landlord). In case of the death of a debtor or creditor the contract ended and neither the credit nor the debt continues for the next generation. Women and children worked as domestic servants. They are also engaged as *khalashi* (fishing labourer) by the Machhi and the Mangela on contract basis for per season. They get their remuneration in cash plus food. Abolition of the feudal system, provision for the mechanisation of agricultural implements, distribution of agricultural land, abolition of bonded labour, distribution of fishing boats under Tribal Sub-Plan and development of the industrial complex and job reservation have provided the Dublas to enhance their economic conditions.

Social control is fully regulated by their *gnyat panch* (traditional caste council) at two levels viz. the *faliya panch* (hamlet council) and *gnyat panch* (village council). The *gnyat panch* regulates their daily activities within a *faliya* or village. The *falia panch* comprising of one member called *faliya* Patel (chief). The *gnyat panch* comprises of *faliya* Patel as *panchas* and headed by a Patel (chief) and assisted by one *avaldar* (messenger) who are elected by voice vote. The *faliya panch* takes care of the social problems within the *faliya* while the *gnyat panch* deals with the problems, not solved by the *faliya panch*, specially the inter-caste marriage, premarital relations, adultery, divorce, betrothal and remarriage. *Nat bar* (excommunication) is the form of punishment imposed by the *panch*. An offender expiates after providing community dinner. Planning and implementation of welfare and developmental activities are the role of modern statutory panchayat. Political organisation of the Dubla have under gone a change after liberation. The adult franchise has generated fraction among them. Though the periodical elections have given new lease of life to fraction among the Dubla but it has not succeeded in upholding the system of social control by the *faliya panch* or *gnyat panch*.

The Dubla profess tribal religion. Their religious beliefs and practices recognize the existance of two different sources of supernatural power viz. the spirits and the deities based on the Hindu mythology. Barham Dev is their house deity, Holi Mata is their family deity. Ashper Dev is their village deity. Their other deities are Malhwada Mata, Sitla Mata (goddess of smallpox), Mohavhu Mata (deity of pimple), Akashi Mata (deity of sky who protects from evil eye on the children), Bamania Bhoot (king of spirits residing near crematorium), Pet Fori Mata (protects from abortion), Kakawaliya (smallpox god), Marki Mata (deity of plague), Kansari Devi (deity of corn) and Khokholi Mata (deity of Cough). Dev (deity of corn) is worshipped on every festive occasions and in the begining of any auspicious work. *Bhagat* or *bhua* (magico religious specialist) is responsible for all the magico-religious pratices like protection from the malevolent spirits, to mediate between the Dublas and their deities and to cure chronic diseases. He is one of the respected persons in village to have special retained power through whose aid the forces of evil spirits or sorceries are countered. They worship also the Hindu deity, the Hanuman. Their main festival is Divaso, which is associated with the *dingla- dingla- lagan* (mock-marriage) ceremony by the unmarried girls. It signifies the sence that every Dubla girls expect to marry, the observance of the festival provides of acquaintance with the marriage rituals. It is celebrated between Jeth-Ashad months and the date is fixed by the Patel. They also celebrate other Hindu festivals like Navratra, Holi, Divali, Makar Sankranti and Dusehra, with full vigour. Some of the Dublas of Daman are active disciples of Swaydhay Parivar in the socio-religious movements started by Pandurang Sastri at Madhav Bag Pathshala at Bombay in 1987 with the aim and objective of self realisation, social service for the upliftment of the illiterates through the religious preaching of the *Geeta*. Faith on Jorawar Peer (mousoleum of a prophet) which is located in the Jogwad village of Valsad district of Gujarat, is the part of change that took place after the interaction with the Dublas of Gujarat.

They have the musical instruments and tattooing marks. *Sarangi* (violin), a musical instrument, made by themselves for the time pass recreation with the help of a musical bow which is made of bamboo sticks and hair of buffalo and skin of frog is used to make the strings of the violin. The nonmaterialistic object of culture is represented by *chundar* (tattooing marks), used by men and women which are made on arms, hand with red and black pigments. It is done with a fine needle or thorn of *babul* (accacia aribica) with the mixture of lamp black, a decoatation of beawood bark and juice of green leaves of *val* (creeper). After tattooing turmeric powder, believed to have antiseptic effect, is applied to the portion punctured and the person is advised not to apply water on the parts of the body so as to prevent from painful swelling. The most commonly used tattoo marks include a *buneli* (mark), *choful* (leaf shape mark) *morla* (peacock), portrait of deities and self name. *Gheriya* is the main folk dance enjoyed by men and women during marriage and Divaso festival.

The traditional linkages of the Dublas of Daman are specially with the Koli-Patel, Kamli and Dhodias for whom they worked as *hali* (agricultural labour). They accept water, *pucca* and *kacha* food from the Koli, Kamli, Mitna, Machhi, Mangela, Baria and Sagar. They consider the Mahyabanshi as unclean and of lower rank with whom they do not live. They consider themselves Hindu and do not accept food from the Muslims and the Christian. They have their own water sources, crematorium and temple. They are allowed to enter the kitchen of the above mentioned communities due to their long association and inter dependence at economic level. The Dublas of Vimpore participated in the liberation Movement in 1960. They have teachers and members holding white collar jobs. The periodical election of statutory panchayat and Assembly, land lord tenant relationship, employer- worker relationship in agricultura have given them the chance of modern linkages with other communities.

Their attitude towards the development programmes is positive. The literacy level has gone up. Both boys and girls study upto High school and drop out as they have to earn to contribute to their family income. They avail of the facilities of primary health centre, family planning (welfare), drinking water, training centre for self- employment through ITI, free electricity, midday meal for the children in the school under ICDS, public distribution system, revision of minimum wage policy. The Dubla who own land make use of chemical fertilizer and insecticides which they get from the government agencies. Though they avail of the banking facilities, they also depend on their landlords and employers when they need money. They are exposed to mass communication through radio, cinema.

N.K.Sinha

REFERENCES

Enthoven, R.E., *Tribes and Castes of Bombay*, Vol. I, 1920, Bombay, The Government Central Press, Reprint; Vol. I, p. 341, 1975, Cosmo Publications, Delhi.

Francisco, Antonio, *Noticas - E - Documentas - Para, A Historia De Damao*, Bastoria (Goa), Vol. II, page 128, 1904.

Raghavaiah. V., *Tribal Revolt*, Andhra Rashtra Adim Jati Sevak Sangh, Nellore, 1971.

Shah, P.G, *The Dubla of Gujarat*, Bharatiya Adim Jati Sevak Samaj, Delhi, 1958.

Sinha, N.K., 'Dubla Ethnography: Structure and Process,' Unpublished report submitted to An.S.I., 1983.

HADI

The Hadi are one of the Scheduled Caste communities. In the existing literature they have been described in general and they are distributed throughout the country, viz. Andhra Pradesh, Bihar, Gujarat, Maharashtra, Mysore, Orissa, Rajasthan, U.P. and West Bengal. Thurston (Vol. II C-1, page 313) says that the name was derived from '*haddi*', a latrine or '*hada*', bones, as members of the caste who collect all sorts of bones and trade in them. They trace their origin from the rishis of Pauranic period. The rishi once carried the body of a dead animal on his shoulder to throw out and was made untouchable by other members. Since then they were named as Hadi. Russell and Lal (1916 Vol. IV, page 216) described Hari synonymous with Hadi in Bengal which is supposed to derive from '*hadi*' 'a bone' and is the bone-gatherer and was familiar to early settlers of Calcutta. They further (Vol. IV, page 217 and Vol. I, page 367) described Hadis as the sweepers and the sub-caste of Mehtar of Bengal. Bhattacharjee (1968-page 249) has described Hari as scavengers and the carriers of nightsoil. According to Das, Roy Chowdhary and Raha (1966, page 40): "Hari is a menial and scavenging caste of Bengal whom Dr. Wise identifies with Bhumalis and regards them as the remnant of a Hinduized aboriginal tribe who were driven into Bengal by the Aryans or Mohammedans". According to *Brahmavaivarta Purana*, the Haris are born of the union of Let father and Chandal mother. Hadis in the territory perceive their distribution in the villages of Vanakvada, Ghoghla, Buchadwada and Gandhipara hamlet of Diu. They are also found in the neighbouring districts of Gujarat. The total population of Hadi in Diu district is 747 (including Bhangi, census of India 1971). Gujarati is the language as well as the script used by the Hadis. Besides Gujarati a few of them speak Portuguese and Hindi in relation to others.

Food habits of the Hadi are largely governed by the ecological condition, in which plenty of fish are available and being non-vegetarian they relish it. *Machhee* (fish), *chokha* (rice), *rotla* (bread of *bajra*) and pulses form the major part of their food. The available vegetables are also consumed. Fruits are taken occasionally. Alcoholic drinks and *neera* (toddy) are commonly used by them available in the market and which are considered as the digestive. The special food viz. *puri, lapsee* (paste like preparation), *pla* (biryani of rice and fish or mutton) and *potaya* (made of wheat flour, sugar, toddy after frying in groundnut oil) are made use of on the festive occasions.

Goter or *got* (clan) is the basis of social division among them. There are eight clans viz. Chauhan, Yadav, Waja, Jethwa, Makwana, Chudarma, Parmar and Rathod, found among them. They suffix the *goter* names to their names. They do not have stratification. The main function of clan is to trace the descent, to regulate the marriage alliances, role during the election of their Patel and worship during their life cycle rituals. They consider themselves higher to the Bhangis and lower to all other Hindu communities excluding the Vankars. They are aware of the *varna* and recognise their place as Shudra. The Hadi resort to community endogamy and *goter* exogamy. Cross-cousin (MBD) marriage is permitted. A marriage cannot take place without the permission of *gnyat* Patel, the chief of the traditional council. They practise adult marriage which was started recently. Marriage is settled by negotiation. They practise monogamy and the marriage symbol is *kanku* (vermilion) and *kach-korh-chudi* (bangles made of turtle-shell). *Dej* (bride price) is prevalent among them which is fixed to Rs. 500/- by the Patel. Patrilocal is the rule of residence for them. Seeking *chhutta-chheda* (divorce) is considered as social offence by them and is discouraged. *Ghad-ghada* is the local term for the remarriage which occurs only in case of death of either of the spouse. This is not a regular form of marriage and no rituals are performed. Approval from the *gnyat* Patel is ascertained and a paper is signed by the interested man and woman and a feast is given to the *gnyat panch*.

Kutumb is the local term for family. Extended and nuclear families are common. Respect, reverence and obedience for elders is reciprocated by love, affection, sympathy and assistance for youngers. The Hadi have the rule of male ultimogeniture to inherit the residential land and male equigeniture for other movable and immovable properties at present. If mother is alive, half of the property goes to her and rest is distributed among the sons. She has full right to give her property to any body during her life time. In absence of son, brother's son is adopted through the official procedures in court. Eldest male member of the family is regarded as the head of the family. After the father's death eldest son suceeds to the authority. In practice, the eldest son dominates the domestic scene so far the succession is concerned. Interfamily linkages become the natural phenomena for the Hadis in the birth, marriage and death, election of Patel, on religious festivals and economic activities. The joint and extended families have lost their significance giving way to nuclear family. Respect and obedience for the elders and for the head of the family have weakened.

Women have a role in economic, social ritual and religious spheres. They help their male members in family management and contribute to family income by doing labour and services. They have specific roles in the life cycle rituals specially during *nam pari*, (name-giving ceremony) of a child and marriage. Though men and women are equal partners in day-to day economic activities but status of women is considered lower than that of man and due to this their women do not find any place in the political activities.

The life cycle rituals are common to all other Hindu communities which have been already discussed in the Introduction.

The economy of the Hadis has been solely dependent on service since the Portuguese rule. They were employed by the Portuguese in police services and in their houses for cooking purposes. They are mainly a landless community. Their primary source of income now is through government service, mainly in Police Department, although the traditional occupation was bone-gathering and skinning of dead animals. The female folk engage themselves in the preparation of beds and quilts for which they get cash. Repairing of these are also to be done by them. In present situation their primary occupation consists of services viz. police, teacher, clerk, peon and jobs of casual labourer in building construction. Agricultural labour is their other means of livelihood. The extent of landlessness has influenced the rise in the number of labourers working in Diu and in the neighbouring districts of Gujarat. Payment of wages varies according to the nature of job. An agricultural and a casual labourer in P.W.D. receive their wages as per the approved government rates.

Social control is exercised by their traditional council. The traditional caste council, *gnyat-panch*, is at the village level only which is fairly effective in dealing with social disputes. The body consists of five elderly members of the community who elect the Patel (chief) by voice vote. The Patel is elected from the community on the basis of high social standing. The council functions at *baithak*, the fixed place. Social disputes pertaining to marriage, adultery, elopment etc. are referred to it for settlement. The *panch* imposes fines in cash which are some times awarded as compensation to the aggrieved person. Punishment is given in the form of excommunication also and the expiation of the person is done through feast to the community people. Seduction of an unmarried girl is also severly punished unless the boy is an eligible Hadi in which case marriage is insisted upon. After the liberation, the whole set up of administration and political organisation have undergone change. The village panchayat is introduced which does not have any interference with the traditional council. Of course, the periodical elections for panchayat and assembly have some linkages with the caste panchayat where the Patel is approached by the political parties. Thus the *gnyati-panch* widely effective authority in regulating caste affairs. Since obedience to the customs of the community is ensured, disputes are settled and reforms can be introduced by the *gnyati-panch*. The tenure of Patel stands for two to five years. Patels are elected from each clans on alternate tenure as per the norms of the community.

The Hadi believe in Hinduism. Their religious belief, rituals and practices recognize the existence of two supernatural powers, i.e. belief in spirits that inhabits certain localities and the belief in deities chiefly on Hindu myth. They have two types of deities, viz. clan and village deities. Ram Deva Pir is their village deity. Chamunda, Khodia, Sonal, Bhawani and Ghel Mata are the clan duties who have specific roles during birth and marriage. They are worshipped during these occasions. They have the temple of Ram Deva in the village which is maintained by the *panch* and religious duties are looked after by the community itself. They have belief in Kalika Mataji, located in the Patelwadi which is considered as shrine by them and where they fulfill their vows. The Hadi consider Somnath, Prachi and Delwada (temples of Lord Shiva in Gujarat) as their major centres for pilgrimage where they visit during Shravan month. Images of other Hindu deities viz. Shiva, Hanuman, Durga and Lakshmi are placed for worship. They offer coconuts to their deities and also make cash offerings. Goat is sacrificed to Kalika Mata occasionally to clear the *badha* (vow). *Bhua*, the magico-religious specialist, who cures ailments by envolving evil spirits while violently shaking their bodies. The acts of evil eyes, spirits are pacified by the *bhua*. *Darah*, a death ritual, discussed earlier, is a magico-religious practice to pacify the spirit. Their major fairs are Shravani

Poonam in Nagao village and Poonam Mela (full moon of the Chaitra month) near the Kalika Mata temple in Patelwadi. These two fairs are attended by all the Hindu communities. Ganesh Chaturthi, Janmashthmi, and Holi are the major festivals considered by them. The observance of these festivals are general to all other Hindus communities. They do not have fairs and festivals of their own except Ramapir Agiyarash. The change in the religious behaviour took place only after liberation when the Hadis were allowed to enter the Lord Krishna temple in Nagoa and Kalika Mata's temple at Patelwadi under the Protection of Civil Right Act, 1955.

The cultural elements are wall paintings during festive occasions and *chunder* (tattooing) etc. The tattoo marks used by Hadis are *choful* (leaf), *trishul* (trident), *marlo* (peacock) and figures of Lord Shiva and Hanuman and the names of husband and wife vice-versa. The tattoo mark is made just above the right hand wrist with the help of lamp black, beawood bark and juice of green *val* leaf (creeper), with the help of *occasia* thorn, a locally available thorn. Folk songs and folk dances are common to all other Hindu communities of Diu.

They maintained traditional linkages with the other communities at economic and social levels. They were economically dependent on the services to the Portuguese government where they had interaction with the officers. For necessary provisions they had to depend upon the Vaniyas. The Hadi play the role of drum-players during marriage, death and magico-religious rituals for other Hindu communities and get remuneration in kind. The feeling of untouchability has lessened and the Hadi are invited by the high castes during birth and marriage ceremonies, but they do not interdine. The relationship is maintained only upto exchange of gifts. The periodical elections for statutory panchayat, Assembly and Parliament seats have been the route of interaction for the Hadis with other communities and the political leaders of Diu district through *gynat-panch*. Participation in the multicaste religious fairs, festivals and visit of sacred centers like Somnath, Prachi and Delwada are the changes after liberation. *Gormaraj*, from their community, are called to perform the marriage rites and rituals and remunerations are paid in kind and cash. They accept water, *pucca* and *kacha* food from all the communities except the Siddi and Bhangi.

Their attitude is positive towards the development programmes introduced by the Union Government which have influenced their social and economic life. Socially, the feeling of untouchability has lessened. Economically, the Hadi are well benefited from the development programme initiated during the sixth five year plan in education, housing, employment (Reservation Policy), financial aids under IRDP for the self employment, health and medical care. Supply of drinking water, electrification, nutrition programme in running Balwadi under ICDS, provision of ration shops, construction of matalled roads and development of GIDC to give more job opportunities are the other facilities availed of. The administration is constitutionally committed to improve the quality of life of the Hadi. Each beneficiary family of the Hadi is provided with a copy of the *Vikas Patrika* (Identity card) and a duplicate copy of the same and is maintained in the Office of the B.D.O at Diu for the record. Fire-wood, cow dung cakes and kerosene oil are the fuel sources. They are exposed to mass communication by radio, cinema etc.

N.K.Sinha

REFERENCES

Bhattacharjee, J.N., *Hindu Castes and Sects*, Editions India, Calcutta, Page 249, 1968.

Census of India, Part X-A&B Series - 28, Goa, Daman and Diu, Panaji, Goa, 1971.

Das, A.K., B.K. Roy Chowdhary, and M.K Raha, *Handbook of SC & ST of West Bengal*, Director of Tribal Welfare Department, Govt. of West Bengal, Calcutta, page 40, 1966.

Hutton, J.H., *Caste in India*, Oxford University Press, Oxford, page 282, 1961.

Russell, R.V. and Hira Lal, *Tribes and Castes of the Central Provinces of India*, Vol. I & IV. 1916, London, Macmillan Company; Reprint, Vol. I & IV, pp. 367. 216-217, 1975, Cosmo Publications, Delhi.

Thurston, Edgar, *Castes and Tribes of South India*, Vol. II, 1909, Madras, The Government Press; Reprint, Vol. II, p. 313, 1975, Cosmo Publications, Delhi.

KAMLI

The Kamli, also known Kamaliya, are an agricultural community. No information regarding the origin of the community is available in the existing literature except that Anotonio Francisco (1904-128) has described them as the sub-group of the Koli. They, however, identify themselves as an independent community. According to their legend they migrated from Dwarka prior to the Portuguese established their rule and have a myth that they fought against Arjuna during the Mahabharata war. They are distributed in Varkund, Bhimpore, Magarwada and Dabel panchayats in Daman and Valsad district of Gujarat. Some, however, migrated from Daman to Mozambique during the middle of Portuguese rule where they occupied themselves in various jobs.

They are non-vegetarian and their staple food includes rice, *rotla* (bread of rice and *jawar*), *nagli* and fish. Pulses of *tur* (red gram) *mag* (grean gram) and vegetables are supplement to their staple food. Alcoholic drinks and toddy are enjoyed by the community regularly. *Lapsi, puri,* and *sire* are the special food used on the festive occasions. Nonvegetarian dishes are now common after their immigration.

The Kamli of Daman are divided into about two hundred exogamous divisions identified as *kutumb* (lineage). The basis of differentiation of *kutumb* is social through which they trace their descent. The chief function of lineage is to regulate the marriage alliances. There is no stratification among the lineages. They suffix 'Patel' to their names. They introduce themselves as Kamli Patel rather than Kamli. They perceive their position as inferior to the Brahman and Koli Patel and superior to the Machhi, Bhandari, Sagar, Bari, Mitna, Mangela, Dhodia, Dubla, Mahyavanshi, Christian and Momin in the regional social hierarchy. They are aware of the *varna* system and recognize their place as Kshatriya. They resort to community endogamy. Marriages are prohibited between the members of same lineage and between the four ascending generations for both the father's and the mother's sides.

Marriage is settled by negotiation and traditionally intiative was taken by boy's father. Now initiative is taken by girl's father. They practise monogamy. Adult marriage is the practice where the age of boys ranges from 22 to 25 years and that if girls from 18 to 20 years. A married woman wears *kali kanthi* (marriage pendant) as her marriage symbol. The practice of brideprice was the traditional norm and was fixed for rupees fifteen. Dowry in cash is permitted which ranges from Rs. 2000/- to Rs. 2500/-. *Chhute-chhedi* (divorce) is granted to both man and woman. It is granted by the *samaj* (traditional council) and the post-divorce maintenance is borne by her parents or brother. It is ascertained from the husband and the wife that they are not willing to continue living together. The usual grounds for the divorce are adultery, impotency, cruelty and insanity. Whosoever approaches for divorce, he/she has to pay a fine imposed by the *samaj*. They allow *natra* (remarriage) between widow and widower and the divorcees. *Deyar- batu* (junior levirate) and *saree- batu* (junior sororate) are permitted. Parents and brothers of the woman take the responsibility of getting the ceremony done. A feast is given to *samaj* and *kanku* (red mark on forehead) is put by the oldest female member of the bride side. If either of the spouses is a bachelor, the regular form of marriage is resorted to in full. They practise patrilocal rule of residence. Adult marriage, *prem lagna* (self-arranged marriage), decrease in divorce cases, bride price to dowry and matrimonial alliances with the Kamli of Gujarat are the recent changes in the institution of marriage.

Extended and nuclear families are common among them. They have prescribed kinship usages viz. Joking and avoidance relationships. It is the customary obligation to bring *maushals* (marriage dresses) and play the role of *anvario* (accompanier) by sister's husband during marriage. Conflict and confrontation arise after son's marriage and father's death in financial matters. Tensions among the family members result into breaking up of extended family into nuclear families. A widow also acts as the head of the family till the son/sons grow up. Inter-family linkages are maintained during the life cycle rituals, economic activities, religious functions and during election of samaj *Patel*.

A Kamli woman has a low status in the soceity. Right of inheritance is not granted to them. They assist in day to day life. Their roles are restricted to religious, social and economic fields. They are forbidden to interfere in political matters except to cast their votes in periodical elections. *Fui-* (father's sister) plays an important role during *barse* (naming) and *chaula* (head-shaving) ceremonies.

Rakhadi and *simant* are the pre-birth rituals performed in the fifth or seventh months of pregnancy and the expectant mother leaves for her parents for the first delivery. *Chhathi* is the first post-birth ritual performed on the sixth day after birth, followed by *barse* (naming) on the twelfth day by the *fui*. *Botan* (Ist cereal feeding) is performed in the sixth month followed by *chaula* (tonsure) in the third or fifth year after birth. They observe birth-pollution for forty days when a mother is restricted to enter the kitchan and to visit the sacred places. After that she returns to her husband. After the marriage alliance is settled, the first comes the *adarni* (betrothal) which takes place at the house of the groom one month prior to *lagan* (marriage) in the presence of *samaj*. Marriage is the matter of three days which takes place before the rain starts. The three days rituals starts with the erection of *mandva* (marriage booth) and installation of *gotrej* (lineage deity) on the first day. The maternal uncle brings *maushala* (customary gift of marriage dress) on the second day followed by *barghori* in the afteernoon. *Pithee* (mixture of turmeric and groundnut oil) is rubbed on the bodies of both the bride and the bridegroom for three days at their respective houses. The *jan* (marriage party), with the groom, arrives at the bride's village and are given *janivas* (separate lodging). The groom with the *jan*, arrives at the bride's house where he is received by the bride's mother near *toran* and *jaimal* (exchange of garland) is performed with the help of bride's brother's wife and *harwan* (groom's sister's husband). The principal ceremonies connected with marriage are *hast-milap, kanyadan, mangalfera*, wearing of *mangalsutra* and worship of *gotrej*. The family priest officiates at the marrriage ceremonies. The marriage dinner is given by the bride's parents and *jan* with the couples, returns back next day. In case of marriage ceremonies in day time, the *jan* returns on the same day in the night. *Ana* (return of the bride) takes place after three to five days which was earlier with an interval of one year. The Kamli cremate their dead with the exception of children below eight years and death casusing of smallpox are buried. The rites connected with death is performed by the eldest son, the chief mourner, who disposes off ashes and bones into the sea in the vicinity on the third day after cremation. The ceremonial impurity is observed for the first ten days after death. *Shraddhas* (ancestors' worship) are performed on tenth day (offering of rice ball to the departed soul), Eleventh day (shaving of head and noustaches and offering of a ball of cooked rice to the dead) and twelfth day (various utility articles designated for the use of the departed soul are presented to the family priest and caste dinner is given) and the funeral rites come to and end. They observe death pollution for ten days.

Land is the major economic resource for them. They are mainly a landowing community and the land is controlled by the individual proprietors. Agriculture is the present day primary occupation as well as the traditional occupation. Agricultural activities include the production of crops viz. rice, *jowar, ragi,* pulses of *tur* and *mog* at subsistence level. The agricultural implements possessed by them are indigenous. They are mainly dependent on rain water. The crop calendar is divided in to three parts namely *siara* (winter), *unadu* (summer) and *chaumasa* (rainy months). Apart from these they also produce vegetables which they sell in daily regulated market at Daman in cash and in exchange of kind. Masion work, carpentary, agricultural labour and casual labour are the other means of their livelihood. Land tenure system is also prevalent, locally termed as *bhagidar*. The cultivator's share varies from 40 to 60 per cent but landowner has to bear the cost of seeds and ferrtilizers. Wages are paid in cash for a labourer and for a mason. Salt production and establishment of small scale industries are the changes took place in their economic activities.

Their *samaj* (caste council) operates at two levels viz. *Kamli samaj* at village level head by Patel and assisted by five *sabhya* (members) and Samast Kamli Samaj at regional level headed by a Pramukh assisted by *upapramukh, karbhari* and fifteen Patels of the villages of Daman and Gujarat. The heads of the councils are elected by voice vote. Social problems partaining to the deviation from the traditional norm, marriage, interfamily disputes are dealt with at the village level and the religious and social reforms are dealt with at the regional council. Excommunication and cash fine are the forms of punishment imposed by the *samaj*. Plan implementation and welfare and development activities are the role of modern statutory panchayat.

The Kamli are Hindus. They worship all Hindu deities and observe all the Hindu fasts and feasts but their favourite object of worship is Lord Krishna. They also believe in ancestral worship. The lineage deity is called *gotraj*. Holi Mata, Laxmi Mata are their village deities. The newly married couple are supposed to pay homage to the said deities, next day of marriage. *Gotrej* is worshipped in a special manner on the *athem* of *maha* (Magh month). Other deities, worshipped, are Kanhari before harvesting, Vaghyo (before the onset of harvesting), Ravli (prior to start of evening) and Mahhar Deo (protection of crops from diseases). Dwarka in Gujarat is their main sacred centre. Their main festivals are Diwali, Holi, Balley (Raksha Bandhan) Janmashtami and Bhai Duj. Another festival is Shravani Poonam, lies on the full moon of Shravan month, associated with the worship of sea-god. The sacred specialist is from other community who helps them in paying homages and in officiating at life cycle rituals. They do not have any specific element of art and culture except *satiya* (floor design) and *chundar* which are common to all the Hindu communities of Daman and *Koli* dance which is also common to the Machhi and Mangelas. Both men and women participate in dance. Folk-songs related to birth and marriage are sung by women only.

Economy has been the prime factor in their traditional linkages with the other communities specially with the Dubla, Koli Patel. They have the relationship of receiving and rendering of services with the Koli Patels. Landlord-tenant reltionship exists with the Koli Patel, Dubla and Dhodia. Brahman is invited to officiate at life cycle ritals. They accept water, *kacha* and *pucca* food from the Brahman, Koli Patel, Bhandari and Vania. *Dharma behan* (putative kinship) is maintained with the Koli Patel and Machhi. They share the water resources with the other communities. They have their own crematorium and temple. They took part in political movement for the liberation of Goa, Daman and Diu in 1958. The periodical elections have opened the route of the modern linkages with the other communities. The community has businessmen. Political leadership has emerged at village panchayat.

The literacy level among the boys has gone up. They study upto secondary level and drop out if there are economic reasons. They do not send the girls to school after seventh standard due to socio-economic reasons. They avail of all the civic facilities, viz. electricity, education, water, health and family welfare, public distribution systems, post office, organic manure and chemical fertilizer, mid-day-meal scheme for the children, ICDS and banking. The development of small scale industries has provided them with opportunities for self-employment.

N.K.Sinha

REFERENCES

Francisco, Antonio, *Noticas-E-Documentas Para, A-Historia De Damao,* Bastoria (Goa), Vol III, page 128, 1904.

KHARWA

The Kharwa are said to be the original fishing community of Diu. The Gujarati term '*kharwa*' denotes 'sailor' or 'sea-man'. Others, at the same time, consider the 'Kharwa' as the dwellers near the *kharapani* (saline water). Their legends say that they are the descendants of the Rathod Rajputs who, on destruction of Kannauj, migrated from Rajasthan to the coastal areas of Sourashtra region of Gujarat viz. Bhidiyaplat, Verawal, Madwad, Mul Dwarka, Kodinar, Sutrapada, Dhamrech, Hirakat and settled there. In course of time, some of them migrated to Diu piror to the Portuguese established rule in the region. Subsequently, due to geographical and other ecological conditions the migrants took to the occupation of fishing and sailing. At the same time the term 'Kharwa' came into existence (Sinha, 1980). Sherring (1881) has described them as one of the exogamous groups of Tanwar/Tawar Rajputs as well as the exogamous group of Rathods of Rajputana. They are distributed in Ghogla and Vanakbara villages. Majority of Kharwa population from Vanakbara village migrated to the coastal areas of Saurashtra region viz. Madhwad, Muldwarka, Sutrapada and Veraval. The Kharwa from Ghoghla migrated to Navabunder, Bombay, Okha and Mithapur after the relation between the Government of India and Portugal became tense and the area of sea-hunt was restricted in 1954. They are also distributed in the coastal areas of the adjoining districts of Gujarat. Gujarati is the language within the community of Ghoghla which is pronounced defferently. English is also spoken by a section of the community. But the people are conversant more with Hindi and Gujarati. Gujarati is their script.

Food habits of the Kharwas are largely governed by the ecological conditions where plenty of fish are available. They are non-vegeterian. They eat egg, fish and meat of goat and fowls. Fish, rice and *bajra* form the major contents of their food. They also consume pulses like *tur* (red-gram) and *urad* (black gram). Consumption of vegetables viz. *bateta* (potato), *ringna* (brinjal), *dudhi* (pumpkin) is very low and that too on three days, viz. second day after *poonam*, *amabashya* (moonless night) and *chaudas* (fourteenth day after *amabashya*). Fruits viz. *kel* (banana), *jamruhh* (guava), *sitafal* (custard apple), *keri* (mango) and *darham* (pomgranate) are taken occasionally. Alcoholic drinks are commonly used by them daily as a digestive and for tiring jobs which they purchase from market. They also take beverages like tea, milk and butter milk daily. *Puri* (fried bread), *farsan* (pakoda), *lapsee* (pastelike preparation of wheat flour and ghee), *pla* (biriyani of rice, fish/meat/vegetable), *potaya* (prepared of wheat flour, sugar, toddy after frying in groundnut oil) and *dudhpag* (porridge) are made use of on the festive occasions like Dulhandi, Ujjani, marriage and Diwali.

They are divided into 27 exogamous groups based on *got* (clan) which are suffixed as their *atak* (surname). These are Kotiya, Gohel, Daree, Anjani, Fanjaree, Lodhani, Tawadi, Dalki, Khokani, Kudai, Doria, Fofandi, Mashani, Khapandi, Motivarsh, Shiyal, Vandarvola, Morvi, Vandaria, Khoraba, Solanki, Homania, Chudasama, Baria, Kamalia, Patelia and Kapadia. Out of these Kotiya, Gohel, Daree, Anjani, Panjari, Lodhari, Tawadi and Dalki are residing in Vanakbara while Solanki, Bamania, Chudasama, Baria, Kamalia, Patelia and Kapadia are in Ghogla. The basis of differentiation of *gots* is at social level through which they trace their descent. The chief functions of these sub-divisions are to regulate marriage, to trace descent and to participate in the life cycle rituals. There is no hierarchy among these groups. They were not allowed to add their surname during Portuguese rule and gradually they forgot their *got* names; but maintained their *gotrej* (*got* deity) in their house which restricted the chance of marriage within the *got*. They could recollect their *got* names after the liberation when situation permitted their interaction with the Kharwas of the coastal area of Saurashtra region of Gujarat. They perceive their status as inferior to the Brahman, Vania and Salat. They are aware of the *varna* system and recognize their place as Kshatriya. They practise adult marriage and the age ranges from 22 to 25 year in case of boys and 18 to 22 years in case of girls. A difference of three to four years between a boy and girl is maintained. Marriage within the village is preferred. They practise monogamy. Polygyny is permitted in case of issueless wife or if she is bounded by certain physical weakness or disease. They allow *devarbatu* (junior levirate) and junior sorrorate. These are not strict rules and the consent of the spouse is necessary for such union. *Kanku* (red vermilion mark on the forehead) and *bangdi* (bangles of turtle shell and ivory) are marriage symbols of women. Besides, a newly married girl is recognised with her colouring of teeth with some locally available fruits which lasts for six months. They have the practice of *dej* (bride price) in kind only. *Chhutta-chhedi* (divorce) is granted to both man and woman by the Patel (chief) of the *gnyat-panch* (caste council). Who soever approaches for divorce he/she has to pay the fine imposed by the Patel. Out of the total fine, one third is to be paid to him/her and two third to the *gnyat-panch*. In granting divorce the *lagna-no-kagaj* (marriage bond), signed by the husband and wife during their marriages, isreturned to the husband by the wife or her guardian. The usual grounds for divorce are quarrelsomeness at home, adultery, neglect of household duties and the sterility of either of the spouse. In case of sterility, insanity and incurable diceases, the divorce is granted easily by the Patel without any fine. The postdivorce maintenance is carried by her brother/parents. *Natra* (remarriage) takes place through *devar-batu* and *sartee-lagna* (junior sororate). But the most common form of remarriage is between a *randel* (widower) and *randeli* (widow). In this form of marrriage if either of the spouses is unmarried, the regular form of *lagan* (marriage) is resorted to in full. A girl after marriage goes to stay with her in-laws. A few changes have been reported in marriage rules i.e. increase in marriage age, emergence of neolocal residence and matrimonial relation with the adjoining coastal are as of Gujarat.

Kutumb is the local term for family. They have extended and nuclear families. Men and women are equal partners in every day economic activities and social and other perviews. The relation between a husband and a wife remains cordial. Respect is duly paid to the elders. Elders assist and look after the youngsters as part of obligation. Joking relationship is maintained with elder brother's wife, wife's younger sister/brother, wife's younger sister's husband, sister's husband's sister/brother and younger brother's parent-in-laws. Avoidance relations are maintained with wife elder brother, husband's elder brother, mother's brother's wife and parent-in-laws vice-versa. Female members are supposed to veil their face from whom they observe avoidance. Confrontation and conflicts start after father's death and after son's marriage in property matters. This tension scale, among the family members, results in the breaking of joint family into nuclear family. Sister's husband has prescribed role of *harvan* (accompanier) during marriage. Male equigeniture is the rule of inheritance for them. In absence of son, female equigeniture is followed. Mother's brother sends the marriage dress, *maushala*, to his sister's son/daughter's marriage. Eldest son succeeds the authority. Inter-family linkages are maintained during the life-cycle ceremonies, economic activities and during the election of *gnyat* Patel. The significant change in the institution of family is the formation of nuclear and nascent families due to the confrontation after father's death. A Kharwa women has a low status in the society. Men and women are equal partners in every day economic activities. *Fui* (father's sister) performs the *nam-pari* (naming) and *bal-maudi* (tonsure) ceremonies. The folk songs and *garba* folk dance are performed by female folk only. They also have a role in social and religious rituals. They do not have any role in political organisation except to cast their vote in the periodical elections in consultation with their male members.

Life-cycle rituals are common to all the Hindu communties and this has been discussed in the Introduction. Some of the funeral rites are performed only among them and the Koli. If a child dies within a week after birth, *tutko* is performed so that the next baby may not face the same fate. *Neel* (ghost marriage) is performed by the sacred specialist to pacify the soul in case a boy dies without marriage. In the process, a cow is ceremonially married to a bull. In case of an unmarried girl a *kwarkan* (stone pillar) is installed near the house. Prachi (in Gujarat) is fixed for the *neel* which is part of addition after liberation. When a person dies in sea and his body is not recovered, all the funeral rites are performed in absentia as usual during the fishing off season when all the relatives and the *got* members remain in the village. A date is fixed for the cremation by the *gnyat* Patel and an effigy, representing the dead, is made of banana plant, oyster and pomegranate which is carried in funeral procession and finally cremated. Inter-caste marriage (with Vanja and Koli) is a part of change, though in such case the Kharwa excommunicate the boy/girl.

Water is the main resource for the Kharwas which is under the control of government. Fishing and sea-manship are the present primary occupation for the community. Both fishing and sea-manship are their traditional occupation. It has already been discussed earlier that they are the original fishermen of Diu. They have three forms of fishing equipments viz. *jhar* (net) *khunti* (hook) and *jharee* (small net) with the help of unmechanised and mechanised boats. The surface drift nets, bottom set gill nets and *ojha* (Japanese style net) are used for fishing with *lodhiya*, *machaa* (big boats) and *hodi* (small boats). The fishing expeditions are carried out for 24 to 48 hours which require four to five members of the crew viz. a *tandal* (captain) and *khalasis* (labourers). They do not carry their catch from the boat to their houses but deliver it out right to the agencies with whom they have entered into contract for the year. They take the money in advance and supply the catches on their return from expedition right at the jetty. Castlelock Company of Bombay and Konkard company of Goa are having their agents in Vanakbara and Ghogla. The average yield is about 3000 to 6000 pieces per expedition. *Bichiro* (pomfret), *palwa, titan* (lobster) and *jambo* (prawn) have great demand in Japan, Iran, Canada and other European countries where the fish are exported by the companies. The trade of dry fish, viz. *tora* (perch fish), *datree* (red snapper), *kanti* (rajor edge) and *bumla* (Bombay Duck) is carried upto the required places in the country. The owner of the boat enters into contract for *tandel* and *khalasis* for the whole season who get their remuneration in cash every month excluding three times food a day. Fishing women labourers are required only after the return from the expedition. They also receive their wages in cash on monthly basis plus two time food daily and full body garments per season. In case of joint fishing the total catch is divided in seven parts. Two parts of the catch go to the owner of the boat and engine and remaining five parts are distributed among the members of the expedition.

Sea-manship is the other occupation for them. This occupation takes them to all parts of the world. Though they went only up to East and South African during Portuguese time, now they are taken to Middle East and South East Asia, Europe, America, China and Japan. This occupation does not always give them work all the year round. They have their names registered in the Employment Exchange at Surat and the Sea-men's Employment Office in Bombay after getting three months training at Navlakshmi (Gujarat), Vishakhapatnam (Andhra Pradesh) and at Calcutta. Preference for such type of training is given to boys belonging to sea faring families. Sea-faring among the Kharwas of Ghogla goes on generation after generation, and naturally has its repercussion on their mental attitudes and social atmosphere. It brings young and enthusiastic persons directly in contact with the people of other countries which makes them smarter and broadens their outlook. Almost every Kharwa family in Ghogla has sea-men. Due to the closure of most of the private shipping companies, the unemployment problem for the sea-men has aggravated not only in Diu but through out India. They have therefore adopted the occupation of fishing and fishing labourer as the secondary one. Teaching and services in government offices are other means of livelihood. The Directorate of Fisheries, in order to improve the fish production in Diu, introduced a scheme for the mechanisation of fishing craft viz. in and out bord engines, manufactured by Kirloskar (India), Torpelo (Yugoslavia), Yama (Japan) and Ruston (India) in 1969. The facilities for the mechanisation of the fishing craft have been provided on loan-cum-subsidy basis. The indigenous method of fishing is used only during off season for shore fishing.

The traditional caste panchayat regulates their daily activities within a *chora* (hamlet) or village or at regional level. Each *chora* has its Patel (chief) from the community. The *gnyat panch* of the village consists of Patel and *sabhya* (members) who are also the *chora* Patels. Patel is elected by voice vote. *Mehta* (accountant) and *mukadam* (messenger) are nominated by the Patel from the community. The tenure of Patel changes every year. The meeting and the proceedings take place at the house of the Patel. A turban is tied on the head of the Patel after his election. The traditional caste council at regional level is called *Bargam-Khrawa gnyat* with its headquarters at Porbandar, represented by the Patels of twelve places of Gujarat and Diu. The chief is called Banat. The function of the *gnyat panch* is to link the members of the community, to punish the miscrants, to prevent breach of customary laws, and to adjudicate on civil and other social squables which may upset the equilibrium of the community. They also take decisions in economic and religious matters. Excommunication and cash fine are the forms of punishment imposed by the *gnyat panch* in case of the breach of traditional norms and rules by the organisation regarding inter-caste marriage, adultery and avoiding the order of the Patel. Cash reward has been introduced recently to encourage the students who secure first and second positions in their classes. The *gnyat panch* still holds the Kharwa population of Diu in its thrall. Even the developmental programmes of the statutory panchayat cannot be carried out without taking into confidence the *gnyat panch*. Inter-caste marriage is the prime offence for them. The *bargam gnyat* is called to discuss any social problem pertaining to their traditional norms and values.

As Hindus their religious belief and ritual practices mostly centre around Hindu mythical deities. Gomti Mata is their village deity which is fully maintained by them. The *goter* deities are Lunai Mata, Khetra Pad, Bhawani Mata and Harsiddhi Mata who are worshipped during life cycle rituals and before doing any auspicious work. Kalinki Mala is the regional deity at Buchadwada for them and the newly married couple is supposed to pay homage next day after marriage. Gupta Prayag, Somnath, Amba Mata and Harsiddhi Mata (all in Gujarat) are the major sacred centres for them. The sacred specialist helps them in making religious offering and homages during the visits. Maghi (associated with the worship of lord Shiva and Parvati) and Narial Poonam are the major festivals, associated with the worship of sea-god, for them which falls on the fullmoon day of Sharavna month. Ujjani, another festival is celebrated on Ashadh Poonam in the form of picnic by the unmarried boys and girls. The *got* deities are worshipped by the married men and women at the respective temples in the morning and the picnic is organised there after. *Namiya* is the festival connected with fishing, which is celebrated after the interval of six months every year, on the boat, for their safty and better sea-catch. The magico-religious practices of the Kharwas are based on the belief in both the malevolent and benevolent spirits living around the villages which can be made subservient to human needs if care is taken not to offend the spirit. *Karbhar* is associated with this which is performed by the *bhu* (magico-religious specialist) on Chaitra Shukla Chaturthi. *Bahan* is performed the same day in the night to ward off the malevolent spirits from their villages. Magico-religious activities are observed throughout the life cycle rituals. They celebrate other Hindu festivals like Diwali, Holi, Janmasthami, Navratra and Ramnavmi with full vigour. Poonam Mela is the most important religious fair celebrated at Kalinki Mata temple at Buchadwada on Chaitra Poonam which is common to all the Hindu communities of Diu.

The tattoo marks *(chundar)* are made on arms, hands, feet and chest with the greenish, black and red pigments. It is done with the help of a thorn of *occasia* and a mixture of lamp black, a decotation of beewood bark and juice of green leaves of *val* (creeper). The tattoo marks include *choful* (leaf-shaped mark), *trishul* (trident), *satia* (a holy mystic symbol), *morlo* (peacock) are tattooed to ward off evils by the potency of these names and marks. *Dandia Ras* and *garba* are the folk-dances enjoyed by them which are common to all other Hindu communities during the festive occasions.

They accept water, *pucca* and *kachha* food from the Koli, Brahman, Vania, Soni Salat and share with the Koli only. They share well and water with all the Hindu communities except the so called untouchables. They share crematorium with the Koli. They are traditionally linked with the

Kolis in economic sphere. Inter-community linkages are maintained during the Poonam Mela which stresses the relationship of brotherhood with all the Hindu communities of Diu. The periodical elections for statutory panchayat, Assembly and Parliamant establish modern linkages with other communities. Brahman's assistance is sought during the life-cycle rituals. Hadis are invited as the drum-beaters during the life-cycle ceremonies and the magico-religious practices. They have doctors, engineers, teachers and other members holding white collar jobs. Political leadership has emerged at regional level.

Their attitude towards development programmes is positive. Though education up to Higher Secondary is favoured for both the boys and girls but the girls drop out of school going due to socio-economic reasons. They make use of both traditional and modern medicare and methods of family planning. They avail of the facilities of water and electricity supplies within their localities. The provisions for loan-cum-subsidy have enabled them in the mechanisation of fishing industries. They use firewood, cowdung cakes, kerosene oil and LPG as fuel resources. They appreciate the government nutrition programmes. They avail of the facilities of ration shop, child and mother-care under ICDS and self employment. The construction of Thud bridge between Diu and Gujarat has provided them transport facilities for their trade in fish. One of the significant features in the life and culture of the Kharwas is their *gnyat-panch* having its own constitution which has largely remained unchanged for centuries. The most powerful one is of the Kharwa *gnyat-panch* of the Ghogla village. Various government agencies, while implementing programmes, always take the *panch* into confidence for getting better results.

N.K. Sinha

REFERENCES

Cabralesa, Mario, "Beyond Freedom and Dignity," Times of India Publication, Bombay, *Illustrated Weekly of India*, November 3, page 58, 1985.

Chib, Sukhdeo Singh, *This Beautiful India*, The Union Territories of India, Light and Life Publication, New Delhi, page 93, 1977.

Sherring, M.A., *The Hindu Tribes and Castes*, Vol. III, 1879, Calcutta, Thakar Spink & Co.; Reprint, Vol. III, pp 27 & 46, 1974, Cosmo Publications, Delhi.

Sinha, N.K., "Funeral Right Among the Fisherfolk of Diu", Indian Anthropological Association, Delhi, *Indian Anthropologist*, Vol. 9, No. 1, pp. 35-40, 1977.

Sinha, N.K., 'Study of Ethnography and Change in a Diu Village,' Unpublished report submitted to Anthropological Survey of India, 1980.

KHOJA

The Khoja are a community of Muslim traders. The meaning of the word '*khoja*' in Sindhi or '*khwajah*' is 'traders'. They perceive their origin from the Hindu trader castes of Sindh who were converted to the Ismailia Sia sect by Muhmmad Sadra-ud-din, the *pirtan* (saint), after discovering divine power in him during their journey for trade. Pirtan Sadr-ud-din, a converted Hindu servant of Imam Hasan, the third successor of Hasan Saheb, came to India from Iran about 700 years ago and proceeded to Kathiawad, Gujarat. Later, Khojas settled in different parts of India. Sherring (1975-Vol.II-241) says that the Khoja are the converted Hindu of Bhatia caste. While Russell and Lal (1975:461) say that the term 'Khojah' is a corruption of the Turkish 'Khwajah' meaning 'lord' which is supposed to be a Muhammaden equivalent for the title Thakur applied to the Lohanas, the Hindu trading caste of Sindh who were converted by Pir Sadr-ud-din, an emissary, who preached that his master Hasan was the Nishkalanki or the tenth incarnation of Vishnu. The Khoja of Diu immigrated from Kotra, Timbi and Kodinar in Gujarat. Suleman Jeeva was the first to settle down in Vanakbara village about four generations ago. They are distributed in the villages of Ghogla and Vanakbara of Diu and also in Gujarat. They use Gujarati for reading, writing and speaking. They are also conversant with English and Hindi. They dress like Gujarati Hindus.

The Khoja are non-vegetarian who take fish and the meat of goat and fowl. Though taking of beef is not prohibited but they do not take it. Their staple food includes *bajra*, wheat, *chokha* (rice) and pulses of *urad* and *tur*. They moderately use vegetables. Fruits are taken occasionally. Men take alchoholic drinks and toddy regularly. They also take beverages like tea, milk and buttermilk. They are fond of chewing betel and smoking cigerette. *Biriyani* (fried rice with meat or fish), *kurma* (meat or chicken curry), *lapsee* (wheat flour fried in ghee mixing sugar and boiling in water) and *dudh-pag* (porridge) are the special food preparations made on the festive occasions.

They are endogamous and belong to one lineage of Suleman Jeeva through whom they trace their descent. They consider the Brahman, Salat, Sangharia, Vania, Kharwa, Koli and Vanja as superior and the Kumbhar, Vankar, Hadi, Bhangi and Siddi as inferior to them in regional social hierarcy. They resort to exogamy at sibling level. Both cross-cousin and parallel cousin marriages are permitted. They practise adult marriage. Marriage is settled by negotiation. *Sarhee-lagna* (junior sororate) is permitted. *Kanku* ((red mark on forehead) *kadedy* (finger ring) and *bangri* (bangles) are the marriage symbols for women. They have practice of *mehr*, which is fixed at Rs. 5000/- and is paid on demand if divorce takes place. Rule of residence is patrilocal. *Chhutta* (divorce) is permitted. Either men or women can approach for divorce to the *jamat* (traditional council) who has authorrity to grant it. Adultery, maladjustment, cruelty and insanity are the reasons for divorce. Compensation is given to the aggrieved party as decided by the *jamat*.

Avoidance relationship is maintained between a daughter-in-law and father-in-law, with younger brother's wife and with husband's elder brother. Joking relationship is maintained between elder brother's wife and younger brother, with wife's elder brother and wife's younger sister. Conflict and confrontations arise in property matters after father's death. All sons get equal share in the property. Women, in the family, have roles in collection of fuel, bringing potable water and doing other household jobs. They participate in the economic activities and contribute to family income by doing teaching etc. They are forbidden to interfere in political affairs. *Fui* (father's sister) plays an important role during *nampari* (naming) and *balmaudi* (tonsure) ceremonies.

The interesting feature of their life-cycle is that they retain some of the Hindu customs. *Kholo-bharo* is the prebirth ritual performed in the seventh month of pregnancy and the expectant mother leaves for her parent's village. *Dayan* (traditional local nurse) attends to the delivery. *Chhathi* (sixth day ritual after birth) is followed by *nampari* (naming) by the *fui* (father's sister) in the evening. They observe birth pollution for forty days. The first pollution bath takes place on sixth day after birth followed by baths on tenth, 20th, 30th and 40th days. *Bal-maudi* (tonsure) is performed by the barber after the completion of one year with the help of *fui*. *Sunnat-sadi* (circumcision) is performed after the completion of five to six years by the barber who gets his remuneration in cash and kind. A community feast is given in the night. A girl in her menses observes pollution for five days. *Sagai* (betrothal) takes place one year prior to marriage. *Lagan* (marriage) is a simple affair of a day only which is solemnized at the *khojakhana* (sacred place). *Pithee* (mixture of turmeric and groundnut oil) is rubbed on the bodies of both the bride and the groom before the marriage. Marriage takes place in May at *khoja-khana* during the religious gathering of the community. The gathering is called at the different places of Gujarat and at Vanakbara village in Diu as decided by their Chief Councillor of inter-regional traditional council. Both parties arrive at the *khoja-khana* or *jamat-khana* on the auspicious day where the bride and the groom are seated opposite each other in front of the portrait of His Highness the Aga Khan, their Imam. Missonary (sacred specialist) recites the marriage acceptance which is repeated by the bride and the groom. Marriage contract is prepared as per the Holy Constituion (Article 9) of the Shia Imami Ismailia, the Pavitra Bandhana, in triplicate and signed by the bride, the groom, fathers of both, the Missionary and witnessed by the Mukki (chief of traditional council). Bride and the groom exchange finger-ring and after that the *barmal* (exchange of garland) is performed. Marriage dinner is given jointly by both the parties. This is a community marriage initiated by the Khoja to avoid expenditure and save on time. Sometime *sagai* (betrothal) also takes place at the religious gatherings. In case the marriage is solemnized at their respective houses, the marriage dinner is given by the bride's parents. During the marriage at *khojakhana*, marriage fee is collected from both the parties and is sent to His Highness the Aga Khan by the Mukhi through All India Federal Council of Ismailia at Bombay. The consummation of marriage takes place at the groom's residence. They bury their dead. The funeral procession reaches the *khojakhana* with the corps for the prayer for the peace of the departed soul. The funeral rites are performed by the eldest son who acts as the chief mourner. While burying, two small peices of round silk cloth are kept over the eye of the corps. The *samuhik-lagna* (community marriage), held at *khojakhana* during the religious gathering, is a post-liberation arrangement to minimize the marriage expenses where rich or poor can afford easily.

Business and trade are their traditional and present day primary occupation. They are enterprising businessmen who have extended their trade in various parts of Gujarat and Bombay and also in Middle East countries. They had trade links with other Portuguese colonies in Africa till 1961. Their main trade is of dry fish and transportation of fresh fish to the bigger fishing agencies in Gujarat and Bombay. Kirana shops, hotels and service in different government offices are their other means of livelihood. They have direct link with the daily market and the transaction is made in cash.

Traditional councils operate, namely *jamat* at village level, council at district level, council at regional (state) level and council at national level. *Jamat* is headed by Mukhi (chief) assisted by a *kamada* (accountant). Mukhi also works as the religious head of the village. The district council comprises the Mukhis of all *jamats* in the district of Diu. It was previously a part of Una (Gujarat) council which was included in Junagadh council after 1961. The regional or state council is headed by the President which has five boards namely Audit Board, Welfare Board, Youth Board, Religious Ismailia Association and Housing Board to look after various problems of the community. The All India Federal Council at national level is headed by His Highness Prince the Aga Khan with its headquarters at Bombay who also appoints the Presidents of regional councils. They have well defined Holy constitution which consists of 180 Articles called *Pavitra Bandhana*. Excommunication was the earlier form of punishment. Presently expulsion form all the religious activities is the form of punishment. Plan implementation and welfare and development activities are the other activities of modern statutory panchayat.

The Khoja are the followers of Siya Imami Ismailiya sect. His Highness Prince the Aga Khan, 49th descendent of Imam Hazrat Ali, is the religious head of the sect which was founded by Hasan Sahab. As mentioned earlier one of their *pirtans* (emissary), Mohammed Sadra-ud-din, came to India from Iran and converted the Lohanas and preached that the master Hasan was the tenth incarnation of Vishnu. He also studied Hindu religion and its sacred books and Gujarati language in Kathiawad. *Khojakhana*, in the respective villages is their sacred centres where they pay visit daily with their family members in the evening for the prayer in front of the portrait of Prince the Aga Khan. The proceeds of the purchase and sale of the food preparations are given to the *khojakhana*. *Deedar* (meeting) and blessings of His Highness Prince the Aga Khan is considered sacred. Mukhi of the *jamat* also acts as their sacred specialist in paying homages. The religious gathering is called once is a year at any place in the state which is decided by the President of the regional council. Ujaini (picnic) is also celebrated by the community members in Ashadhmonth. Id-ul-zuha and Id-ul-fitr are their major festivals. They have the tradition of singing folk song for marriage, birth and prayer in praise of the Aga Khan.

Trade and business has been the prime factor in their traditional linkages with all the communities specially the Koli, Kharwa and Vania. They accept water, *kachha* and *pucca* food from the communities other than the Hadi, Vankar, Bhangi, Kumbhar, Dhobi and Siddi. *Dharm behan* (putative kinship) is maintained with the Koli when they visit the house of the putative kin for tieing *rakhi* on Raksha Bandhan. They have their own religious places and burial grounds. They participate with the Koli, Kharwa, Vania and Vanja in marriage ceremonies. They share drinking water sources with other communities. The Hadi play the role of musicians during their marriage ceremony. Employer-worker relationship exists with the Koli. Political leadership has emerged at regional level. The community has enterprenuers and teachers.

Their attitude towards formal education is positive for both boys and girls. Boys study up to postgraduate level and drop out from studies as they have to support their family. Girls also study up to graduation level and drop out from studies due to social reason. They make full use of the system of modern medicare. They do not favour family planning and prefer to have four or more children. They avail of the facilities of drinking water through dug well and piped water, self employement in general merchandise, transport and contractorship, electricity, midday meal under nutrition scheme, ICDS and ration distribution system. Firewood and kerosene oil are their fuel resources. Their attitude towards saving is favourable and they avail of the facilities of banks for loan and saving purposes. The network of road has linked their villages with Diu to the Municipal area and the places of Gujarat for transportation. They are exposed to the mass communication.

N.K. Sinha

REFERENCES

Russell, R.V., and R.B. Hiralal, *The Tribes and Castes of the Central Provinces of India*, Vol. III, 1916, London, Macmillan and Company; Reprint, Vol. III, p. 461, 1975, Cosmo Publications, Delhi.

Sherring, M.A., *Hindu Tribes and Castes*, Vol. II, 1879, Calcutta, Thakar Spink & Co.; Reprint, Vol. II, p. 241, 1974, Cosmo Publications, Delhi.

Sinha, N.K. 'Study of Ethnography and Change in a Diu Village', Unpublished report submitted to Anthropological Survey of India, 1980.

KOLI

The Koli, also known Machhi Koli, are a fishing community. They explain that the term 'Koli' has been derived from the Roman word 'coolie' which means porter. They were employed as porters, carriers, sea-man and fishing labourers by the Kharwa community during the Portuguese regime. Another version tells as that the word '*korhi*' means robber. Sinha (1980) says that Ramnik Lal, a retired school teacher in Diu, derived the Koli from the word '*kol*' meaning 'machhava' or boat. They were well-known as sailors since the ancient times. They were described as notorious sea-pirates operating from their bases on the long and conveniently broken coast line of Saurashtra and Gujarat. Whenever piracy was rendered difficult or impossible by organised efforts of the government they fell back upon farming the land. They claim to be descendants of Rajput. One of the then states of Gujarat was ruled by a Koli king in 1583 who repulsed the attack of Portuguese. Their legends say that they are the descendants of Pandavas who spent one year of the exile in this island. Their surnames and *goter* (gotra) names lead to the inference that they were connected with the Rajputs. These statements, regarding their history of origin, were supported by Enthoven (1920), Russell and Lal (1916), *Gazetteer of the Bombay Presidency*, *Census of India* (1961) and Baines (1976). Regarding their migration to Diu they recall that after invasion of Mahmood Ghazni on Gujarat, some of them left the state of Patan and Kathiawad and settled in the coastal region of Saurashtra, i.e. Okha, Porbandar, Verawal, Jamnagar, Dwarka and island of Diu. Some of Kolis, however, migrated temporarily to Mozambique during the middle of Portuguese rule, where they occupied themselves in various jobs, viz. dock porters, massons and mine labourers and after making a sufficient fortune, returned to their places to spend the evening of their lives.

They are divided into three endogamous divisions on the basis of occupation viz Rajput Koli (fisherman), Khedut Koli (agriculturist) and Kadia Koli (mason). They are distributed in Vankakbara, Bucharwada,

Ghogla, Fudam and Diu municipal area. They are also distributed in the coastal areas of the Saurashtra region of Gujarat. Gujarati is the language as well as script for them. They speak Hindi, English and Portuguese

Food habits of the Kolis are largely governed by the ecological condition. They are nonvegetarian. As Diu is located on the seashore, it has provided them with plenty of fishes. They eat egg, fish, meat of goat and chicken. Fish, rice, *gehu, bajra* form the major content of their food. They also consume pulses like *tur* (red-gram) and *urad*. The consumption of vegetables is very low and that too permitted on three prescribed vegetarian days, viz. second day after *Poonam* (full moon), *Amabashya* (moonless night) and *Chaudash* (14th day after *amabashya*). Fruits are taken occasionally. *Daru* (liquor), is commonly enjoyed by them daily as a digestive. They also take beverages like tea, milk and butter milk daily. *Puri* (fried bread), *farsan* (pakoda), *lapsee* (pastelike preparation of wheat flour and ghee), *pla* (viriyani of rice, fish/meat/vegetables), *potaya* (prepared of wheat flour, sugar, toddy after frying in groundnut oil) and *dudhpak* (porridge) are made on the festive occasions like Dhulendi (Holi), Uijani, marriage and Diwali.

In all they have fifteen exogamous sub-divisions based on *goter* which are common to all the three endogamous sections of the Koli. They are Bariya, Bamania, Solanki, Chudasama, Waja, Rathod, Damya, Vaishya, Chawda, Charaniya, Sikotariya, Gathla Waja, Banslemti, Kathi, Fatla and Jethwa. They suffix the *goter* with their names. The basis of differentiation of the *goter* is at social and territorial level through which they trace their descent. The chief functions of *goter* is to regulate marriage, trace the descent and help participation in the life cycle rituals. Machhi Koli consider themselves superior to Khedut and Kadiya Koli being economically sound and they consider themselves as heir of Rajput Koli. There is no stratification among the *goter*. During the Portuguese rule the government ordered them not to suffix the *goter* to their names. In course of time they forgot their *goter* names but maintained their *gotrej* (clan deity) in their houses. The chances of marriage within the *goter* did not take place as all the *goters* have their own deities. They could recollect the *goter* names after the liberation when opportunities arose for their interaction with the Kolis of the coastal areas of Gujarat, viz. Jamnagar, Verawal, Okha, Porbandar, Kodinar and so on. They perceive their position as inferior to the Brahman, Vania, Sangharia and Salat. They are well aware of the *varna* system and recognize their place as Kshatriya.

They resort to community endogamy and *goter* exogamy. They practise adult marriage and the age ranges from 22 to 25 years for boys and 18 to 22 years for girls. A difference of age by three to four years between a boy and a girl is maintained. Marriage within the village is preferred. Monogamy is the most familiar way of acquiring mates. Polygyny is permitted only in case of issuless wife or if she is afflicted by certain physical weakness or diseases. They practise *dervatu* (junior levirate) and junior sororate. *Kanku* (red vermilian mark on the forehead) and *bangdi* (bangles of turtle shell and ivory) are the marriage sysmmbols. Apart from these a newly married girl is recognised through the colouring of teeth by some locally available fruits which lasts for six months. They have practice of *dej* (brideprice) in kind only. *Chhutta-chhedda* is the local term, used for divorce and the right is granted to both men and women by the Patel (chief) of *gnyat panch* (traditional caste-council). Who so ever approaches for the divorce, he/she has to pay fees imposed by the Patel. Out of the total fees, one third is to be paid to him/her and two third to the *gnyat panch*. In granting divorce the *lagna-nokagaj* (marriage bond), signed by the husband and wife during their marriage, is returned to the husband by the wife or her guardian. The usual grounds for the divorce are the quarrelsomeness at home, adultery, neglect of household duties and sterility of either of the spouses. In case of sterility, insanity and incurable diseases, the divorce is granted easily by the Patel without any fees. The post-divorce maintenance is carried by her brother/parents. *Gharagharu* (remarriage) takes place through *der-batu* (junior levirate) and *sarhee-lagna* (junior sororate). But the most common form of remarriage is marriage between a *randela* (widower) and a *randel* (widow). In such marriages if either of the spouses is a bachelor, the regular form of *lagan* ((marriage) is resorted to in full. Patrilocal is the rule of residence. In changing situation marriage age has increased, emerging out of neolocal rule of residence, and matrimonial relations are maintained with the adjoing areas of Gujarat.

The Koli consider *kutumb* (family) as consisting of members living, eating and working jointly in a house. It is very vague term and includes, in its ambit, the nuclear family, the extended family, the joint family and a still larger group comprising the near kins on the paternal side. Nuclear and extended types are common. Men and women are equal partners in every day economic activities both in fishing and agriculture and social or other problems. The relation between husband and wife is cordial. Respect is duly paid to the elderly members. Elders assist and lookafter the youngsters as part of their affection and obligation. Joking relationship is maintained with the elder'brother's wife, wife's younger sister, wife's younger sister's husband, sister's husband's sister, brother and younger brother's parent-in-law. Avoidance relationship is maintained with the wife's elder sister, parent-in-laws vice-versa, mother's brother's wife. Female members keep their face veiled in front of the avoidance relatives. Conflict and confrontation arise among the family members after son's marriage. The sense of rivalry, jealousy and quarrel start among the brothers and sisters-in-law on property after the death of father . This tension scale in the family results into breaking of extended family to nuclear family. Sister's husband plays the role of *harvan* (accompanier) during marriage. Male equigeniture is the rule of inheritance for them. In absence of son, it is the rule of female equigeniture. A person has heavy obligation towards his old mother and people will remind him about it repeatedly. Mother's brother sends the marriage dress to his sister's son/daughter. Eldest son succeeds to the authority in the family after the father's death. A widow also acts as the head of the family when her sons are immature. Inter-family linkages are sought during the life cycle ceremonies, economic activities and during the election of *gnyat* Patel. The significant change in the institution of family is the formation of nuclear and nascent families due to family tension after the death of father. A Koli woman has low status in the society. Though their involvement in economic activities is quite important but they do not have decision-making powers. They have roles in fishing and agricultural operations. They also have roles in social finctions, rituals and religious sphare. *Fui* (father's sister) has important roles in *nampari* and *balmaudi* (tonsure) ceremonies. Folk songs are sung by the female members only. They do not have any role in political sphare except to cast their votes in the periodical elections with the consulation of their male members.

The rites-de-passage are common to all the Hindu communities of Diu which has been discussed in Introduction. They do not perform sacred thread ceremony. Marriage season of Rajput Koli differs from Khedut Koli. Rajput Koli perform marriage during rainy season (fishing off season) while the Khedut Koli perform before the rain starts. This season is also associated with their nature of occupation. The important feature of death rites is that all funeral rites are performed in absentia if a person dies in sea and his body is not recovered. An effigy of the deceased is made from banana plant, oyster and a pomegranates, carried in funeral procession and finally cremated as per the date fixed by the *gnyati* Patel. They perform all other death rituals so that the departed soul would no longer remain agressive to the fishing parties.

Land and water are major economic resources for the Koli. Fishing is the primary job for the Rajput Koli and for Khedut Koli, it is agriculture. The control of water resource is exercised by the government. The community have a combination of both the landowning and landless. It has been already discussed earlier that the three occupational divisions of the Koli have different primary occupations for them, viz. fishing and allied activities, agriculture and massonary. Traditionally the Koli were sea-men and fishing labourers. They shifted to fishing when the loan-cum-subsidy facilities were provided by the government after liberation. They have three forms of fishing namely by *jhar* (met), *khunti* (hooks) and *jharee* (small net) with the help of mechanised and non-mechanised boats. Tralling boat, *lodhiya* (big boat) and *hodi* (small boat) are used for fishing. The first mechanised boat was introduced by the Rajput Koli of Vanakbara in 1971. They go for fishing expedition from 24 hours to 48 hours with four to five crews viz. one *tandel* (captain) and *khalasis* (fishing labourers). The Rajput Koli do not carry their catch from the boat to their homes but deliver it out right to the agencies with whom they entered into contract for the year. Castlelock Company of Bombay and Konkad Fish company of Goa, Pithadia, Kana Sham etc., have their agents in Vanakbara, Ghogla and Diu municipal area. The fishermen take the money in advance and supply the fish after their sea-hunt. The trade runs for both the fresh and dry fishes. The average yield is about 3000 to 6000 pieces of different varieties per expendition. Pomfret, lobster and prawns have great demand in Japan, Iran, Canada and other Europeon countries where the fishes are exported by the companies. The trade of dry fishes viz. *tora* (Perchfish) *datree* (Red snapper), *kanti* (Rajor edge) *bumla* (Bombay duck) are carried to these demanded places in the country. The total catch is divided into seven parts. Two parts of the total catch go to the owner of the boat and engine, and remaining five parts are distributed among the five crews. Some time wages is paid in cash to the five crews by the owner.

The present day primary occupation of the Khedut Koli is agriculture and its allied activities. Agricultural labourer, fishing labourer and sea-men are the secondary one. Traditionally they held the land as the tenant of the Vanias who paid the revenue after collecting it from the Khedut Koli. The tenant had to pay 100 *escuda* (Portuguese currency) as the yearly rent to the Vanias. Apart from that, half of the total produce went to the landowners. The agricultural implements possessed by them are indigenous. The crop calendar is divided in the three parts, viz. *siara* (winter), *unadu* (summer) and *chaumasa* (raining season). Wheat, *bajra* (millet), *jowar* (barely) pulses like *tuar* (red gram), *urad* (black gram), *sing* (ground nut), *mardiya* (sweet potato) and vegitables like *ringna* (brinjal), *dudhi* (pumpkin), *turiya* (sponge gord) and *gwar fali* (beans) are grown during the above crop calender. They are mostly dependent on rain as the sea ecology has provided the saline water in the region. The Progressive Goa, Daman and Diu Mundakar Act in 1976 protected the right of tenants and the Khedut Koli became the owner of land. The Kadia Kolis have massonory work as the primary occupation. Casual labourer is the secondary occupation. Kadia Kolis from Diu have been working in Mojambique and Lisbon since Portuguese time. Vegetables and sea-products are directly sold in the markets in Diu and the negibouring areas of Gujarat, viz. Kotra, Una, Kodinar and Verawal by the producers itself. Change after liberation with the mechanization of fishing implements, from indigenous method to Japanese method of sea-hunt, freedom for deep sea-hunt, the feudal system abolition, supply of chemical fertilizer and good quality of seeds from the government agencies and cooperative societies have played an important role in the Koli's economy. Interaction in the field of economy in the large areas was accorded.

Their social control was studied under the formation of traditional councils and their function. The village organization of the traditional council, i.e. *gnyati panch* (caste council) which regulates their daily activities within a *baithak* (ward), *wadee* ((hamlet) and village or Diu as a whole. Each *baithak* has a Patel (chief) from the community. Each villages has a *gnyati panch* represented by the Patels of *baithak* and *wadee*, as the *sabhya* (member) who elect the President (chief) of Samast Koli Rajput Gnyati (caste council at village level) by voice vote. *Mahamantri* (accountant) and *kotwal* (messenger) are nominated by the Patel out of its members. The tenure of Patel remains for two years. *Samaj bhavan* is the place in the villages for meeting. After the election of Patel, a turban is tied on his head. Samast Koli Gnyati Samaj, (regional council) is represented by the villages of Diu, Madhvar, Kotda, Veraval, Sutrapada, Ghogla, Porbunder, Kodinar who elect a Chief Patel by voice vote. Social problems pertaining to inter-caste marriage, adultery, disobeying of the Patel's order, breach of the traditional rule are dealt by the *gnyati panch.* They also take decisions in religious and economic activities i.e. looking after fishing and agricultural matter and organize the religious fair and gatherings, excommunication and cash fine, ranges from Rs.1000/- to Rs.5000/- are the form of punishment imposed by the *gnyati panch.* Apart from the traditional caste council the traditional village *panchayat* is also in existence which is represented by the Patels of different *gnyati panchas* (caste councils) where inter-caste disputes and issue pertaining to periodical elections are solved. Plan implementation and welfare and development activities are the role of modern statutory panchayat. Political organization of Koli have under gone changes after liberation. The adult franchise has generated divisionness among them and is not held as conductive for the caste unity. Though the periodical elections have given new lease of life to faction among the Kolis but it has not succeeded in upholding the system of social control by *gnyati panch.* The traditional council seems to more powerful than the village statutory Panchayat.

The Koli profess Hinduism. Their religious beliefs and ritual practices recognize the existence of two different sources of supernatural forces namely the spirits and the deities based on Hindu mythology. Gomti Mata, Vadli Mata, and Holi Mata are the village deities. Their *Gaur Matas* (clan dieties) are Moti Samadh Mata, Khodiya Mata, Shikotar Mata, Gadhechi Mata, Nani Samodh Mata, Som Mata, Vadli Mata and Jethwa Mata who are worshipped in the life cycle rituals and before doing any auspicious work. Kalinki Mata, at Patelwadi, is the regional deity for them. The newly married couple are supposed to pay homage to the deity next day after marriage. They consider Gupta Prayag, Som Nath and Amba Mata (all in Gujarat) as the major sacred centeres. The sacred specialist help them in the religious offerings and homages during their visit. Their major festivals include *Gaur Mata* festival which is considered as Nav Durga and which lies on Prathama, Duitiya and Tritiya of Shukla Paksha in Chaitra month with the significance of *goter* deities worship. This is the festival of the Koli only in Diu. Narialpoonam/ Shrawani Poonam/Mahi Bij, another major festival celebrated on fullmoon of Shravna month with the significance of worship of sea-god. Ujjani is celebrated on Ashadh Poonam and extends for seven days in the form of picnic by the unmarried boys and girls. Seven days are fixed for the seven religious places in village where the married men and women worship different deities namely Kala Pani Mata, Bhawani Mata, Maha Kaleshwar, Hanumanji, Gomti Mata, Wadli Mata and the unmarried girls and boys enjoy the days with special food preparation and folk dance. *Bara Murat* and *Namiya* are the festivals connected with fishing for the Rajput Koli celebrated after every six month on the boat for safety and better sea-hunt. The magico-religious activities of the Koli are based on the belief in supernatural being living in and around their villages which can be made subservient to human needs if care is taken not to affend the spirit. *Karbhar* is associated with this, which is performed on Chaitra Sukla Chaturthi by the *bhu* (magico-religious specialist). Same day in the night *bahan* is performed when the *bhua* calls the spirit on his body so that no malevolant spirit enters their villages. Magico-religious activities are observed in the various walks of life right from pregnancy, birth, marriage and death. They celebrate the other Hindu festivals like Diwali, Holi, Janmasthmi, Ram Navami with full vigour. Poonam Mela is the most important religious fair celebrated at Kalinki Mata temple on Chaitra Poonam. This is the common festival for Diu. The Koli, from the neighbouring villages of Gujarat and even those are working in Mojambique visit the temple on this auspicious day. Importance of Jala Ram Satadhar, a saint from Gujarat is the recent change in the religious life of the Koli of Diu. The saint was from Lohana caste and was great devotee of Lord Krishna and Rama who died at Birpur in Junagadh district of Gujarat. The Koli consider the place as the centre for pilgrimage. They consider *pujari* and *bhua* as the sacred specialists who look after the temple and their worship and supernatural being of nature and spirits.

The Koli do not have any materialistic cultural element. The non-materialistic cultural element possessed by them is *chundra* (tattooing). The tattoo marks are made on arms, hand, feet and chest with the greenish, black and red pgiments. It is done with a fine needle or a thorn of *ocacia* with the help of a mixture of lamp black, a coat of bea-wood bark and juice of green leaves of *val* (creeper). After the tattooing, turmeric powder, considered as an antiseptic effect, is applied to the portion punctured and the person is advised not to apply any water for some time to the parts of the body, tattooed, so as to prevent from painful swelling. The tattoo marks include *choful* (leavf shaped mark), trishul (trident), *sathiu* (a holy a mystic symbol), *morlo* (peacock), *kunda-ne-ful* (pot with flower plant). Images and names of deities are tattooed to ward off evil by the potency of these names and marks. *Dandiya Ras* and *garba* are the main folk-dances enjoyed by both the male and female separately on the festive occasions which is common to all the Hindu communities.

They accept water, *pucca* and *kacha* food from the Kharwa, Brahmin, Vania and share with the Kharwa. They share well and water with all the Hindu communities except the Hadi, Vankar, and Bhangi. Traditionally they are linked with the Kharwa, Vania and Soni in the fishing and agricultural activities. They share the crematorium with the Kharwa. The Kadia Koli maintained the relation with all the communities of Diu in economic sphere due to the occupation of masonry. Inter-community traditional linkages are sought in religious sphere during the Poonam Mela which brings a relation of brohterhood with all the Hindu communities. The Brahman priest attends to the life-cycle rituals. The Hadi are invited as the musician during the life cycle rituals and magico-religious practices. In political sphere, the traditional village *panchayat* brings the route of interaction of the Koli with the Kharwa, Soni, Vanja and Vania. The periodical elections for panchayat, Assembly and Parliament have given the route of modern linkages with the other communities and the political parties. They maintain production relation with the Kharwa in fishing activities. The Khedut Koli have become the owner of land and they employ Vankars as agricultural labourer during peak agricultural season. The feeling of untouchability has lessened. They have doctors, engineers, advocates, teachers, businessmen and members holding white collar jobs. Political leadership has emerged at the regional level. Members of the community actively pasticipated in the liberation movement of Diu in 1960-61 specially Dr. Bawa Rama Solanki.

Their attitude towards the development programme is positive. Literacy has gone up both among the boys and girls. Boys study up to college and postgraduate level and drop out from study as they have to earn to support their family. Girls study upto secondary level and drop out of school going due to socio-economic reasons. Though the modern medicare is favourable for them, they make use of both modern and traditional medicare (magico religious practice). They favour family planning programme and prefer to have three children. They avail of drinking water facilities through piped water and wells and make use of electricity. The provision of loan cum subsidy has provided the Koli in the mechanization of fishing industry and modernization of agricultural activities. They use fire wood and cowdung cakes for cooking.

Kerosene oil and cooking gas are the addition fuel resources after liberation. They are mainly dependent on rain water. In absence of rain even the well, dug by themselves or by the government agencies becomes dry. They make use of chemical fertilizer and insecticides from the Agriculture Department and the officials visits them time to time for the demonstration. They avail of the facility of child and mother care under ICDS, ration distribution system. The construction of Thad bridge between Diu and Gujarat has provided them transport facilites for the trade of fish, vegetables and food grains to the markets in Gujarat. Other media of mass communication are radio, T.V., newspaper and cinema, etc.

N.K. Sinha

REFERENCES

Baines, Sirathelastane, *Ethnography: Caste and Tribes*, Concept Publishing Company, Delhi, page 53, 1976.

Census of India, *Village Survey Monograph of Magdalla of Surat District*. Vol. V, Part VI, No. 2, page 35, 1976.

Enthoven, R.E., *Tribes and Castes of Bombay*, Vol. I, 1920, Bombay, The Government Central Press, Reprint, Vol. I, p. XVIII, 1975, Cosmo Publications, Delhi.

Gazetteer of Bombay Presidency - *Thana*, Vol. XIII, Part II, Bombay, Pages-453-544.

Russell, R.V. and R.B. Hiralal, *Tribes and Castes of the Central Provinces of India*, Vol. III, 1916, London, Macmillan and Company; Reprint, vol. III, p. 532, 1975, Cosmo Publications, Delhi.

Sinha, N.K., 'Funeral Rites Among the Fisher Folks of Diu', *Indian Anthropologist*, Delhi, Vol. 9, No. 1, pp. 35-40, 1979.

Sinha, N.K., 'Study of Ethnography and Change in a Diu Village', Unpublished report submitted to Anthropological Survey of India, 1980.

KOLI PATEL

The Koli Patel are also known Koli. They suffix 'Patel' to their names as their *atak* (surname). They explain that the term 'Koli' has been derived from the English word 'coolie' meaning 'porter' or from Gujarati word '*kori*' meaning 'robber' as they were employed as porters and carriers in the shipping dock during the Portuguese regime. They are well known sailor and sea pirates since the ancient times. They claim to be descendants of Rajput. Once the region (part of Ram Nagar state) was ruled by a Koli chief who was defeated by the king of Chittorh. *Gazetteer of Goa, Daman and Diu* (part-II:16) says that the Rajput king Ramashah, after losing his ancestral patrimony from Udaipur during the Muslim conguest, came down to south and seems to have defeated the Koli chief Nathoaut and established himself in the hilly tract at Asheri or Assersata near Daman about A.D. 1262. They fought against the Portuguese and caused heavy loss to them during their invasion. Roy (1983 : 29) has discussed the episode. Their *got* (clan) names lead to the inference that they are somehow connected with the Rajput. Sherring (1879:308) says that in the sixteenth century the king of Ahmednagar had Koli soldiers in the armies. Enthoven (1920:XIII) and Baines (1976 : 53) have discussed the origin of the Koli. They have been residing in Daman prior to Portuguese established their rule which has been supported by Antonio Francisco (1904 : 128). Some of them however, migrated temporarily to Mozambique during the middle of Portuguese rule where they occupied themselves in various jobs. They introduce themselves as Patel as the term 'Koli' refers to 'coolie' or porter. They perceive their distribution in the village of Vimpore and Kadaiya. Some how they are also distributed in Maharashtra and Gujarat. Gujarati is the language as well as the script within the community. They are also conversant with Hindi and Portuguese in relation to others.

They are non-vegetarian. They eat egg, meat of fish, and goat and fowls. Their staple food include rice, wheat, *jawar*, fish and pulses of *mag* (green gram) and *tur* ((red gram). They also consume vegetables, viz. *bateta* (potato), *ringna* (brinjal) *dudhi* (pumpkin) etc. Fruits are taken occasionally. Alcoholic drinks are enjoyed by the community men regularly while the women folk take *tadi* (toddy). They also take beverages like tea and butter-milk. *Puri* (fried bread), *dudh-pak* (rice boiled in milk), *sira* (porridge), *lapsi* (paste-like preparation of wheat flour sugar and ghee) and *pla* (fried rice) are made use of on the festive occassion. They are fond of smoking *bidi* and cigarette and chewing betel.

The Koli Patel are divided into seven exogamous sub-divisions based on *kul* (clan) namely Mor, Sarwaria, Chowdhara, Jogi Rathor, Solanki and Agri. The basis of differentization of the *kul* (clan) is social through which they trace their descent. The chief functions of the sub-divisions are to trace their descent and participation in the life cycle rituals. There is stratification among the *kuls*. They perceive their position inferior to the Brahman in the social hierarchy and consider superior to the Kamli, Bhandari, Baria, Sagar, Machhi, Mitna, Mangela, Dhodia, Dubla, Mahyabanshi, Muslim and Christian. They obviously have a high status due to their traditional occupation of settled agriculture. They are well aware of the *varna* system and recognize their place as Kshatriya in the *varna* order. They resort to community endogamy and *kul* and *faliya* (hamlet) exogamy. They practise adult marriage and the age for boys ranges from 20 years to 25 years and that for girls from 16 to 21 years. A difference of three to four years of age between a boy and a girl is maintained. Marriage is prohibited within the four ascending generations from both the sides. Monogamy is the form of acquiring mates. Marriage is settled by negotiation and initiated by the girl's party. *Kanku* (vermilion mark on the foreahead) and *kali-kanthi* (marriage pendant) are the marriage symbols for women. *Dej* (dowry) is paid in kind and cash viz. clothings, ornaments and furniture and amount ranges from Rs. 1000/- to Rs. 5000/-. *Far-gati/Chhutta-chhedi* are the local term for divorce. The right is granted to both man and woman. It is granted by *samaj* (traditional council) and the post-divorce maintainance is carried by her parents/brother. The usual grounds for divorce are quarrelsome nature at home, adultery and sterility of either of spouses. *Natra* (remarriage) takes place between a widow and a widower and the divorcees. It also takes place through *dever-nata* (junior levirate). Generally the parents and brothers take the responsibility of getting the ceremony done. A drink party is given to *samaj panch* and a *tika* (red mark on the forehead) to the woman by the eldest member of the female side. If either of the spouses is bachelor, the regular form of marriage is resorted to in full. Matrimonial relations with the Koli Patel of the neighbouring areas of Gujarat and adult marriage are the part of changes that have taken place recently.

The Koli Patel consider a *kutumb* (family) as consisting of members living, eating and working jointly in a house. They have practice of extended and nuclear families. Men and women are equal partners in every day economic activities. Joking relationships are maintained with one's elder brother's wife, wife's younger sister/sister's husband and younger brother's parent-in-laws. Avoidance relationship is maintained with wife's elder sister/husband's elder brother, parent-in-law vice-versa, mother's brother's wife. Female members are supposed to cover their head from the avoidance relatives. Conflict and confrontation arise among the family members after the son's marriage and the father's death in property matters. The tension scale in the family results into breaking of extended family to nuclear family. It is the customary obligation of sister's husband to play the role of *anvario* (accompanier) and mother's brother gives *maushala* (marriage dress gift) in marriage. Inheritance follows the rule of male ultimogeniture for the residential land and male equigeniture for other property. Eldest son succeeds to the *karta* (authority) in the family after his father's death. A widow also acts as the head of the family till son/sons grow up. The inter-family linkages are maintained during the life cycle rituals, economic activities, religious functions and during the election of *samaj* Patel (chief of traditional council). A Koli Patel woman has a low status in the society. Though their involvement in economic activities is quite important, they do not have decision making powers. They have role in agricultural operations. They also contribute to family income after doing teaching jobs. They look after the household jobs. They are forbidden to interfere in political matter except to cast their votes in the periodical elections. *Fui* (father's sister) plays an important role during *barse* (naming) and *chaula* (tonsure) ceremonies.

The life-cycle rituals connected to birth, childhood and marriage are common to all the Hindu communities of Daman which has been already discussed in the Introduction.

Land is the major economic resource for the community. They are landowning community. Agriculture is their traditional as well as their present day primary occupation. Agricultural labour, service in different government offices, fishing labour and wine shops are their other means of livelihood. Agricultural activities among these people include the production of crops, mainly on subsistance level. They are mostly dependent on rain as the sea ecology has provided the saline water in the region. However, some of them, avail of the facilities of electrically operated pump and tube-wells for irrigation.The crop calendar is divided into three parts viz. *siara* (winter) for *tur*, *mag* and wheat cultivation, *unadu* (summer) for rice and *jowar* and *chaumasa* (rainy season) for *ragi*. Apart from these, they also produce vegetables viz. *ringna* (brinjal), chillees, bean and zinzer. The economically sound Koli Patel sell pulses and rice to the Vanias of Daman and Vapi who come in contract with the Koli Patel before the harvesting. Vegetables are directly sold in the markets of Daman and Vapi by women folk. The land tenure system, prevalent, is locally termed as *bhagidar*. The cultivator's share varies from 40 to 60 per cent, but the land owner has to bear the cost of seeds, and fertilizers. They take the services of the Dubla and Dhodia as *hali* (agricultural labourer) against the loan credited to them and the wages are paid in cash and kind. Supply of chemical fertilizer, introduction of electrically handled pump and good quality of seeds from the government agencies and cooperative societies have played an important role in the economy of the Koli Patel.

Their traditional councils operate as a two-tier system namely *samaj* at village level and Samast Koli Samaj at district level. The *samaj* consists of five *sabhyas* (members) headed by Patel (chief) and assisted by one *karbhari* (accountant) who are elected by voice vote. The election criterion being the age of the man, his popularity among the community men and knowledgeability regarding the worldly affairs of the community. The Samast Koli Samaj is headed by Pramukh (chief) and assisted by *upapramukh*, *mantri* (secretary), *khajanchi* (accountant) and fifeen *sabhyas* (members). The *samaj* regulates their daily activities. Social problems partaining to deviation from the traditional norms, inter-caste marriage, adultery, divorce are dealt with by *samaj*. The Samast Koli Samaj takes care of the problems not solved by the *samaj*. Excommunication and cash fine are the forms of punishment imposed by the traditional councils. An offender is expiated in the community after paying the fine and giving the community dinner. They have their own voting system in the council to elect a suitable candidate to fill the nomination for the statutory panchayat so that fraction may not occur. Plan implementation and welfare development activities are the role of modern statutory panchayat.

The community profess Hinduism. Their religious beliefs and practices postulate the existence of two different sources of supernatural forces viz. spiritual power and the deities based on Hindu mytholoogy. Holi Mata and Lakshmi Mata are the village deities. The newly married couples are supposed to pay homage to the deity next day after marriage. *Gotraj* is the term for their *kul* deity who is worshipped in a special manner on the *atham* (eight day) of 'Maha'(Magh) month. They also worship other deities namely Lord Shiva, and Lord Vishnu. Maha Lakshmi temple near Dhanu in Maharashtra, Ranchor Rai (Lord Krishna) temple at Dakor in Gujarat and Dwarka are their main shrines. They have other deities associated with their agricultural practices who are worshipped during their agricultural operation. They are Kanhari (before harvesting), Vaghyo (before the onset of harvesting), Ravali ((prior to the start of sowing), Mahhar dev (protection of crops from diseases) and Mawli (after sowing to avoid the ill-effects). The sacred specialists help them in the religious offerings and paying homages during their visit to the sacred centres. Their major festivals include Maha Atham associated with the worship of the kul deities which lies in the month of Magha (January-Februrary), and Nag Panchami associated with the worship of snake which is celebrated in the month of Kartik (October-November). They also celebrate Makar Sankranti, Bhai Beej, Janamastami, Ujjani, Diwali, and Holi with full vigour. Another festival is Shravani Poonam associated with the worship of sea-god which falls on the full moon of Shravan (July-August) month. Satya Narayan katha is performed before doing any auspicious work. Their main fair is held at the lord Shiva temple in Palsana, near Udwada railway station in Gujarat on Maha Shivratree day. The Koli Patel from Daman and the neighbouring villages of Gujarat pay offerings to Lord Shiva on this occasion. The plants viz. *aghora*, *amb* (mango), *apta.*, *aunla* and *khopra* (coconut) are of religious importance which are used on the religious performances. Importance of Jala Ram, a saint from Gujarat, is the recent change in the religious life of the Koli Patel of Daman. The saint, a devotee of lord Rama, died at Birpur in Junagudh district of Gujarat.

The members of the community do *satiyo* (floor design) and *chundar/tarjwana* (tattooing). The tattoo marks are made on ridges and back of the palm by the men while women on face, neck, forearms and back of the palm. The marks includes flowers, birds and figure of gods and goddesses. Their folk dances are *koli* and *garba* which are enjoyed on the festive occasions specially after harvesting.

They have their traditional linkages related to their occupation of agriculture with the Dubla, Dhodia, and Vania. The Brahman officiates at their life-cycle rituals and religious practices. They share well and water with all the Hindu communities except the Scheduled Castes. They have their own crematorium and temples. Inter-community linkages are maintained in religious spheres during the Shivratri fair and Shravani Poonam. The Bhangis are invited as musicians during marriage and for sending information of death to the community men. *Dharam Behan* (putative kinship) is maintained with the Machhi. Cultivator-labour and landlord-tenant relationship are maintained with the Dubla, Dhodia and Kamli. They accept water and *kacha* food from the Brahman, Bhandari, Kamli and Machhi. They have engineers, advocates, teachers and other members holding white collar jobs.

The development programmes have made an impact. Literacy level has gone up among both boys and girls. Though the education is favourable upto college for both the boys and girls, but girls drop out from the study due to socio-economic reason. They make use of both the traditional and modern medicare. They avail of the facilities of drinking water through piped water and wells. They make use of electricity with the facilities within their localities. They use firewood and cowdung cakes, kerosene oil and LPG gas as their fuel resources. They make use of chemical fertilizer and insecticides. They avail of the facilities of midday meal for the children under ICDS, IRDP, ration shops and banks. They are exposed to mass communication by radio, television, cinema.

N.K. Sinha

REFERENCES

Bains, Strathelstane, *Ethnography: Caste and Tribes*, Concept Publishing House, Delhi, page 53, 1976.

Enthoven, R.E., *Tribes and Castes of Bombay*, Vol. II, 1920, Bombay, The Government Central Press; Reprint, Vol. II, p. XVIII, 1975, Cosmo Publications, Delhi.

Francisco, Antonio, *Noticas-E-Documentas-Para, A Historia De of Damao*, Bastoria (Goa), Vol.I, page 128, 1904.

Gazetteer of India, *Gazetteer of the Union Territory of Goa, Daman and Diu.* Panaji, part-2, Daman, page 18, 1979.

Roy, Shibani, *Koli Culture*, Cosmo Publications, New Delhi, page 29, 1933.

Sherring, M.A., *Hindu Tribes and Castes*, Vol. II, 1916, Calcutta, Thakar Spinks & Co.; Reprint, Vol. II, p. 308, 1974, Cosmo Publications, Delhi.

KUMBHAR

The Kumbhar, a community of potmakers, are also known as Kumbhi or Prajapati. The literal meaning of the word 'Kumbhi' is the maker of earthen pot, the Sanskrit word being 'Kumbhakara'. According to their legend they recall their origin from Kashyap rishi, a mythical sage and claim their descent from Daksha Prajapati (father-in-law of Lord Shiva), who migrated from Himalaya, settled in different parts of India and adopted the occupation of pot making. The Kumbhar of Diu are the immigrants from Amreli (Gujarat) and Govind Bhai Chouhan was the first to settle in Vanakara village before the Portuguese established their rule. They are divided into three occupational endogamous groups nemely Marhu Kumhar (Cultivator), Kadia Kumbhar (Mason) and Sadaria Kumbhar (Cultivator), though these three groups are primarily pot makers. They are mainly distributed in Vankabara village of Diu. They are also distributed in the different parts of Gujarat. They use Gujarati for reading, writing and speaking purposes. They are also conversant with Hindi in relation to others.

They are non-vegetarian who take fish and the meat of goat, chicken and fowls. Their staple food includes *rotla* (bread of *bajra*), *bhat* (rice) pulses of *tur* (red gram) and *urad* (black gram). They also take plenty of vegetables. They take fruits occasionally as per the availability. They enjoy alcoholic drinks regularly which they purchase from the local market. Apart from that they also take tea and butter milk. Their special food preparations are rice fried in ghee mixing with fish, *lapsee* (poridge), *potaya* (wheat flour fried with groundnut oil mixing with toddy and jaggery) and *dudhpag* (rice boiled in milk mixing sugar) which are consumed during marriage and other festive occasions. They use groundnut oil as their cooking medium.

The internal structure of the Kumbhars has thirteen exogamous divisions based on *goter* which are common to all the three endogamous groups. These are Chauhan, Solanki, Jethwa, Chowda, Kamalia, Tank, Lodwa, Saravia, Parmar, Wala, Rathod and Chitorah. They suffix their *goter* to their names as *atak* (surname). The above mentioned *goters* do not have any stratification. The basis of differentiation is social and their function is to trace the descent, to regulate marriage alliances and to participate in the life cycle rituals. They are well aware of *varna* system and recognize their place as Kshatriya. They consider the Brahman, Salat, Sangharia, Bania, Vanja, Kharwa and Koli as superior to them.

They resort to community and sub-group endogamy. Marriage is prohibited within the same *goter* and within the four ascending generations from mother's side. Early marriage was the traditional norm. In present day situation they practise adult marriage where a boy and a girl are married at the age of twenty one and nineteen years respectively. Marriage is settled by negotiation and the maternal uncle from both the sides play an important role as mediator. They practise monogamy. A married woman uses *kanku* (red mark on forehead), *bangdi* (bangles of turtle shell, ivory) and *mangalsutra*. They have practice of *dej* (briideprice) in kind only which is settled during the negotiation. A bride goes to stay with her groom's parents after marriage. The Kumbhar society recognize *chhutta-chheda* (divorce) and it is granted by the traditional caste council. Whosoever approaches for divorce, he or she has to pay Rs. 1500/- to Rs. 2000/- as the divorce fee to the council. Adultery, maladjustment and cruelty are the reasons for divorce and compensation is given to the aggrieved party. The post-divorce maintenance is borne by both as per decision of the council. They allow *natra* (remarriage) through *devar batu* (junior levirate), *saree-lagna* (junior sororate) and between widow and widower.

The institution of family consists of extended and nuclear types. They have prescribed kinship usages of avoidance and joking relationships. Avoidance relationship is maintained with mother-in-law and son-in-law, daughter-in-law and father-in-law, with younger brother's wife and with husband's elder brother. Joking relationship exists between elder brother's wife and husband's younger brother and with wife's younger brother and sister. Sister's husband plays the role of *harvan* (accompanier) and maternal uncle brings *maushala* (customary marriage gift) during his/her marriage. Conflict and confrontation among the family members arise after son's marriage or after father's death on property matter. All sons get equal share in father's property but the eldest son succeeds authority after father's death. A Kumbhar woman has a low status in her society and her role is restricted to household jobs, viz. collection of fuel, bringing potable water, assisting in economic activities, social functions, rituals and religious activities. She is forbidden to interfere in political affairs. *Fui* (father's sister) plays an important role during *nampari* (naming) and *bal-maudi* (tonsure) ceremonies.

Life-cycle rituals, right from the pregnancy to birth, childhood, marriage and death are common to all other Hindu communities of Diu. Marriage rituals are performed at both the places of the bride and the groom and is solemnised at the bride's residence, but the consummation takes place at the groom's residence.

Making of earthen vessel is their traditional and present day primary occupation. For pottery special black soil is obtained from the neighbouring district of Gujarat. They apply indigenous methods of pot making with the help of *chak* (wooden wheel). They mix sea water with the clay to increase its cooling capacity. Mainly they make *handa/ bedan* (pitcher), used for storing and collecting water. Apart from this they make all types of earthen vessels required for household use. The importance of the Kumbhar is noted during all the life cycle rituals for the supply of specific earthen vessels like *ghad* (pitcher) and *kadia* (lamp) during Diwali. Their link with market exists directly at the weekly *hat* (market) in Diu and the adjoining areas of Gujarat. The transaction is in cash as well as in exchange. They get one *mund* (measuring unit) for the supply of four *ghads*. Service in different government offices is their other means of livelihood which is part of change in their economic activities after independence.

The community do not have any formal caste-council at village level and the social problems are dealt with by the elderly members when and where needed. They also seek the help of Sarpanch of the statutory panchayat if their problems are not solved by the elderly members. Bargam Prajapati Mandal, the post-liberation organization is their political organization at regional level which comprises the representation from 42 villages of Diu and Gujarat. The regional council consists of a Pramukh (the chief), one *mehta* (accountant) and one *mukadum* (messenger). The chief is elected by voice vote who nominates *mehta* and *mukadum*. Cases pertaining to inter-community marriage, adultery, social reforms, divorce fee and excommunication are decided by the Pramukh. *Gam Panch* is another organization at village level which comprises all the communities headed by a Patel. Problems perttaining to inter-community disputes are dealt with by the *gam panch*. Plan implement and welfare development activities are the role of modern statutory panchayat.

The Kumbhar are Hindus. Gomti Mata is the village deity which is common to all the Hindu communities. Their *goter* deities are Chamunda Mata, Khodiar Mata, Butai Mata, Sindhvi Devi and Mahakali Mata. Their prime tool of production, *chak* (wheel), is worshipped as a representation either of Lord krishna or of Prajapati being their emblem or reproduction. They consider Somnath as their major sacred centre. Their sacred specialists are from the Brahman community who help them in making religious offerings and conducting other religious and life cycle ceremonies. Their main festtival is Shiv Ratri associated with the worship of Lord Shiva. The fair at Gangeshwar temple in Fudam on Shivratree is considered a major one. They also celebrate other Hindu festivals namely Navratra, Diwali and Holi. Poonam Mela is common fair, held at Buchadwada, for all the Hindu communities.

Pottery is their craft. *Handa* (pitcher), *tanki* (water container), *tawdi* (hot plate), *kodia* (lamp) and *ghad* (renhut used for irrigation) are the main products of the craft industry, used in domestic work and during festive occasions. They also make various kinds of ornamental pottery viz., toys, images of deities and the like and sell them in the village of Diu and the adjoining areas of Gujarat. The oral traditions are common to all the Hindu communities living in the region.

They accept water, *pucca* and *kuchha* food from the Brahman, Vania, Salat and *sidha* from all the Hindu communities of Diu except the Hadi, Vankar and Bhangi. The communities, placed higher in social hierarchy, accept only water from the Kumbhar as their water container is an earthen vessel which is considered as pure; but they do not dine with them. They have their own place in cremation ground. They have their own temple, but are allowed to visit the temples of other communities. They participate in Poonam Mela, an important fair, with other communities. They share well and other water sources with others. The community members are holding white collar jobs and also working as teachers.

The various development programmes initiated by the government agencies have made an impact on their life style, especially in terms of education, health and medicare, job opportunities and the various avenues of mass communication.

N.K.Sinha

REFERENCES

Sinha, N.K., 'Study of Ethnography and Change in a Diu Village', Unpublished report submitted to Anthropological Survey of India, 1980.

MACHHI

The Machhi, also known as Tandel, are fishermen and sailors of Daman. The literal meaning of the word 'Machhi' denotes 'fishermen'. The Gujarati word 'Machhi' and Tandel denote head of fishing expedition. According to their legend, they trace their origin from Dhimars of Dwapar Yug, one of the mythical periods. Enthoven (1920, page-328) has called Dhimar a sub-division of the Machhi. They immigerated from Mehri and Bharooch in South Gujarat about 200 years before, when the State was under the clutch of drought, and settled in the coastal areas of Daman. Paul (1978) says that Machhi deserted Mehri village and settled first in Kadaiya village and subsequently in other coastal areas of Daman after Portuguese attacked the village during the period of king Balmi of Ramnagar. Antonio Francisco (1904) has called Machhi as an independent group of Daman. They are distributed in the village of Kadaiya, Bhimpore and the Municipal area of Daman district. They are also distributed in Surat and Valsad districts of Gujarat and Thana district of Maharashtra. Population figure is not available.

Food habits of Machhi are largely governed by the ecological conditions and their nature of occupation where plenty of fish is available. They are non-vegetarian. They eat egg, fish and meat of goat and fowls. Their staple food includes rice, wheat, *jowar*, fish and pulses of *mag* (green gram) and *tur* (red gram). Vegetables are taken on three restricted days, viz. *poonam* (full moon), Amavasya (moonless night) and Igyaras (eleventh day after Amavasya) when fishing is forbidden. Fruits are taken occasionally. *Daru* (alcoholic drinks) and *toddy* are enjoyed by the community regularly, but the female folk take it occasionally. They take it as digestive and it protects them from sea-wind while on fishing expedition.

The community is divided in to two sections, i.e. Suryavanshi and ChandraVanshi. The basis of difference is social. They say that a SuryaVanshi performs marriage in day time while a Chandra-Vanshi performs after sunset. They are divided into more than 200 exogamous divisions, based on *kutumb* (lineage) out of which they could trace only six viz. Dhan Bhai. Barlewali, Ghantiwala, Malwani, Prabhakar and Ravia which are added as their surname. Tandel is the changed surname adopted recently. There is no stratification among the divisions. The chief function of *kutumb* is to trace the descent and to regulate the marriage. They consider the Brahman, Koli, Kamli, Baria and Bhandari superior to them in the social hierarchy. They are well-aware of the Varna system and recognize their place as Kshatriya in the Varna order. Economically and numerically they dominate in Daman. They resort to community and section endogamy (whether Suryavanshi or Chandravanshi division) and *kutumb* exogamy. Marriage is settled by negotitation only and boy's father initiates. The form of marriage is monogamy. Child marriage was the traditional norm but now they practise adult marriage and the age for boys ranges from 20 to 25 years and that for girls from 16 to 21 years. *Kanku* (red mark on forehead) and *kanthi* (mangalsutra) are the marriage symbol for a married woman. *Dej* (dowry) is given in kind only, which includes ornaments, dresses and utensils. Patrilocal is the rule of residence for them. They allow *natra* (remarriage), where a widower can marry a widow as well as a divorcee or unmarried but a widow can marry only a widower or divorcee. Marriage with mother' s brother's daughter and mother's sister's daughter is permitted. *Devar batu* (junior levirate) and *saree batu* (junior sororate) are permitted on usual conditions. The right of *fargati* (divorce) is granted to both man and woman by traditional council. The usual grounds for divorce are maladjustment, cruelty, chronic sickness and insanity. The post divorce maintenance is carried by her parents or brother. Matrimonial relations are maintained with the Machhi of Gujarat and Maharashtra after liberation. *Samuhik lagna* (community marriage) is a post liberation introduction which is performed at the *samaj* temple to minimise the expenditure and time.

The common form of family is vertically extended and nuclear types. They have prescribed kinship usages, viz. avoidance and joking relationship. Avoidance is maintained between mother-in-law and son-in-law, father-in-law and daughter-in-law, between younger brother's wife and husband's elder brother. Joking relation exists between elder brother's wife, and husband's younger brother, wife's elder brother, and elder and younger sister, and with wife's younger brother. Mother's brother and sister's husband play important roles during marriage. Conflict and confrontations arise after father's death and sons' marriage in property matters. They practise the rule of male ultimogeniture for residential and male equigeniture for other properties. Eldest son succeeds the *karta* (authority). A widow also acts as the head of the family till sons is/are immature. Inter-family linkage are sought during the life-cycle rituals, political activities and religious spheres, economic activities. The significant change in the institution of family is the formation of the nuclear family. The Machhi women enjoy a low status in the community. No right of inheritance is given to the women. They assist in day to day life. They are assigned the job of fishing activities such as preparation for sale after the men folk return from the fishing expedition, bringing potable water, ritual observance and religious activities. They look after the household job. Some of them support the family income after doing teaching job. They are forbidden to interfere in the political matters. *Fui* (father's sister) plays important roles during the naming and head shaving ceremonies.

The rite-de-passage of the Machhi are common with all other Hindu communities of Daman except a few like Dubla, Dhodia and Mahayavanshi which been has already discussed in Introduction.

Water is the major economic resource for them controlled by the government. A few of them are landowners. Fishing and sea- manship are the traditional as well as the present primary occupation of the Machhi. Toddy tapping, wine shops, agriculture, and service in different government offices are the subsidiary occupations for them. They use both the indigenous and mechanized methods for fishing. Different boats, viz. traller, *horha, horhi* and *kotiya* are used for fishing with the help of fishing companies like Ruston, Leyland and Yamaha Motors. The fishing expedition lasts for ten to fifteen days in deep sea. The main sea catches include prawns, pomphrate, Bomby Duck, solmen fish and lobster which are exported to Liverpool, Singapore, Japan and Canada through the exporting companies at Porbandar, Bombay and Ernakulam. Muslims of Daman are the agents of these companies who collect the catches from Daman. Export of *pota* (fish moss) of *darah* (solemon fish air bladder) and wings of *mogra* (shark) at the rate of Rs. 550/- and Rs. 1000 per kg. should be arranged to the aforesaid countries. Fishmoss is now used to prepare thread for stitches after operation in Japan, America and other foreign countries. The total catches for the seasons ranges from the value of Rs. five crore to rupees six crore. An expedition requires nine crews which include one *tandel* (captain) and eight *khalasis* (labourers) who get Rs. 1000/- and Rs. 5000/- to Rs. 8000/

- as their season (eight months) remuneration. About four hundred mechanized and 15 to 20 sailing boats are now in action after a scheme for the mechanization of fishing craft was introduced in 1963 for the purchase of boats, engines on loan-cum-subsidy basis. The Machhi of Daman have Matsya Udyog Bind Sahkari Society to assist the poor in fishing with its five hundred members and Kalyan Bhai Ravia as the Chairman. The sea-men going abroad, work on the dock and in the engine department, to Middle East and South East Asia, Europe, America, China and Japan. Due to the closure of most of the private shiping companies the unemployment problem for the sea-men has taken a shape and they are truning towards fishing.

The Machhi Mahajan Samaj (traditional council) operates at district level headed by a President who is elected by voice vote in the interval of three years. The other office bearers include Vice-Presidents, six *karbharis* (secretaries) treasurer, joint- treasurers and twenty one *sabhyas* (members). Social problems pertaining to deviation from the traditional norms, inter family disputes, social reforms, religious matters, assistance to poor and educational facilities are dealt with by the Samaj. Excommunication and cash fine are the forms of punishment imposed by the *samaj*. An offender expiates in the community after paying the fine. They have their voting system in the council to elect a suitable candidate to file the nomination for the Councilor seat so that the fraction may not occure. No Machhi can give the mandate in the periodical elections against the decision of the *samaj*.

The Machhi are Hindus. They believe in gods and goddesses of Hindu pantheon. But their favourite deities of worship are Lord Vishnu and Lord Shiva, whom they visit and worship in the temples daily. Sangliya Mata is their *gotrej* (family deity). They also have belief on N.S. Dos Remedious (Lady of Remedy) one of the shrines of the Catholics whom the Machhi consider since Portuguese period as one of the seven sisters of goddess Lakshmi who lost her caste. They pay homage to the shrine once in a year in the end of June with a spirit of deep gratitude for the protection in fishing expedition and good catches. Mothers place their newly born infants on the altar steps of the church for seeking blessing. Antonio Fransisco (1904, p. 219) has discussed the same. Somnath and Bhuleshwar temples in Gujarat are their main sacred centres. Their main festivals are Diwali, Ujjani, Bhai Bij, Makar Sankranti and Shravani Poonam. Holi and Navratras are also celebrated by them. Satyanarayan *katha* is performed for any new expedition. The principal fair is Shivratri. The plants of *aghora, amb, apta, aula* etc. are of religious importance which are used on the religious performances. They worship the *barh* (banyan tree). The magico-religious practice of the Machhi are based on the belief of both the malevolent and benevolent spirits living near the sea coast which can be made subservient to human needs if care is taken not to offend them.

The folk art and culture of the Machhi are represented by *chundar* (tattooing) and *satiya* (floor - design) which are common to all the Hindu communities of Daman. *Satiya* is a type of decoration design made in front of the outer door of the house to welcome the deity of prosperity in the morning with the help of white stone powder. The *koli* folk dance is the nonmaterialistic element of Machhi and Mangelas culture enjoyed during marriage, Ujjani and Mahi Bij ceremonies by both men and women.

Economy has been the imporatant factor for their traditional linkages with all the communities specially the Mangela, Dubla and Muslim of Daman related to the occupation of fishing. The Mahyavanshi do the jobs of musicians during the life-cycle rituals. The Brahman officiates the life cycle rituals and religious ceremonies. They accept both *kachha* and *pucca* food from the Brahman, Koli Patel, Bhandari, Kamli, Sagar and Baria, and do not accept from the Mahyavanshi, Dubla, Dhodia, Momin Muslim and Christian. The belief on Lady of Remedy has made the traditional linkages with the Catholic in religious spheres. They share well with all the communities except the untouchables. They share the crematorium with the Mangelas. They have their own temple. The periodical elections have given the route of modern linkages with the other communities. Political leadership has emerged at regional level. The community has business men, teachers, doctors, engineers. The majority of Machhis are employed in different government offices.

The Machhi avail of all the civic facilities regarding development programmes by the government agencies. The fishing department takes care of the problems of the fishermen and facilitate them with loan-cum-subsidy to purchase boat and other appliances for fishing. They are linked with the mass communication through radio, television, newspapers, etc. What the community feels is that while the mechanization of fishing industry in Daman has developed but not upto the mark as in Gujarat and Maharashtra, viz. facilities of harbour, establishment of fishing research laboratories to find out the fish belt, transmission arrangement with the fishermen in the deep sea in case of any accident etc. Licence for the export of fishmoss, side and tailwings of shark should be provided to help the fishing industries which would provide foreign currency to the government.

N.K. Sinha

REFERENCES

Enthoven, R.E., *The Tribes and Castes of Bombay*, Vol. III, 1922, Bombay, The Government Central Press, Vol. III, 1975, Cosmo Publications, Delhi.

Francisco, Antonio, '*Noticas -E- Documentas-Para A Historia De of Damao*'. Bastoria (Goa), Vol. I & II, Page 219 & 128, 1904.

Paul, J., 'Study of Ethnography and Change in Daman Village', Unpublished report submitted to Anthropological Survey of India, 1978.

MAHYAVANSHI

The Mahyavanshi, also known the Dhed, are one of the Scheduled Castes. The new nomenclature of 'Mahyavanshi' was given to the Dhedh of Bombay Presidency by Govt. of Bombay, General Department Memo No. 9330 of December 1939 (item No. 12), to give justice and relief to the community from the curse of untouchability. This was due to the efforts of Shri Kanhaiyalal Maniklal Munshi, the then Home Minister of Bombay and Dr. Purushottam Solanki, representative of the Depreessed Classes of Gujarat in the Bombay Legislative Council who stressed that the Mahyavanshi were the descendants of the Rajput. Subsequently, the Dhed of Daman were given the name of Mahyavanshi, after its liberation, by the government of Goa, Daman and Diu vide the notification No. DF-1-SCT/64 dated 19th February, 1968. Enthoven (1920) and Sherring (1974) have discussed the Dhed of Gujarat while Antonio Francisco (1904:129) has discussed the Dhed of Daman. According to their legend they trace their origin to a Rajput named Maya of Rajasthan who sacrificed his life to bring down the rain during a drought in Rajasthan in the immemorial times. Supporting the legend Parmar (1987, page 25) says, "during the time of Sidh Raja of North Gujarat (A.D. 1094-1143) a Dhed named Mayo was beheaded in the Sahastraling taluk at Patan for rain and at the time of death Mayo begged that Dhed should not be forced to remain at a distance from the village as a reward for his sacrifice and the King asserted the privilege afterward." He further (page-86) says, "It was written in 'Prithvi Raj Raso' that there were originally five branches of Kshatriyas, viz. Parmar, Rathod, Jadhavan, Chauhan and Solanki which later developed into nine branches and Mayavat was the twentieth branch, sprung from Parmar from which the Mayhavanshi trace their origin." There is no information regarding their migration. They are distributed in the seventeen villages of the different panchayats with their concentration in the Varkund village of Daman. They are also distributed in Pardi and Umbergam in Valsad District of Gujarat and in Thana district of

Maharashtra. Their total population in Daman, according to census of India, 1971, is 1361.

They are non-vegetarian who take the meat of goat and fowls. They also consume locally available vegetables. They consume fruits occasionally. They enjoy drinking liquor, toddy which they purchase from market. They smoke *bidi* and cigarettes. The special food preparations namely *puri* (fried bread), *lapsee* (porridge) *dudhpag* (rice boiled in milk mixing sugar), *biryani* (fried rice mixing mutton or fish) and *potya* (fried wheat flour mixing with toddy and sugar) are consumed on the festive occasions.

The Mahyavanshi are divided into ten exogamous *got* (clan) namely Pardinar, Danania, Kantharia, Barodia, Chasia or Surti, Gohel, Parmar, Rathod, Wadekar and Vaghela. The basis of differentiation is at territorial level, i.e. the place from where they migrated and at social level. All the divisions are exogamous resembling the Rajput-like clan names. There is no stratification among these divisions. These names are suffixed to their names as their surnames. 'Contractor' is a surname recently adopted by them. Its chief function is to trace their descent, to regulate marriage alliances and to help in the life cycle rituals. They are well aware of the *varna* system and recognize their position as Kshatriya. Though they claim a Rajput origin but their centuries old, ill-treated and degraded position when they were forced to live in segregated localities as untouchables, has made them perceive their position as inferior to the Brahman, Koli Patel, Bhandari, Kamli, Machhi, Bania, Sagar, Mangela, Mitna and Dhodia. They perceive their position as superior to the Bhangi in social hierarchy.

The rule of endogamy is observed at community level while exogamy is applied to *got*, at village level and to the three ascending generations from mother's side. Marriage is settled by negotiation with the help of wife's brother. *Panch* (caste council's) permission is taken after the negotiation for *adarmi* (betrothal). They practise monogamy, but in case there is no issue, a husband can marry another girl by prior permission of the wife and the *panch*. Child-marriage was the traditional norm when a girl was married before attaining puberty. Now girls are married not before they are eighteen and boys not before they are twenty-five. The territorial restrictions imposed by the Govt. of India from 1954 to 1961 was one of the factors for their practice of adult marriage. The Mahyavanshi then could not contract matrimonial alliances outside Daman. A married woman ties *kanthi* (marriage pendant) round her neck and uses *kanku* (red vermillion) as marriage symbols. They have practice of *dej* / *pallu* (bride-price) which is fixed by the traditional council in cash at Rs. 30/- Though the community was using *escude* (Portugese currency) during the Portugese regime yet during the time of alliances bride price was fixed in rupees. One had to exchange *escude* for rupees from the Vania of Daman on commission basis. The brideprice is given at the time of marriage by the bride groom's father to the bride. They practise patrilocal rule of residence. Though they allow *chhutta* (divorce) but they do not encourage this. The reasons for divorce are adultery, impotency, cruelty and insanity. A man cannot divorce without any reason and the *gnyat panch* has right to punish the husband in such cases. Whosoever approaches for divorce, he/she has to pay Rs. 101/- to the *panch*. The custom of *natra* (remarriage) is permitted. A man or women can remarry in case of the death or divorce of either of the spouses. According to the norm a man cannot remarry after divorce till the divorced wife is alive or remarried. *Pallu* (bride-price) is also paid during the *natra*. A divorced woman can go for *natra* with the permission of *gnyat panch*. A woman remarries symbolically a *samri* tree and then goes to stay with the man. Children are the liability of mother in dovorce cases and post-divorce maintanence is given to the aggreived party. *Devar batu* (junior levirate) and *salivatu* (junior sororate) are permissible. Child marriage was one of the reasons for divorce. The rise in marriage age has caused the decline in divorce cases. *Pallu* in kind, i.e. a silver *hansadi* (necklace), a silver *kanthi* (nose stud) and one *sari* are gradually taking the place of *pallu* in cash.

The common forms of family among the Mahyavanshis are nuclear and extended ones. They have prescribed kinship usages i.e. avoidance and joking relationship. Avoidance is maintained between mother-in-law, daughter-in-law and father-in-law, with younger brother's wife and husband's elder brother. Joking relationship exists with elder brother's wife, husband's younger brother, wife's elder and younger sisters and wife's younger brother's wife. The sister's husband, *behnevi*, plays an important role and *mama* (maternal uncle) brings *maushala* (ceremonial marriage gift) during marriage. Conflict and confractations in the family arise after sons' marriage and father's death in financial and property matters. Male primogeniture was the tradition for inheritance during the Portuguese regime. Now they have the rule of male equigeniture. In absence of male child, the daughter's or brother's son is adopted as *dattak* to inherit the property. After father's death the division of properties is done equally in the presence of five community men. Eldest son succeeds to the authority and becomes the *karta* after father's death. Inter-family linkages are maintained during economic activities, life-cycle rituals and the election of *gnyat panch.* According to their norms it is obligatory to stay jointly with the elder brother, after father's death, till the sisters' marriages are performed. Women have low status. Though right of inheritance is not granted to the daughters but a widow is elegible to inherit half of her deceased husband's property, provided she does not remarry. They have roles in agriculture, animal husbandry, collection of fuel, bringing potable water, social functions, rituals and religious spheres. They also assist in economic activities and contribute to family income. They do not interfere in political matters except when they cast their votes during the periodical elections in consultation with their menfolk. *Fui* (father's sister) has an important role during naming and *badhautaravi* (head shaving) ceremonies while *mami* (maternal aunt) has role during marriage. The folk songs, on the festive occasions are sung by the women only.

The life cycle rituals right from *kholubharo* or *agharni* (lap filling ceremony) to death are common to all the Hindu communities of Daman. They have some specific rituals, the *chhathi* (sixth day ritual) after birth for female child, is performed on fourth day, birth pollution is maintained for fifteen days, clan deity is worshiped on the marriage day at the groom's house and on third day before marriage at the bride's house, the bride and the groom make four rounds of the *chouri* (sacrificial fire in marriage booth) and *dapu* (a sort of cash amount) is paid to the various community men for their services in marriage. Practice of both burying and cremation and performance of *dakhado* by the in-laws. on thirteenth day to remove the grief, caused due to the death of family members.

As it has been discussed earlier, they were Dhed and, being considered untouchable, they were associated with unclean activities such as tanning of the dead animal and skinning them. After the Portuguese occupied the area, there was change in their economic activities. The sense of untouchability prevailed and no higher Hindu castes employed them as private servants except those who worked as agricultural labour. They got their remuneration in kind, i.e. seven *matta* (a pither containing sixteen seera) of *jawar* per season. Portuguese employed them, the then Dhed, as private servants specially as cook. A few of them were provided land against their services. The services of the community were taken over by the British in Bombay from Portuguese where the Mahyavanshi were engaged as cooks, butlers and house-servants in Bombay. A number of the Mahyavanshis migrated to Bombay for the said occupations. The Christian, Koli Patel and Kamli also employed them as farm hands to til their land. Land was alinlated after 1961, the Mahyavanshis became tenants to landowners. Agriculture is now their primary occupation. Service in government offices in Daman as well as in Bombay, carpentry and tailoring are other means of their livelihood. Agriculture labourers receive their wages both in cash and kind.

Social control is exercised by their *gnyat panch* (traditional caste council). Any person violating the customary norms is dealt with by the council. They have a three tier system of counncil namely *gnyat panch* at village level, *chaura* (comprising of eight villages) and *bahuteri*, (comprising of 72 villages of Daman, Gujarat and Maharashtra) are post liberation organizations. The *gnyat panch* comprises five *sabhyas* (members) headed by a Patel (chief) and assisted by a *khajanchi* (accountant) and a *kotwal* (messenger) and the Patel is elected by voice vote. *Chaura* is represented by all the Patels of *gnyat panch* and headed by a Patel. The Patels of *chaura* elect a Pramukh (chief) of *bahuteri* who nominates a *upapramukh*, a *khajanchi* and a *kotwal*. The traditional council has made their own *kayada* (customary rules) to maintain their social system. Social problems partaining to divorce, marriage, remarriage, adultery, intra and inter-family disputes are dealt with by the *panch*. *Shiksha* (excommunication) is the form of punishment imposed by the *gnyat panch* to an offender. The statutory panchayat takes care of the plan implement and welfare development activities.

The Mahyavanshi profess Hinduism. Majority of them are active followers of Sanatan Dharma sect started by Shri Shiva Nath for Nath Sect in 1971-72. Irrespective of their affiliation to this sect, they worship all the deities held sacred by the Hindus of Daman, viz. Hanuman, Ganpati etc. Their favourite deities are Lord Shiva and Hirva Devi. Apart from them, they have *gotrej* (clan deity) who is worshipped during life cycle rituals and religious festivals. The principles of Nath sect are brotherhood, love, kindness, *bhakti* and meditation to avoid taking of meat and wine. They have their own temples in which the images of their favourite deities are enshrined. Their major sacred centres are Bhuleshwar temple in Palsana village in Gujarat and Ashram of Nath Sect in Chardod village in Varoda District located on

Narmada river where they visit once in a year in Chaitra month for religious discourse. Their festivals are Chaitra Navratri, Diwali and Shivaratri. To fulfill once's promise, they sacrifice goat or cock in the name of *gotrej*. They also observe other Hindu festivals, viz. Ganesh Chaturthi, Holi and Bhai Bij. The Mahyavanshi takes out the image of Lord Ganesh to celebrate Ganesh Chaturthi festival. It is ceremonially immersed in sea which is also participated by other Hindus of Daman. *Garoda* is the sacred Brahman specialist who performs life-cycle rituals and helps in religious performances. They also believe in spirt and evil eye and to pacify the malevolent spirits they take the help of *bhua*. Tatooing, floor design, folk dance and folk songs are common to all.

Their occupation has been the prime factor in their traditional linkages with all the communities of Daman especially with the Koli Patel, Kamli, Muslim, Machhi and the Christian of Daman and Bombay. They accept water, *kacha* and *pucca* food from all the communities. They have their own water resources, temples and crematorium. Landlord-tenant and employer-worker relationship exists with the Koli Patel and Dhodia in agricultural activities. The Christian employ them as cook and house servant. Services of *Garoda* (Brahman) are sought during religious activities and life-cycle rituals. They participate in other Hindu festivals and fairs. They perform the role of musicians in religious festivals. The establishment of educational institutions and implementation of various development programmes have provided the routes of modern linkages with the other communities. They have teachers, members holding white coller jobs. The political leadership has emerged at regional level where members are actively working with the bigger political parties as part of their social awakening.

They have a positive attitude towards the development programmes. They avail of the facilities of education where boys and girls study up to college and drop out from studies as they have to earn to support their family and girls are married. They make use of both the modern and indigenous medicines and prefer to have three children. They avail of other civic facilities, common to all, provided by the Daman Administration. The Sectoral programmes, for S.C. and S.T. have provided them with more avenues for job under IRDP and GIDC. Few, who have land, avail of the facilities of irrigation through tubewell, organic manure and chemical fertilizers. They are exposed to mass communication by radio, television, newspaper, cinema.

They are well aware of the Mahyavant Rajput movement, which

provides the historical basis for linking their caste name with Rajput, Kshtraiya and Mahyavanshi, as started by Makanji Kuber Makwana and Patel Purshotamraj, Govind Singhji Solanki (member of Bombay Bahuteri Panch and Mayavat Rajput Sabha about 50 years ago. The long association with British and Portuguese officers has also changed their way of life through education and living pattern.

N.K. Sinha

REFERENCES

Enthoven, R.E., *The Tribes and Castes of Bombay*, Vol. III, 1922, Bombay, The Government Central Press; Reprint, Vol. IV, p. 322, 1975, Cosmo Publications, Delhi.

Francisco, Antonio, *Noticas - E - Documentas - Para A Historia De of Damao, Bastoria*, (Goa), Vol. II, page 128, 1904.

Parmar, Y.A., *The Mahyavanshi: The Sucess Story of a Scheduled Caste*, Mittal Publications, Delhi, page 26, 1987.

MANGELA

The Mangela are said to be the original fish trading community of Daman. The term 'mangela' denotes their occupation of fishing, i.e. '*mang*' means fishing net and '*ela*' means working with. Enthoven (1922) has described them as synonymous with the Mang or Dhimar. According to their legend, they trace their origin from the family of Satyavati or Matsya Gandha, the grandmother of the Pandavas and relate themselves to Dhimars or Mallahas. Antonio Francisco (1904-128) has called them Mangela as well as Bois and has discussed their habitation. They are distributed in the coastal villages, viz., Jampore, Kadaiya, Mangelwad and Moti Daman of Daman. The community has its concentration in the Thana and Valsad districts of Maharashtra and Gujarat. In all, they are distributed in 56 villages of Daman, Gujarat and Maharashtra. Mangeli is the spoken dialect within the community. Gujarati is the script for them. Besides Mangeli, some of them are conversant with Gujarati, Hindi and Portuguese.

They are non-vegetarian and their food habits are largely governed by the ecological conditions where plenty of fish are available. They take fish and the meat of goat and chicken. Their staple food includes rice, *bajra*, wheat, *sag* (curry of vegetable and meat), pulses of *tur* (red gram) and *mag* (green gram). Tea and butter milk are availed of. Fruits are taken occasionally. *Daru* (alcoholic drinks) and *toddy* are considered as digestive in accordance with climate and water. The special food viz. *puri*, *lapsee*, *potoya*, and *biriyani* are consumed on the festive occasions.

They are divided into 40 exogamous divisions and out of those six, namely Raut, Dhanu, Marigyl, Goodkar, Mihir and Ambir are found in Daman and are identified with the *kul* (clan) which they suffix to their names. Enthoven (1922, Vol. III- page- 1), has discussed ten traceable *kuls*. They belong to Kashyap Gotra. There is no stratification among these subdivisions. The function of *kul* is to trace their descent and to regulate marriage alliances. The basis of differentiation among the *kuls* is social. Though they are aware of the *varna* system, they can not confirm their position in *varna* order. They perceive their position as superior to all the communities, except the Brahman.

The rule of endogamy operates at community level, while they practise exogamy at *kul* and village level. They do not allow consanguineous marriage as practised among the Machhi. Child marriage was the traditional norm, but now they practise adult marriage. However, marriage age ranges for the boy from 20 years to 25 years, while that for girls from 18 years to 22 years. Marriage is settled by negotiation and initiated only by boy's parents. The form of marriages is monogamy. Married women use *kanthi* (marriage pendant) and *kanku* (red vermilion mark on forehead) as the symbol of marriage. They have the practice of *dej* (brideprice) in kind which includes ornaments and marriage dress. If a girl develops sexual intimacy within the community, the boy is bound to marry her. Sexual involvement outside the community is punished with excommunication. *Chhuta- chheda* (divorce) is granted to both men and women by the *samaj*. Adultery, maladjustment and cruelty are reasons for seeking divorce. Child-marriage was also one of the reasons for the maladjustment. Now they do not encourage divorce. *Diyarbatu* (junior levirate) and *saree-batu* (junior sororate) are permitted on usual conditions provided both the party agree for. *Natra* (remarriage) is allowed for widow, widower and divorcees. It is widow's parents who initiates for marriage which is performed near *samrhi* (cotton) tree and the hems of the partner are tied into a knot by the priest in the presence of *samaj* Patel. A bachelor willing to marry a widow is married first to *shamri* tree. In case of a widower willing to marry an unmarried girl, the regular form of marriage rituals is fully observed. Adult marriage, self arranged marriage, decline in divorce, practise of bride price in cash are some of the recent changes in the institution of marriage. *Samuhik lagan* (community marriage) is a post-independence addition which was arranged first on 1.6. 86 keeping in view the need to minimise the expenditure and time. For this marriage a place is fixed by the traditional council comprising 56 villages once in year during the off fishing season where both the parties assemble for marriage.

Their institution of family includes extended. Avoidance and joking relationship are well-defined. Avoidance is maintained between mother-in-law and son-in-law, father-in-law and daughter-in-law with younger brother's wife and husband's elder brother. Joking relationship exists with elder brother's wife and husband's younger brother, with wife's elder and younger sisters and with wife's elder and younger brothers. Conflict and confrontations in the family arise after father's death between the sons in property matters. They practise rule of male ultimogeniture for the residential land and male equigeniture for other properties. In absence of son, brother's son is adopted through the official procedure in court. Sister's husband has an important role to play as *harvan* (accompanier) and maternal uncle brings *maushala* (customary right to present marriage dress), during the marriage and head shaving ceremonies. Elder son succeeds as the *karta* (authority) after father's death. Inter family linkages are maintained during the life cycle rituals, economic activities, religious and social function and during the election of traditional council chief. The significant change in the institution of family is the breaking up of extendeed family.

Though the women assist the men in day to day life, they have low status. No right of inheritence is allowed to them. Their roles are restricted to religious, social and economic fields. They contribute to family income from buying the sea catches from the Machhi and selling in the market, service in different government offices and working as *khalashis* (fishing labour). They do fishing for the small catches in the coastal area of Daman. *Fui* (father's sister) plays an important role during naming ceremony. They are forbidden to interfere in the political matters except to cast their votes during the periodical elections.

Srimant is the pre-birth ritual performed for the safe delivery at the closing of seventh month of pregnancy, and the expectant mother leaves for her parent's house. *Chhathi* is performed on the sixth day after birth followed by *khijra/barse* (naming ceremony) on twelfth day by *fui*. The pollution bath takes place on eleventh day but the pollution period extends upto fortieth day. *Botan* (first feeding of cereals) is performed in the sixth or eighth months after birth followed by *chaula/mundan/badha-utaravi* (tonsure) in the third or fifth years after birth by the barber, with the help of maternal uncle. *Charenaganthwanu* (betrothal) takes place one month prior to *lagan* (marriage) at the bride's residence in the presence of *samaj* Patel. Marriage is a matter of three days and the rituals are performed at both the houses and solemnised at the groom's residence. The three-day ritual starts with the erection of *mandava* (marriage booth) and installationn of *devak medh* (*kul* deity) on first day with the worship of Ganapati and *kul* deity. *Bar- Ghodi* (taking a round of the village in the marriage dress by the groom) on second day. *Maushala* comes on second day. On third day, the bridegroom comes to the bride's house with fruits and sweets and takes back the bride with her relatives to his house for marriage. *Ghana* is performmed and *pithi* is rubbed for three days to both at their respective houses. The principal ceremonnies in connection with marriage are *kanyadan*, *jaimal*, *hast-milap*, *mangalfera* (four circumambulation of the celestial fire in *mandava*), wearing of *mangalsutra* and putting of vermilion, *kanku* on bride's forehead and *ashirvad* by the participants. The Palsha Brahman officiates at the ceremonies. The bride returns to her house after marraige in the evening. Four step *mangalfera* ceremony is supposed to be the binding portion of the marriage. *Ana* is performed after five days. The rites connected with death are common to all other Hindu communities of Daman.

Water is the main economic resource for the Mangela which is under the control of Government. They are a landless community. Their occupation is associated with fishing and its allied activities. Fishing is their traditional as well as present primary occupation. Service in different government offices and fishing labour are the subsidiary occupations for them. Selling of fish in cash is done only by the female members on cash transaction. The Mangela are employed as *tandel* (captain) and *khalisi* (fishing labour) by the Machhi and get rupees 10,000/- and rupees 5,000/- to rupees 8,000/- per season, i.e. eight months. Their sea hunt includes pomfret, Indian Solmon, prawn, perches, and Bombay Ducks. A scheme for mechanization of fishing craft in the form of grant of loan cum subsidy from 1963 has been introduced to provide impetus to fishermen by the government of Goa, Daman and Diu.

Social control is fully regulated by their *samaj* (the traditional caste council) at four levels, viz. six villages level, twelve villages level, eighteen villages level and 56 villages level. The regional council of 56 villages is represented by the Patels of all the villages. The *samaj* consists of five *sabhyas* (members) headed by a Patel (chief) and assisted by one *karbhari* who are elected by voice vote. Social problems pertaining to deviation from the traditional norms, inter-family disputes and breach of rule are dealt by the *samaj*. They also take decisions on religious and economic activities. Inter-communities disputes are settled in consultation with the the Patels of each community. Excommunication and cash fine of rupees 501/- are the forms of punishment imposed by the *samaj*. An offender is accepted back in the community after paying the fine. The regional council of 56 villages is the post-liberation formation. Plan implement and welfare development activities are the role of modern statutory panchayat.

The Mangela have faith in Hindu religion and they are followers of the Sanatan Dharam Sect. They worship all Hindu deities and their favourite deity of worship, *isht devta*, is Lord Shiva who is also the village deity. Khandoba, Bhaidoba, Cheda, Narsha and Gangud are their clan deities. They have also belief in N.S. Dos Remedious (Lady of Remedy), one of the shrines of the Christians erected by Portuguese whom the Mangela consider as one of the seven sisters of Goddess Lakshmi who lost her caste. They visit the said shrine once in a year in the end of June by spirit of deep gratitude for the safe fishing expedition and good catch and make offerings of bread, vegetables and eggs. Mothers place their new born babies on the altar steps of the church for the blessings. Antonio Francisco (1904, p.219) has discussed the same. Somnath and Bhuleshwar temple in Gujarat and church of the Lady of Remedy are considered major sacred centres. Their main festivals are Diwali, Ujjani, Bhaibij and Shravani Poonam. The principal fair is Shivratri. They are active disciples of Swayadhaya Parivar of the socio- religious movement started by Pandurang Shastri at Madhav Bagh Pathshala, Bombay in 1967 with the aim and objective of self immunization, social service for the upliftment of the poor and the illiterate through the religious preaching of Geeta and community marriage which are examples of their activities. Their art and culture viz. tattoing, *satio* (floor design) and folk-songs are common to all the Hindu communities but the *koli* folk dance is the cultural element of the Mangela and Machhi only, where both men and women participate jointly on festive occassions.

Economy has been the important factor in their traditional linkages with all the communities, specially the Machhi of Daman related to their occupation of fishing. They accept water, *kachha* and *pucca* food from all the communities except the Mahyavanshi, Dubla, and Muslim. They have their own temples. Belief in Lady of Remedy has provided the linkages with the Christians in religious sphere. *Dharma-bahan* (putative kinship) is maintained with the Machhis, Vanias, Sagar and Bhandari. They share the crematorium with the Machhis. They have their own wells and water sources. Palsha Brahman is invited during the life-cycle rituals who accept *sidha* or cash as his remuneration. Modern linkages are fostered during the periodical election and social functions with the other communities, especially during Holi and Narial

Poonam. Receiving and rendering of service and patron client relationship exists with the Machhis. They have members holding white collar jobs and teachers.

They have a positive attitude towards the development programmes initiated by different government agencies. They send the girls to school who do not continue for higher studies due to socio-economic reasons. They avail of all the civic facilities provided after independence. They are linked to mass- communnication through radio, television, newspaper, cinema etc.

One of the significant features in the life and culture of the Mangela which shows the impact of Christianity is their religious belief in the Catholic church of N.S. Dos Remedios in Moti Daman whom they consider the sister of Goddess Lakshmi, the deity of wealth and prosperity and who protects them in deep sea during their sea-hunt. This was built by Ruy-de-Mello-Sapario, Captain Governor of Daman under Portuguese in year 1607. Another significant feature in their life is that marriage is solemnised at groom's residence.

N.K. Sinha

REFERENCES

Antonio, Francisco, *Noticas-E-Documentas-Para, A Historia De of Damao*, Bastoria (Goa), Vol. I, page 219, 1940.

Enthoven, R.E., *The Tribes and Castes of Bombay*, Vol. III, 1922, Bombay, The Government Central Press; Reprint, Vol. III pp. 1-5, 1975, Cosmo Publications, Delhi.

MITNA

The Mitna are a salt-making community of Daman. The Gujarati term 'mitna' means salt, thus the literal meaning of the word 'mitna' denotes salt-maker. The community does not have any legend, nor is history available in the existing literature about their origin and migration except that Enthoven (1922:56) and Antonio Francisco (1904:128) have described Mitna as a sub-division of the Machhi. They however, identify themselves as an independent community. They are distributed in the villages of Varakund, Nani Daman and Moti Daman of Daman district. They are also distributed in Umbergaon Taluka of Valsad district in Gujarat. Population figure is not available.

They are non-vegetarian and eat fish and meat of goat and fowls. Their staple food includes rice, wheat, *jawar*, pulses of *tur* (red gram) and *moong* (green gram). Vegetables are taken according to availability. Fruits are taken occasionally due to economic condition. Toddy is commonly enjoyed by men and women folk while alcoholic drinks are taken by men only, purchased from the local market. The special food preparations are *sira* (porridge), *lapsee* (wheat fried in ghee mixed with sugar), *puree* and *bhajya* are taken on the festive occasions.

The Mitna of Daman are divided into four exogamous groups which are identified with the *kutumb* (lineage), viz. Mota Kutumb, Nana Kutumb, Vathi Kutumb and Katha Kutumb. There is no stratification among the divisions and the basis of the differentiation is social. The function of *kutumb* is to trace their descent, to regulate marriage and to participate in the life cycle rituals. The name of the community, Mitna, was earlier suffixed as their surname which has taken the place of 'Patel'. They perceive their position in social hierarchy as inferior to the Brahman, Koli Patel, Kamli, Bhandari and Machhi in regional social hierarchy. They are aware of the *varna* system and place themselves as Kshatriya in *varna* order. They resort to community endogamy and *kutumb* exogamy. Marriage is settled by negotiation only and the form of marriage is monogamy. *Kanthi* (marriage pendant) is the marriage symbol for women. Earlier, *dej* (dowry) was fixed for Rs. 4.50 only, now it ranges from Rs. 12000/- to Rs. 15,000/-. Marriage with mother's brother daughter and mother's sister's daughter is permitted. Junior levirate and junior sororate are permitted on usual conditions. The rule of residence after marriage is patrilocal. *Chhutta* (divorce) is granted to both men and women by the *samaj* (caste council) and the post divorce maintenance is borne by her parents or brother. It is ascertained from the husband and wife if they are not willing to continue living together. The usual grounds for divorce are adultery, impotancy, chronic sickneess, and cruelty. They allow *natra* (remarriage) between widow, widower and divorcee. Parents of the women take the responsibility of getting the ceremony done. The oldest female member of the village put *kanku* (red vermilion mark) on her forehead. A feast is given to the *samaj*.

The common forms of *kutumb* (family) are extended and nuclear types. They have prescribed kinship usages viz. avoidance and joking relationship. Important role is played by mother's brother and sister's husband during marriage. Conflict and confrontation arise after father's death in financial matters. Inheritence follows the rule of male ultimogeniture for the residential land and male equigeniture for other properties. Eldest son succeeds to become *karta* (authority) after his father's death. Inter family linkages are maintained during the life cycle rituals, religious ceremonies and during the periodical elections. The Mitna women have a low status in the society. They assist in day to day life. They look after the household jobs and also contribute to family income by doing labour job. They assist their male members in salt production. They also have roles in agriculture operation, collection of fuels, bringing potable water, ritual observances and religious practices. They are forbidden to interfere in the political matter. *Fui* (father's sister) plays an important role, during *barsee* (naming) and *chaula* (head-shaving) ceremonies.

Rakhawadi and *srimant* are pre-birth rituals performed in the fifth and seventh month of pregnancy for the safe delivery and the expectant mother leaves for her parent's house. *Chhathi* is the first post-birth ritual performed on the sixth day after birth followed by *barse* (naming ceremony), on twelfth day by the *fui*. *Bahda-Utaravi* (tonsure) ceremony is performed in the third or fifth year after birth. The pollution period after birth extends upto forty days. After the marriage negotiation, marriage is finalised and then come *sagai* (betrothal) at bride groom's residence. Marriage is a matter of three days which starts with the erection of *mandava* (marriage booth) and installation of *gotrej* (lineage deity) on the first day. The maternal uncle brings *maushala* (marriage gifts and ornaments) on the second day followed by *barghorhi*. *Pithi* (mixture of turmeric and ground nut oil) is rubbed on the bodies of both the bride and the groom for three days. The *jan* (marriage procession) arrives at the bride's village in the afternoon and are given *janwas* (separate lodging). The groom with *jan*, arrives at the bride's residence escorted by *harvan* where he is received by the bride's mother. *Kanthi* (marriage pendant) is handed over by the groom's father to the bride. The principal ceremonies in connection with marriage are *jaimal*, *kanyadan*, *hasta milap*, *mangal fera* followed by feeding of sweets to each other. The groom with his bride and the *jan* returns back next day where they are received by the groom's mother. Homage is paid to the *gotrej*. Marriage feast is given by the bride's parents. *Ana* (return of the bride) takes place after five days. Brahman officiates at the marriage ceremony. The Mitna cremate the dead with the exception of children below eight years of age and death due to smallpox who are buried. The rites connected with death are performed by the eldest son, the chief mourner, who disposes off ashes and bones in sea on third day after cremation. *Shraddha* is performed on tenth, eleventh and twelfth days. Community dinner is given and the articles designated for the use of the departed soul are presented to the family priest on twelfth day. Family male members, including the chief mourner, shave their heads and moustaches on tenth day. Ghost marriage is performed to pacify the departed soul in case of the unmarried boy. Caste dinner is given after the completion of one year.

Land is the major economic resource for them which is under control of individual proprietor. They have a combination of both the land-owning and landless. Agriculture and salt production are their present day primary as well as traditional occupation. They use indigenous method of agriculture and salt production. They produce salt from the sea water. They were taken for six to seven months to Mozambique (Africa) and Basin near Bombay to work as labourers during the Portuguese regime due to their specialization in salt production. The salt industries have developed recently in Diu and the Mitna of Daman are involved in the production of salt. Agricultural labour, labour in salt industries, casual labour and work in government offices are other means of their livelihood. Payment of wages is made in cash on monthly basis, viz. Rupees 375/- for a labourer and rupee Rs. 600/- for the supervisor. Being expertise in salt production, some of them have migrated to Goa, Bombay, Diu, Madras, Kutch, Bharuch and Thane.

Social control is regulated by Mitna Samaj at village level. The *samaj* consists of five members headed by Patel (chief) and assisted by one *karbhari* who are elected by voice vote. The tenure of Patel runs for three years. Social problems pertaining to divorce, marriage, widow-marriage and deviation from the traditional norms are dealt with by the *samaj*. Inter-community disputes are settled in consultation with the Patel. Excommunication and cash fine of rupees fifty-one are the forms of punishment imposed by the council. The district level traditional caste-council, comprises seven villages, has been disorganized after liberation. Plan implementation and welfare and development activities are the other role of modern statutory panchayat.

The Mitna are Hindus. Their religious beliefs and practices postulate existence of supernatural and spiritual powers. They believe in gods and goddesses of Hindu pantheon but their favourite deities of worship are Lord Vishnu and Lord Shiva. Mahalakshmi and Moti Ma are their lineage deities who are worshipped during marriage birth and during *athem* in Chaitra month. Somnath and Bhuleswar temples are their main sacred centres. Their main festivals are Diwali, Ujjani, Bhai-Bij, Makar Sankranti and Shravani Poonam associated with the socio-religious significance. On Shravani Poonam, they worship the sea-God by throwing liquor, coconut and flowers in the sea. Holi and Navratri are also celebrated by them. Their principal fair is Shivratri. They have magico-religious belief in both the malevolent and benevolent spirits living near the sea coast which can be made subservient to human needs if care is taken not to offend them. Brahman attends to the life cycle rituals and religious practices. They do not have their own elements of art but have the elements common to all the Hindus of Daman. Only women sing songs and participate in folk dance.

This occupation of saltmaking has been the prime factor in inter-community linkages with all the communities specially with the Koli Patel and Kamli of Daman, Gujarat and Maharashtra. Brahman officiates at the lifecycle ceremonies. They accept water, *kacha* and *pucca* food from the Brahman, Koli Patel, Bhandari, Kamli, Sagar, Baria and Machhi. They share well and water resources with all the communities except the Mahyavanshi. They have their own temples and crematorium. Patron-client relationship is maintained with the Koli Patel and Kamli. Cultivator-labour relationship exists with the Dubla.

They have members holding white collar jobs. Political leadership has emerged at village panchayat level.

The literacy level among the boys has gone up. They do not send the girls to school due to economic reasons. Boys study upto secondary level and drop out because of economic reasons. They avail of all the facilities of drinking water, electricity, public distribution system, family-welfare and post office. Midday meal scheme for children and ICDS programmes are availed of. Their economic condition is not sound, and they have to depend on money-lenders and shopkeepers in their needs. The region has a good network of metalled road for transportation. The other medias of communication are radio, T.V., cinema etc.

N.K. Sinha

REFERENCES

Enthoven, R.E., *The Tribes and Castes of Bombay*, Vol. III, 1922, Bombay, The Government Central Press, Reprint, Vol. III, p. 56, 1975, Cosmo Publications, Delhi.

Francisco, Antonio, *Noticas-E-Documentas-Para-A Historia De of Damao*. Bastoria (Goa), Vol.II,page 128, 1904.

MOMIN

The Momin, a Muslim trading community, are also known Meman. They explain that the term 'Momin' has been derived from the word 'mahazarin' which denotes the followers of Hazarat Mohammad. *Gazetteer of Bombay Presidency* (1899: 76), *Gazetteer of the Baroda State* (1923 : 241), Enthoven (1922, Vol. III-62) and Sherring (1974, Vol. II-242 & 273) have reported that the Momins (believers) are Muslim converts of Multani Hindu castes originally from Sindh. Enthoven (1922, Vol. II,62) further reports that they were converted to Islam by different members of Ismailia Saiyads of whom Imam Shah (1449) of Pirana is most distinguished. They migrated from Kathiawad and Nadiad to Daman during the latter part of Portuguese regime. Gulam Nabi Ali Bhai was the first Momin to migrate from Vaso in Nadiad and settled in Daman in 1930 followed by Md. Fazle Karim Momin. They are distributed in the urban areas of Daman and in Gujarat. Population figure is not available. Urdu is their language within family and kin groups and Arabic and Gujarati are the scripts. They are also conversant with Portuguese, Urdu and Gujarati. Their women dress like Hindus and wear saree, Panjabi *kurta* and *paijama*.

They are non-vegetarian who take fish, egg and meat of goat and fowls. They do not take beef. Their staple food includes rice, *jowar*, pulses of *tur* and *mug*. They also take locally available vegetables and fruits. They smoke cigarette and chew betel regularly. *Biriyani* and *zarda* are the special foods made on the festive occasions.

The Momin do not claim to have any social division. They are Muslims and belong to Shia sect, also called as Jafri Saiyeed. They place themeselves in the Sheikh category of their traditional order. They suffix 'Momin' to their names. They perceive their position as high in status within the Muslim fold and higher to the Dhodia, Dubla and Mahyavanshi. They marry within the community and practise adult marriage. The rule of exogamy is applied to the extent that a boy and a girl should not have breast-feeding by one mother. They practise cross-cousin and parallel-cousin marriages. Marriage is settled by negotiation only. Though polygyny is allowed, they practise monogamy only. *Mehar* (mehr) is fixed during the negotiation and is promised in case of divorce. A girl goes to stay with her in-laws after her marriage. Marriage with wife's younger sister is allowed after wife's death. A married Momin woman wears *saree* and bangles which can be considered as a survival of the pre-chang practice before their conversion. *Talaq* (divorce) is granted to husband only. If wife desires divorce, she approaches the *jamat* (traditional council). According to the rule, one has to pass through the stage of desertion for two months, i.e. husband and wife live separately. After two months it is again ascertained by the *jamat* whether they need divorce. If they so desire, the *talak* is granted by the President of the *jamat* in the presence of two witnesses when the word *talak* is repeated three times and the wife is free. The amount of *mehar* is paid to the woman. Children become the liability of father. The reasons for divorce are barrenness and cruelty. They do allow remarriage for the widow, widower and the divorcees. The period of two months for desertion before divorce is taken into consideration to find out if the woman has conceived or if both have decided to live together again. Remarriage takes place according to the *nikah* rules. Till a divorcee woman remarries, post divorce maintenance is borne by the husband.

Avoidance is maintained between the mother-in-law and son-in-law, father-in-law and a daughter-in-law, with younger brother's wife and husband's elder brother. A woman covers her head while facing an avoidance relative. Joking relationship exists with elder brother's wife, husband's younger brother, wife's elder and younger sisters and elder and younger brothers. Conflict and confrontations in the family arise after father's death in property matter. The rule of inheritance follows the Islamic law where one eighth of the property goes to the daughters and remaining is equally distributed among the sons. Eldest son succeeds to the authority after father's death. Intra-community linkages are maintained during the life cycle rituals, in economic activities and during the election of *jamat* Patel (chief of traditional council). A Momin woman has a low status in the society. Their roles are restricted to household where they collect fuel, bring potable water and participate in ritual performances. They are prohibited to take part in the political affairs. They cast their votes during the periodical Assembly and Parliamentary elections.

The expectant mother has to observe restrictions during pregnancy.

The first delivery takes place at her parents' house. The expectant mother is to carry a knife or a piece of iron to protect herself and the child from the evil eye. She does not go outside the house on full-moon day and after the sunset avoids visiting sea. The new born child first of all hears the *takbir* (prayer) to his/her creator which is repeated by father or any elderly member of family in his/her ear called as *azan* (call). *Chhathi* is the first post-birth ritual performed on the sixth day after birth. The child is given name by the father or grand father after consulting Koran. The father looks up the page at random and wherever the first letter of the first word of third line occurs that is taken as the initial of the child's name. Purification bath takes place on the same day. The naming among the Momin starts with Mohammad and ends with Ali. *Aqiqa* (sacrifice) and *mundan* (tonsure) are performed for both male and female children after the completion of three months. *Sunnat* (circumcision) is performed on the male child after the completion of one year. Pollution for mother, after birth, is observed for 40 days. The first Ramjan fast of a boy or girl is initiated after the completion of eight years. *Shagai* (betrothal) takes place one year prior to *nikah* (marriage) at the house of the girl. The exchange of gift takes place between the *shagai* and *nikah*. On the marriage day the bridegroom with the *jan* arrives at bride's village in the evening. When the time comes for marriage, a *sehra* (flower-sheet) is fastened round the head of the bridegroom by his father and the groom rides on a horse with the help of father and relatives. On the arrival at bride's residence both the parties sit in *mandav* (marriage place) side by side. The groom, the agents of the bride and *kazi* ask the bride's agent for her acceptance with certain fixed *mehar*. If she accepts the same is represented to the bridegroom. The proceedings are recorded by the registrar and signed by the groom, the girl's agent and the *kazi*. The *nikah* ceremony ends with the recital of *kalma* from the holy book Koran. A marriage dinner is given by the bride's father. The newly married couple returns to groom's village next day after *nikah*. The consummation of marriage takes place at groom's house. The Momin bury their dead. The body is placed on bier and carried by only the relatives and *namaje zanaja* (funeral prayer) is performed at the gate of the mosque first before the funeral procession starts for the burial ground. *Shayum* (recital of the *Koran Shareef*) is performed on the third day for the peace of the departed soul. *Chaleesi* (fortieth day) is performed to remove death pollution. For forty days no food is cooked in the house of the deceased. The mourning period extends up to six months when no festivals are celebrated.

The Momin are a landless community. Weaving of silk and cotton fabrics are their traditional occupation. Weaving by power-loom, and running small scale industries and cloth shops are their present day primary occupation. General merchandise and service in different government offices are other means of their livelihood. Women assist them in weaving and preparing thread and men weave cloth on handlooms. Now only men do this job. The shopkeepers purchase the clothings from Surat, Valsad and Bombay and sell in daily markets of Daman. They also work as labourers in small scale hosiery industry at Daman and Vapi. They have specialization in the weaving of saree especially for the women fisherfolk which has now given way to tailoring of clothes.

Social control is exercised by Momin *jamat* (traditional council) at village level, headed by a Patel (chief) and assisted by five *sabhyas* (members). The Patel is elected by voice vote. *Sunat jamat* of Momin was formed in 1962. It is headed by a President and assisted by Vice President and twelve members. Social problems, inter-family disputes and financial problems within the community are dealt with by the *jamat*. During the liberation of Goa, Daman and Diu, whole municipal market was destroyed by bombing. The *jamat* acquired the space to run the shops of the community for six months till the shops were reconstructed by the Municipality. Disrespect to the council and inter-community marriage are major social offences and an offender is excommunicated from the community. Plan implementation and welfare and development activities are the other roles of modern statutory panchayat and municipality.

They profess Islam and belong to Shia sect. They belong to the Hanafi school which travelled from Sindh to North Gujarat and then to Bombay and Daman. They believe in the Pir and visit the *majar* (mausoleum) of Jorawar Pir located in Valsad district of Gujarat to fulfil their vowes. Their major shrines are Mecca and Ajmer Shareef in Rajasthan. *Kazi* performs their life cycle rituals. They resort to magic and sorcery. Id-ul-Fitre and Id-ul-Zuha, Shab-e-Barat and Muharram are their major festivals celebrated with zest which are associated with the religious belief. Their art is represented by their traditional occupation of weaving of special *saree* for fisher women folk. Folk songs related to *nikah* is common as in Gujarat.

The Momin accept water, *kachha* and *pucca* food from all the Hindu communities and the Christian except the Mahyavanshi. They have their own burials, mosque, and school for religious preaching and teaching of Arabic. They share well and water resources with all the communities. Employer-worker relationship exists with the Machhi for weaving purposes. The community have businessmen, members holding white colar jobs. Political leadership has emerged at the levels of village panchayat and municipality.

The literacy level has gone up among their boys who study up to college and drop out due to economic reasons and as they have to support their family. Girls study upto primary level and drop out due to social reasons. They make full use of modern system of medicare. Their attitude is not favourable towards family planning and they prefer to have four or more children. They avail of all the civic facilities provided by Daman Administration. They are exposed to mass communication through radio, television, cinema etc.

N.K. Sinha

REFERENCES

Enthoven, R.E., *The Tribes and Castes of Bombay*, Vol. III, 1922, Bombay, The Government Central Press; Reprint, Vol. III, p. 62, 1975, Cosmo Publications, Delhi.

Gazetteer of the Bombay Presidency, *Gujarat Population: Musalaman and Parsis*, Government Central Press, Bombay, Vol. IX, Part II, page 76, 1899.

Gazetteer of the Baroda State, *General Informations*, Times Press, Bombay, Vol. I, Page-241, 1923.

Sherring, M.A., *The Hindu Castes and Tribes*, Vol. II, 1879, Calcutta, Thakar Spinks & Co.; Reprint, Vol. II, p. 242, 1974, Cosmo Publications, Delhi.

SAGAR

The Sagar explain that the term 'sagar' denotes their habitation near *sagar* (sea). According to their legend they trace their descent from Raghunath, the Kshatriya king of Sagaria Bhagirathi of Chapaner in Gujarat who migrated from the place after the Moghul invasion and settled in different parts of Gujarat and fifteen families in Daman before the Portuguese established their rule. Enthoven (1922-311) says, "The Sagars ('sa' means 'with' and 'gar' means 'poison') claim to be the descendant of Sagar, a king of solar race, son of Bahu and great grand-father of Bhagirath born with poison on account of his mother Sumati being poisioned by another wife of his father, whose 60,000 descendants migrated from the Gangetic Valley to Bhilwada and then to Mangrol in Gujarat." Antonio Francisco (1904-128) has discusseed their settlement in Daman. They are distributed in the Damanwada and Pariari villages of Daman. In Gujarat, they are distributed in Gandevi, Surat, Bharooch, Ankleshwar, Tilakwada, and Ahmedabad. Though Enthoven (1922-312) has reported two endogamous groups of the Sagar viz. Gujarat Sagar and Saurathia Sagars, evidently territorial, the Sagars of Daman do not have such divisions now. Population figures are not available.

They are non-vegetarian who take fish and the meat of goat and fowls. Their staple food includes *bhat* (rice), *rotla* (bread prepared of rice and *jawar*) *sag* (curry of vegetables and meat), and pulses of *tur* (redgram) and *mag* (green gram). Fruits are taken occassionally. Toddy is commonly enjoyed by men and women while alcoholic drink is socially approved for men only. The special food, viz. *sira* (porridge), *lapsee* (wheat fried in ghee mixer with sugar), *puree* (fried bread) and *bhajiya* (pakoda) are taken on the festive occasions.

The Sagars of Daman are divided into four exogamous groups based on the *kul* (clan), viz. Bhagirathi, Rathod, Chauhan and Parmar which are identical with the Rajput clans showing their descent from the Rajput. Enthoven (1922: 312) has discussed thirteen groups of Sagars of Gujarat referring to the profession followed by the community. There is no stratification among these groups. The function of the *kul* is to trace their descent, to regulate their marriage and to help in the life-cycle rituals. They suffix 'Sagar' to their names. They place their position in the social heirarchy after Brahmans, Koli Patel and Kamli. They are well aware of the *varna* system and recognize their place in Kshatriya order. They resort to community endogamy and *kul* exogamy. A marriage cannot take place within the three ascending generations from both the sides. Adult-marriage has taken the place of child marriage. Earlier the age at marriage for boys was fifteen years and for girls was twelve years which has raised to 22 and 18 years. Marriage is settled by negotiation only and girl's father takes initiative. The form of marriage is monogamy. *Kanthi* (marriage pendant) presented by the groom to his bride, and *kanku* (vermilion mark on forehead) are the symbols for married women. *Dej* (brideprice) is paid in kind which includes two to three *tolas* of gold ornaments, during *adarni* (betrothal) to the girl by the boy's father. The couple goes to stay at groom's house after marriage. *Chhutta* (divorce) is granted to both by the *gnyat panch* (caste council). Who so ever approaches for divorce she/he has to pay Rs. 51/- to the caste council and the brideprice is refunded. The post-divorce maintenance is looked over by her parents or brother. *Natra* (remarriage) is permitted and degree of prohibition for three ascending generations from both the sides is registered. It is performed at the women's father's house. The *gnyat panch* must be consulted. Junior levirate and junior sororate are permitted. Adult marriage, self arranged marriage, decline in divorce cases and the matrimonial relation with the Sagars of Gujarat are the changes taking place in the institution of marriage after liberation.

Extended and nuclear families are the common types of *kutumb* (family). They have prescribed kinship usages, viz. avoidance and joking relationship. As per the Portuguese Right of Property Act, after father's death, 50% goes to mother and 50% are divided among the sons. In absence of son, the *dattak* (adoption) is taken out of the brother's sons. Eldest son succeeds to the *karta* (authority) and mother's brother plays the role of bringing *maushala* (customary right of gift of the marriage dress) during the marriage. Conflict and confrontations erupts after father's death and son's marriage in property matters. Inter-family linkages are sought during the life-cycle rituals and in the economic activities. Women have low status in the community. Right of inheritance is not granted to women. They have roles in collection of fuel, bringing potable water, social functions, rituals and religious spheres. They also assist their men in economic activities. They also contribute to family income by doing labour works. *Fui* (father's sister) plays an importance role during naming and tonsure ceremonies and sister plays an important role during widow remarriage.

Srimant is the pre-birth ritual performed in the seventh month of pregnancy and the expectant mother leaves for her parent's house. *Chhathi* is performed on sixth day after birth followed by the *chaula* (tonsure) on seventh or ninth day after birth. *Barse/Khijra* (naming) ceremony is performed five weeks after birth by the *fui* (father's sister). Though the pollution bath takes place on seventh day but the pollution period extends upto three months and then only she returns to her husband's house. *Adarni* (betrothal) takes place one month prior to *lagan* (marriage) at the groom's residence in the presence of *gnyat panch* (caste council). Marriage is a matter of three days and rituals are performed at both the places but is solemnized at the bride's residence. Marriage is registered in the office at Daman and a certificate is secured after the betrothal and finally the permission for marriage is given by the *gnyat* Patel (caste council chief). The three days rituals starts with the erection of *mandva* (marriage booth) at bride's residence and installation of *devak modh* (clan-deity) at both the places. *Bar-ghodi* and *maushala* (obligatory gift of marriage dress by maternal uncle) take place on second day. *Pithi* (a mixture of turmeric poder and water) is rubbed on the bodies of the both for three days. The *jan* (marriage party) leaves for bride's village on third day where they are given separate lodging. The bridegroom arrives at bride's residence where he is received by the bride's mother. *Kanthi* (marriage pendant) is given to the bride by the bridegroom's mother or sister. The principal ceremonies in connection with marriage are *kanyadan, jaimal, hast-milap, mangalfera,* garlanding of *mangalsutra,* feeding of sweets by spouses to each other and *ashirvad* by the participants. The Brahman officiates at the ceremonies. The bridegroom returns with his bride in the same night or sometimes on the next day after marriage. *Ana* (return of the bride) takes place after five days. The Sagar cremate the dead. Children upto six year, caste saints, and persons died of small pox and chicken pox are buried which is called *dathna.* Saints are buried in sitting posture. Ashes and bones are collected on the third day and disposed off in the sea. They observe pollution for three days but the mourning period extends upto tenth day and the male members of the family, including the chief mourner, shave their heads and moustaches. *Shraddha* is performed on tenth, eleventh and twelfth days. Caste dinner is given and the articles, designated for the use of the departed soul, are presented to the family priest on twelfth day. Ghost marriage (marriage of a male and a female calf) is performed to pacify the departed soul in case of the death of an unmarried boy.

Land is the main economic resource for the Sagar which is under individual proprietorship. The community have combination of both the landowning and landless categories. Agriculture, specially the growing of vegetables, is their traditional as well as present day primary occupation. Labour job, wine and toddy shops, tailoring and service in government offices are the other means of livelihood. Local market is fully regulated, and they sell vegetables directly to the markets where the transaction is made in cash. Women of the community sell the vegetables also by hawking. Earlier the Sagar were tenants to the Koli Patels and Bhandaris and became land owners after liberation according to the Government Act. Casual labourers receive their remuneration in cash only while the agricultural labourers receive in both cash and kind.

Their traditional council named Sagar Gnyat Panch operates at village level. The *gnyat panch* consists of five members headed by a Patel (chief) and assisted by one *karbari* who are elected by voice vote. The tenure of Patel runs for five years. Social problems pertaining to divorce, marriage, widow marriage and disputes within the community are dealt with by the *gnyat panch*. Inter-community disputes are settled with the consultation of the Patels of each community. Excommunication and cash fine of Rs. 51/-, (earlier it was rupee one and fifty paise), are the forms of punishment imposed by the council. Rigidness about excommunication has lessened now. Plan implementation and welfare and development activities are the role of modern statutory Panchayat.

The Sagar profess Hinduism and believe in Jalaram sect. Though they worship all the Hindu deities but their favourite goddess is Maha Kali. They also believe in exorcism and ordinary omens. Kalika Mata and Dagal Mata are their *kul* deities whose importance are sought during birth and marriage. Birpore in Saurashtra of Gujarat is the major sacred center for the community. A Sagar desires to pay homage to the Ganges once in their life time. Their main festivals are Navratra, Diwali, Holi and Rakshabandhan. Weapons are worshipped in Navratra and agricultural tools during sowing days. The Bajkhedwal Brahmans attend to the job of their sacred specialist. The principal fair is Shivratri at Bhuleshwar temple in Gujarat which is common to all the Hindu communities. The community does not have any element of art of its own and *satiyo* (floor design), tattooing, folk songs and *gherba* folk dance are common to all the Hindu comunities. Men and women participate in the dance separately.

Occupation has been the important factor in their traditional linkages with all the communities specially the Koli Patel and the Bhandari of Daman related to their occupation of agriculture. The services of Bajkhedwal Brahmins are sought during the life cycle rituals. The Mahyavanshis perform the job of drum beating during marriage. They accept water, *kachha* and *pucca* food from the Brahmans, Koli-Patel, Bhandari, Kamli, Dhodhia and Baria. They have their own temple and crematorium. They consider water as pure and cannot carry pollution with it. Modern linkages are established during the periodical elections and other social functions. The political leadership has emerged at panchayat level.

The development programmes do not have much of an impact. Their literacy level which is very low. Boys study up to primary level and drop out due to economic reason. Girls do not study. They avail of the civic facilities of drinking water, electricity, public distribution system, banking, family welfare and post office. The midday meal scheme for children and ICDS programmes are availed of. The community uses organic manure, chemcial fertilizer and insecticides. Sources of irrigations are rain water and tubewells. They are linked to the mass communication through radio, television, newspaper, cinema etc.

N.K. Sinha

REFERENCES

Antonion, Francisco, *Noticas-E-Documentas-Para A Historia De of Damao*, Bastoria (Goa) Vol.II, Page 128, 1904.

Enthoven, R.E., *The Tribes and Castes of Bombay*, Vol. III, 1922, Bombay, The Government Central Press; Reprint, Vol. III, pp. 311-315, 1975, Cosmo Publications, Delhi.

SALAT

The Salat, a community of sculptors, also call themselves Sompura Brahmans. The word 'salat', a derivate of Gujarati word 'salya' means 'stone'. Thus the Salat denotes the stone worker. They recall their origin from the Sompura Brahman who are the priest attached to the temple of Somnath and were instructed by Lord Shiva to start the job of stone cutting. Enthoven (1922 : Vol.III, 316) has desribed the Salat as stone worker. According to their legend Hiradhar and Gangadhar were the first to immigrate from Siddhapur Patan state (presently Sabarkantha and Palanpur) to Diu during the regime of the Turks, i.e. before the Portuguese established their rule. Gradually, the number of the migrants went on rising. In course of time a majority of the Salat migrated back to different places of Gujarat due to lack of interest in their traditional occupation during the Portuguese regime. They are divided into three endogamous subgroups on the basis of occupation namely Sompura Salat (sculpture) Kumbhar Salat (masons or potters) and Talboda Salat (stone sculpture) and out of them, the Sompura Salat occupy the highest position. They are distributed in Diu town and also in Surat, Valsad, Vatod, Palitana, Verawal, Junagadh, Mangrol and Somnath Patan having their main concentration in Porbandar of Gujarat. Gujarati is their spoken language as well as their script within and outside the community. They are also conversant with Hindi in relation to others.

Traditionally they are vegetarian conscious of the fact keeping in the mind that nonvegetarian dishes degrade the purity of the art of stone-work. Taking of nonvegetarian dishes by the men is a way ecological adaptation during the Portuguese regime. Their staple food includes rice, *bajra*, pulses of *tur* and *urad* with jaggery. They also consume vegetables. The locally available fruits viz. *keri* (mango), *jamfal* (guava) and banana are taken moderately. They enjoy tea, milk and buttermilk. They occassionally take alcoholic drinks, which is a recent change. They also enjoy smoking *bidi*, cigarettes and chewing tobacco leaf and betel.

Their special food preparation include *puri* (fried bread), *dudhpog* (rice boiled in milk mixing sugar) and *lapsee* (porridge) which are made use of on the festive occasions.

The Salat of Diu are divided into eight *gots*, exogamous divisions, namely Sompura, Yadav, Maniyar, Hariyal, Dabhi, Jethwa and Parmar on the basis of social differentiation. The chief function of the *got* is to trace descent and to regulate marriage alliances. These *got* names are suffixed to their names. Diwecha is the surname, adopted recently. They enjoy high position in the regional social hierarchy after the Brahmin. They are well aware of the *varna* system and recognize their position among the Brahman. Other consider them between the Brahman and the Kshatriya. They are considered lower in rank to the Salat of Gujarat due to their change of food habits. They resort to community and subgroup endogamy and *got* exogamy. They practise adult marriage which is the changed form of child marriage. They allow cross-cousin marriage. Marriage is settled by negotiation and they practise monogamy only. *Kanku* (vermilion mark on forehead), *bangdi* (bangles of turtle shell and Ivory) are their marriage symbols. They have practice of *dej* (dowry) in kind only, i.e. 30 to 40 grams of gold which is fixed during the negotiation. Rule of residence is patrilocal. They do not allow divorce. *Natra* (remarriage) is permitted which takes place between widow and widower and through *dewar-batu* (junior levirate) and junior sororate. *Natra* is performed in a simple ceremony in the presence of *gnyat panch* (traditional council). Regular form of marriage is observed fully in case of a widower marrying a unmarried girl. One of the significant changes in the marriage rules of the Salat, that took place during the Portuguese, is that they adopted cross-cousin marriage due to the change in food habits (nonvegetarian and taking of alcoholic drinks) and the territorial blockade of the region between 1954 and 1961.

The Salat have prescribed kinship usages, viz. avoidance and joking relationship. They maintain avoidance relationship with mother-in-law, son-in-law, daughter-in-law and father-in-law, younger brother's wife and husband's elder brother's wife. Joking is maintained with elder brother's wife, husband's younger brother, and wife's elder and younger brothers. Property is the main factor for conflict among the family members after father's death. All sons get equal share in the property but the eldest son succeeds the authority in the family. In the absence of son/sons brother's son is adopted as the successor and the inheritor.

Sister's husband has an important role of *harvan* (accompanier) and maternal uncle brings *maushala* (customary marriage gift) during his or her marriage. Women have low status. Their roles are restricted to religious, ritual, social and domestic fields. They also contribute to family income by doing service in different government organizations. *Fui* (father's sister) plays and important role during *nampari* (naming) and *mundan* (head shaving) ceremonies. Inter-family linkages are sought during the lifecycle rituals and the political activities.

Shrimant is the first pre-birth ritual performed in the seventh month of pregnancy to guard the embryo from injury and the expectant mother leaves for her parents next day in the first pregnancy. *Dayan* (local midwife) attends the job of delivery. They also take the service of Government doctor during delivery. Women in pregnancy has to observe certain restrictions. *Chhathi* is the first post-birth ritual performed on the sixth day after birth and *suraj-pujan* (sun worship) is performed in the evening. The mother, with the new born infant, pays homage to the *gotrej* (*got* deity). Caste-dinner is given in the night. *Nampari* (naming) is performed by the *fui*, after procuring the *rashi-name* (zodiac name) from the Brahmin. Horoscope of the child is prepared on the naming day. *Mundan* is performed in the third or fifth month after birth by a barber and *fui* collects the hair and disposes off in the sea. They observe birth pollution for forty five days when the mother is forbidden to visit the religious places and to enter the kitchen. *Yajnopavit* (sacred thread ceremony) is performed in the eighth year of birth and the family priest who invests the boy with a sacred cord made of cotton applying the boy has reached the stage of a *brahmachari*. The priest also whisper the *gayatri-mantra* in the boy's ear. A girl in menses observe pollution for five days. *Sagai* (betrothal) takes place one or two months prior to *lagan* (marriage) at the boy's residence initiated by girl's father and her maternal uncle. Marriage is a matter of three days and the ritual connected with this is performed at both the residences but is solemnised at the bride's residence. The three days rituals starts with the installation *manek-stambh* (sacred pole) stained with turmeric and near it is placed a *kalash* (jar) full of water. Erection of *mandava* (marriage booth) is done at both the houses there after. *Pithi* (a pastelike preparation of barley flour, turmeric and groundnut oil) is rubbed on the bodies of the both for three days at their respective houses. *Maushala* (gift of marriage dress) is presented to both by their maternal uncles on the second day and *jan* (marriage procession) starts for the bride's village where they are given *janiwas* (separate lodging) on their arrival. The *jan* with the groom arrives at bride's house in the evening where *ponkhavan* (reception of the groom) is performed by the bride's mother. *Har-todi* (exchange of garland) is performed at *otah* (inner verandah) and the groom is led to *chauri* (square of sacrificial fire) in the *mandva* and is seated there. The bride is also brought in the *mandava* escorted by her maternal uncle and is seated on the left side of the groom. *Kanyadan* is performed there after when groom is presented a golden ring by the bride's father. The priest recites the sacred verses and their robes are knotted together followed by *hasta-milap*, when the priest joins the right hands of both covered by a piece of cloth with recitation of the verses. *Saptapadi* is the last and the principal ritual performed, and the bride and groom circumambulate seven rounds of the *chauri*. Family deity is worshipped by both in the family oratory and the groom returns to *janavas*. *Chaturthi karma* is performed on the third day in *mandava* and both feeds each other *kansar* (rice boiled in milk mixing jaggery). *Dej* (dowry), in kind, is given to the groom. The groom with his bride pays homage to the village diety and the *gotrej* (family deity). The consummation of marriage takes place at groom's residence. *Ana* (return of the bride) takes place after twenty days or three months. The Salat cremate the dead and rites connected with death are performed by the eldest son, the chief mourner. A *kalash* (earthen pot), full of water and lamp are kept in the house for the use of the deceased during the mourning period which extends upto tenth day. Ashes and bones are collected after cremation and disposed off in the Triveni Sangam near Somnath or Hiran Saraswati or in the sea. They observe death pollution for ten days. *Pind dan* (offering of the holy rice balls to the departed soul) is performed on eleventh day and the family and *got* members shave their heads and moustaches and *got* members are fed. *Pitra dan* (offering of four rice balls to the ancestors) is performed on twelfth day and community dinner is given. *Kriya* (memorial rites) is performed on thirteenth day and the favourite articles of the deceased are donated to the priest, who performs the funeral rites.

The Salat are a landless community. Their traditional occupation was stone-cutting. Besides they were involved in architectural works in house-building, sculpture and stone-made articles of domestic use. They have been expert in portrait paintings. The temples of Somnath in Gujarat and others in Diu were built by the Salat. At present, their primary occupation is service in schools and other government offices. Masonary work is the other means of livelihood. Only one family of the community owns cultivable land in Diu. They engage the Khedut Koli as the agricultural labour on daily wages in cash. They are linked to the daily regulated market to purchase general provisions and the transaction is made in cash.

Social control is exercised by the traditional councils at the local level namely *gynat panch* (village level) headed by a Patel, and Samast Salatak Nate at regional level comprising of six places viz. Porbandar, Somnath, Patan, Verawal, Mangrol, Junagadh of Gujarat and Diu which is headed by a Pramukh with its headquarters at Porbandar. Other office bearers are *upapramukh* and *mantri* (secretary). Both the Patel and the Pramukh are elected by voice vote. Social problems pertaining to deviation from the traditional norms and breach of rules are dealt by the *gnyat panch*. There is a traditional rule that a negotiation for marriage can not be broken after engagement. Inter-family disputes are also solved by the Patel. Excommunication and cash fine are the form of punishment imposed by the Pramukh on the offender. The meeting of the regional council is called once in a year at any of the said places to deal with the social problems and to make reforms on the evil of the system. Plan implement and developmental activities are the role of modern statutory Panchayat.

They profess Hinduism and believe in Shaivism. Their religious belief and practices recognize the existence of the supernatural power viz. worship of natural objects based on the mystry of their growth namely *pipal*, *tulsi* (basil), *vad* (banyan) and *val* (creeper) and devotion to cow is predominent feature. Their Shaiva belief resort to Lord Shiva which is their community as well as the village deity. They also believe in spiritual power living around the village. They keep the regular Hindu fasts and visit the usual places of pilgrimage. Their *got* deities are Mahalakshmi and Modeshwari Mata who are worshipped daily with their community deity and in a special way during the life-cycle rituals. Shivratree is their major festival associated with religion. They also celebrate the other Hindu festivals namely Diwali, Navratri, Rakshabandhan and Holi with full vigour. Mahibij festival is celebrated on Shukla Paksha Dvitiya of Magh month which is associated with the worship of sea-god and adoption of sea ecology. They consider Somnath as their main sacred centre. Their sacred specialists are the Gaur Brahmans who help them in ritual performances and paying homages. Their art and culture is represented by both the materialistic and non-materialistic objects. They have the art of portrait painting and architectural work. Sculpture is their handicraft, and they make the statues of deities and construct temple and palacial buildings. They have folk songs which are sung by the women only. *Garba* and *dandiya ras* are the folk dances and they are performed by women only.

They accept water, *pucca* and *kachha* food from the Brahman, Sangharia, Vania, and Soni. Their occupation has been the main factor for their traditional linkages with all the Hindu communities of Diu. The services of Gaur Brahman is required for their ritual performances and religious activities. Matrimonial alliances with Nagar Brahman, Vania and Soni were permitted during Portuguese regime due to the territorial bindings. They share the crematorium with the Brahman and Vania. Though they have their own temple, they also visit the temples of other Hindu communities. They participate in the Poonam Mela festival of Kalinki Mata temple at Buchadwada with all other Hindu communities. They are invited by all other communities during marriage. They employ the Khedut Koli for their services during cultivation. They have members holding teaching profession. Inter-community linkages are saught during the periodical election at political level.

Their attitude is positive towards the development programmes initiated by the government. Boys study up to college level and girls up to the secondary level and drop out as the boys have to earn to support their family. Girl do not continue higher study as their is no any college in Diu. The majority of them are employed in teaching and government offices. They make use of both the traditional and modern system of medicare. They favour family planning but prefer to have two or three children. They use modern methods of family planning. They avail of the facilities of drinking water by dug-well and piped water. They avail of the electricity facility and ration distribution system, mid-day meal scheme for children and ICDS under nutritional scheme. Firewood, cowdung cakes and kerosene oil are fuel resources. Their attitude towards saving is favourable. The area has a good network of road. They are exposed to mass communication by radio, T.V., cinema, post office, newspapers etc.

N.K. Sinha

REFERENCES

Enthoven, R.E., *The Tribes and Castes of Bombay*, Vol. III, 1922, Bombay, The Government Central Press; Reprint, Vol. III, p. 316, 1975, Cosmo Publications, Delhi.

Sherring, M.A., *Hindu Tribes and Castes*, Vol. II, 1879, Calcutta, Thakar Spink & Co.; Reprint, Vol. II, p. 253, 1974, Cosmo Publications, Delhi.

SANGHARIA

The Sangharia of Diu, are the makers of the turtle-shell and ivory products. The term 'Sangharia' has been derived from the Gujarati word 'sanghar' meaning a tool of polishing the raw material. They also call themselves Brahma Kshatriya. They are said to have migrated from Punjab to Pali in Rajasthan and finally to Diu before the Portuguese established their rule. Nothing much is known in the existing literature about them except some accounts by Enthoven (1920), Crooke (1896) and Rose (1919) who have described the community as an endogamous division of Gandharias who were probably allied to the Chhangar of Punjab or related to Sengar, the Rajput sect. They are distributed in the municipal area of Diu and the adjoining districts of Gujarat. Census figures are not available. Gujarati is their language as well as the script within the community and outside. They are also conversant with Hindi, Portuguese and English.

They are purely vegetarian. Their stapple food includes *bhat* (rice), wheat, *bajra*, pulses of *tur* and *mong*. Fruits viz. *jamrukh* (guava) and *kel* (banana) are taken daily. Milk, butter milk and tea form the part of their daily drink. They do not take alcoholic drinks. The special food preparation viz. *puri*, *lapsee*, *dudh-pag* (porridge) are made use of on the festive occasions like marriage, Ujjani, Diwali and Dhulendi.

The Sangharia are divided into five exogamous groups on the basis of *got*. These are Kumkna, Diwecha, Mainpura, Jajaw and Dhanda. The basis of differentiation is at social and territorial levels, e.g. the Sangharia from Diu are called Diwecha, which they also suffix to their names. The chief functions of *got* are to regulate marriage alliances and to invite members during the life cycle rituals. Verma is the surname adopted by them recently. They perceive their position as inferior to the Brahman and Salat. They are well aware of the *varna* system and recognize their place as Kshatriya. They resort to community endogamy and *got* exogamy. The bride and the bridegroom should not be blood relation for four *pidhees* (ascending generations) from the mother's side. They practise adult marriage and age for marriage ranges from 22 to 25 years for boys and 18 to 22 years for girls. Marriage is settled by negotiation. They practise monogamy. A married woman uses *bangdi* (bangles of turtle-shell) and ties *mangalsutra* round her neck as her marriage symbol. They do not have the practice of dowry. A girl after marriage goes to stay with her in-laws. They do not allow divorce. *Nara* (remarriage) is allowed between a widow and a widower which is solemnised in the presence of *gnyati* Patel (traditional councils chief). Adult marriage has taken the place of child marriage in recent years.

The institution of *kutumb* (family) consists of joint and extended families. Respect is duly paid to the elderly members of the family. It is the duty for the elders to assist and look after the youngestors as a part of the obligation. Avoidence in terms of talking with husband's elder brother and elder male and female in-laws is maintained. Joking is permitted with the elder brother's wife, husband's younger brother and with wife's younger sister and brothers. Mother's brother has an important role during marriage. Sister's husband plays the role of *anwar* (accompanier) during the marriage. Conflict and confrontations within the family arise after sons' marriage and after father's death in property and financial matters. All sons get equal share in father's property. Daughter's son is adopted through the official procedure in the court in case of no male issue. Eldest son succeeds the authority in the family. Inter-family linkages become more close for them during the life cycle rituals, election of the *gnyati* Patel, religious ceremonies and assistance in the economic activities. The Sangharia women have low status in the society. No right of inheritance is granted to the daughters. Half of the properties goes to widow after the death of her husband who has full right to give her will to anybody during her life time. Women's role's are restricted to household jobs, social and religious spheres. *Fui*, (father's sister) plays an important role during *barse baria* (naming) and *balmoura* (tonsure) ceremonies. In political matters, women are forbidden to interfare except to cast their vote in the periodical elections.

The life-cycle rituals right from birth to death are common to all Hindu communities of Diu which have already been discussed in the Introduction. Marriage is solemnized at the bride's residence and is consummated at the groom's residence. In changing situation, marriage rituals have been curtailed from five to three days to save money and time. *Dej* (dowry) was their traditional practice which does not exist now.

The Sangharia are a landless community. Bangle-making from lac, ivory and turtle-shell is their present day primary occupation. Tie and dye was their traditional ocupation. They shifted to the occupation of bangle-making in course of time. They have specialization in the craft of *kachkaru* (turtle-shell) making which they brought from Mozambique, one of the Portuguese colonies in Africa. One of the Sangharias visited there and learnt the craft of turtle-shell making where dishes were being made of. The Sangharia started the ornamental craft of turtle-shell. They have been importing the raw materials from Sri Lanka and Mozambique where special kind or turtle is available for the craft. In addition to this, they produce bangles of phinolic tubes, the artificial raw material or synthetic turtle shell, purchased from a licensed party at Pali who used to import it from Germany. The ivory work was also introduced with the beautiful engraving in all products. They use self made tools viz *pana, barakhi, chens*, emerical wheel and buff machines. The cost of turtle shell products viz; *bangdi* (bangles), *butti* (ear tops), *kudedis* (ring) bracelet, earrings and buttons; ranges from rupees five to Rs. 250/-. The turtle shell raw material costs Rs. 400/- per kg which contains 35 to 40 small pieces. The raw materials for the ivory work are procured from Ahmedabad and cost of a pair of ivory bangles ranges from Rs. 90/- to Rs. 120/-. Service in the government offices is the secondary occupation for them which is part of change in their economy. The area of the turtle shell products and its trade has widened to the national and international level.

The political organization of the Sangharia consists *of gnyati panch* (the traditional caste council) at village level which functions at a fixed place called *baithak*. The council consists of five elderly members as *sabhya* (member) of the community who elect the Patel (chief) by voice vote on the basis of high social standing. The age factor is also an important point. Social disputes pertaining to marriage and disputes with inter and intrafamily are referred to it. Other functions include the maintenance of the traditional norms and values of the community. Excommunication is the form of punishment inflicted by the council. The political organization has gone under change after liberation. The modern statutory panchayat was introduced. Its activities are centered to welfare and implementation of development programme.

The Singharia profess Hinduism. They worship all the leading Hindu deities and observe the principal Hindu festivals. Hing Raj Mata is their village deity as well as their *goter* deity who is worshipped during birth, marriage and before doing any auspicious work. They also worship Kalinki Mata, one of the main deities of all the Hindu communities of

Diu. Every year on Chaitra Shukla Ashtami, the auspicious day, they and the Bhoiraj are the first to visit the deity as per the tradition. Hinglaj Mata is worshipped in a ceremonial manner by them in the month of Jyeshtha every year. They consider Somnath, Gupta Prayag, Dwarka (all in Gujarat), as their major sacred centres. Their sacred specialists are the Brahmans who help them in the religious offerings and homages during the visit. Ujjani is one of the major fairs common to all the Hindu communities of Diu with the significance of the worship of their community deities. Another important fair is held at the Gangeshwar temple in Fudam on the day of Mahashivratri. Diwali, Gopal Ashtami, Holi and Navratra are the major festivals celebrated by them. They have started visiting Amba Mata (Gujarat) and Nath Dwara (Rajasthan) for pilgrimage.

According to their traditional occupation, they had specialization in the art of tie and dye. One of the Sangharia, Jethi Bai, who was the only freedom fighter from the community, prepared the design in a piece of cloth showing the map of Goa, Daman and Diu and the exploitation of the people by the Portuguese Administration, with the help of tie and dye art and presented it to the then king of Portugal during his visit to Goa in 1732. She requested for the reformation which was accepted by the king. Their materialistic cultural elements in the form of ornamental craft of turtle-shell in its own type and uniqueness is not only for India but whole of Asia. It has been already discussed that the use of turtle-shell was borrowed from Africa; but the ornamental craft of turtle-shell is their own creation. Turtle-shell bangles are specially used by the Hindu communities during marriage with the significance that one of the incarnations of Lord Vishnu was turtle, the *Kachhapa avtar*, which protects their married life. Though the motor machines have been introduced to handle the emerical wheel and the buff machine, the production is on decrease gradually. A pair of turtle shell bangles costs Rs. 80/- to Rs. 100/-. They have started the craft of ivory as they can procure the raw material from Ahmedabad easily. They consider that until the government would take some initiative to procure the raw material from Africa or Sri Lanka the ornamental craft of turtle shell will vanish.

They maintain traditional linkages with all the Hindu communities at economic level and with the Bhoiraj and Brahman at religious level. Economically, they have interaction due to the trade of turtle-shell products. They have linkages in religious sphere with the Bhoiraj when both visit the Kalinki Mata alongwith for the worship as per tradition.

In social and religious sphere the services of Brahman is required during name giving, sacred thread, marriage ceremonies and death rites. They exchange food with the Vania and invite the Bhoiraj, Vanjha, Koli, Kharwa, Dhobi, Kumhar during the marriage ceremony. They share crematorium with the Vania. The periodical election for statutory panchayat, Pradesh Council and Parliament seats have been route for the modern linkages of the Sangharia with the other communities and the political parties of the Diu district through the *gnyati panch*. The area of interaction has widened in the field of economy to national and transnational level.

They have a positive attitude towards the development programmes in the field of education, health, family welfare, drinking water, self-employment, electricity, public distribution system, nutritional programme and banking facilities. Other programmes like IRDP and Employment Guarantee Scheme do not have any importance for them as they are restricted to the SC and ST. They desire to be constitutionally classified as a backward class as done by the Bakshi Panch in Gujarat which will facilitate them more to enhance their economic condition. Nutrition programme of the children under Balwadi has been appreciated by them for the mental and physical growth of the children which they avail of. Boys study up to college level and droup out from their studies as they have to support their family. Girls study up to secondary level and drop out from their study due to social reasons. Though economically they are not very sound but they do not depend on money-lenders and shopkeepers in their need. They are exposed to mass-communication by radio, television, cinema, newspaper, etc.

The turtle-shell craft which is a unique art and craft of the Sangharia of Diu representing India in whole of Asia should be preserved after taking the initiative by the government.

N.K.Sinha

REFERENCES

Crooke, William, *The Tribes and Castes of the North-Western Province and Oudh*, Vol. IV, 1896, Calcutta, The Government Press; Reprint, *The Tribes and Castes of the North Western India*, Vol. IV, p. 313, 1975, Cosmo Publications, Delhi.

Enthoven, R.E., *The Tribes and Castes of Bombay*, Vol. III, 1922, Bombay, The Government Central Press; Reprint, Vol. III, p. 355, 1975, Cosmo Publications, Delhi.

Rose, H.A., *A Glossary of the Tribes and Castes of the Punjab and North-West Frontier Provinces*, Lahore, Government Printers, Punjab, Vol.II, page 153, 1919.

SIDDI

The Siddi, also known as Kafira or Landa (this term is derived from the place Lundi in Africa) or Gamtha, are a Scheduled Tribe being a Negrito ethnic group in India with the population of 42 (Census of India, 1971) in Diu. They are themselves conscious of the fact that diverse racial strains, viz. the Vania, Kharwa and Muslim have blended in their blood. The voyages of the Vania, Kharwa and Muslim of Diu in Mozambigue during the Portuguese regime provided the opportunity for them to establish relation with the Negroid women who finally brought their offspring with them to Diu. The local population did not accept them and gave a separate identity as Kafira or Landa or Gamtha meaning the cross breed. Enthoven (1920:332) and Russel and Lal (1916: 409) have called the Siddis as Abyssinian or Negro or Hubshi meaning one comming from Elhabish, the Arabic name for North East Africa, but Siddi has a narrower application for a particular group of people of Negroid origin living on the Western coasts of India. Trivedi (1961) says that the tribe appears to have been brought into India by the Portuguese towards the end of 17th century presumably as slaves. The term Siddi was firstly adopted by the community after liberation finding the community in Gujarat having the same racial features. The constitutional status of Schedule Tribe was conferred on them by the Government of Goa, Daman and Diu. Gujarati is the language as well as script for them. However, the language spoken by them differs somewhat from that spoken by other communities of Diu. They speak with some hoarseness which is called *landi*. Besides Gujarati, they are also conversant with Hindi and Urdu.

The Siddi are non-vegetarian who take meat of goat, fowl and buffallo. Their staple food includes *bajra*, rice, wheat and pulses of *urad*, and *tur*. Alcoholic drinks are commonly used by men which is purchased from the local market. They also take milk and milk products, smoke *bidi* and cigarette, chew tobacco and betel. *Viriyani* (fried rice with fish or meat), *kher-khurma* (curry of meat) and *malida* (porridge prepared of wheat flour fried in ghee and sugar) are their special food preparation's made use of on the festive occasions.

The Siddi of Diu are divided into five exogamous divisions, the *atak*, namely Solanki, Makwana, Chauhan, Mansuri and Siddi without any hierarchy. The basis of differentiation is social. The earlier discussed three subgroups, viz. Gamtha (strain of Vania), Landa (strain of Kharwa) and Kafir (strain of Muslim) were not intermarrying during pre-independence period. It was only after the liberation that all the three subgroups were merged into one and started calling themselves as the Siddi. The chief function of *atak* is to trace the descent and to regulate marriage alliances. They place themselves superior only to the Hadi and Bhangi in regional social hierarchy. Others also consider them as such.

The Siddi follow the norms of community endogamy and *atak* exogamy. They practise only cross-cousin marriages. Adult marriage is in practice. Marriage is settled by negotiation. Though the Muslim scripture permits the polygyny but they practise monogamy. Junior levirate is permitted. They do not have any symbol of marriage. They have the practice of *dej* (bride-price) and *hakmore* (mehr) in cash. *Chhutta-chedi* is granted by the *jamat*. *Natra* (remarriage) is permitted which includes widow/widower and the divorcees. Matrimonial relation with the Siddi of Gujarat is the significant change after liberation.

The institution of family among the Siddi is characterized by mixed extended and nuclear ones. The disputes in the family arise on property division after father's death. Avoidance relationship is maintained between mother-in-law and daughter-in-law. Joking relationship exists with elder brother's wife, husband's younger brother, wife's elder and younger sisters. Property is equally shared by the children and the eldest son succeeds the authority. Inter-family interactions are sought during the life cycle rituals, economic and political activities. Though the women share the burden of day to day life but they have low status. They have roles in collection of fuel, bringing potable water, social function, ritual observances and religious activities. They also participate in the economic activities and contribute to family income by doing labour works. They are forbidden to interfere in the political matters except to cast their votes in the periodical elections. Sister plays the role of *lunari* (harbinger or auspicious omen) in her brother's marriage and perform *ponkhavan* (reception of bridegroom) in her sister's marriage.

The interesting feature of the Siddi's life-cycle is the practice of some of the Hindu customs. *Kholo-bharvo* is the pre-birth ritual performed in the seventh month of first pregnancy for the safe delivery. The expectant mother goes to her parent's house for the first delivery. *Dayan*, local midwife from the community, is called to attend the delivery. *Ajan* (call to a prayer) is recited in the ear of the new born. *Chhathi* is performed on the sixth day after birth followed by *nampari* (naming) on the same day. Pollution is observed for 40 days and post-natal restrictions on mother are also observed. *Aqiqa* (tonsorial ceremony) is performed after completion of five or seven years while *sunnat sadi* (circumcision) is performed to male child between five to six years of birth by the *hajjam* (barbar) and is paid in cash against his services. *Sagai* (betrothal) takes place fifteen days prior to *nikah* (marriage) at girl's house and marriage date is fixed with the mutual consent of both the parties. *Mandava* (marriage booth) is erected at both the houses one day prior to *nikah* and *pithee* (a paste of turmeric and groundnut oil) is smeared on their bodies at their respective houses. A *mindhol* (emetic knot) is tied on their wrist which is a part of Hindu custom. *Jan* (marriage procession) arrives at the bride's village and are provided separate lodging, and thereafter *samaiyu* (reception) is performed. The *jan* with the groom arrives at the bride's residence in the evening where *ponkhavan* is performed at the *mandva* by the bride's sister. *Kazi* ascertains the consent from both the bride and the groom and conducts the marriage as per the Muslim *Shariyat* and recites the *nikah* verses from the Koran. *Hakmore* (mehr) is promised to pay just before *nikah* by the bridegroom, followed by the payment of *dej* (brideprice) by the groom's father. *Logas* (compulsory contribution) is paid to *jamat* (traditional council) by the bridegroom, followed by the *kariyawar* (marriage gift) to the bride by her parents. *Jan* returns with the newly married couple on third day of the marriage. The couple pay visit to the *pir dargah* and untie the *mindhol*, tied on their wrist. The consummation of marriage takes place at the groom's residence. *Ana* (return of the bride) takes place after five days and groom takes her bride back to his village on the first *jumma* (weekly Muslim half day). They bury their dead. *Fatiha* is recited from Koran when a Siddi is on death bed. *Kazi* accompanies the funeral procession upto burial ground. Women are forbidden to accompany the funeral procession. *Kalma* is read by the *kazi* before the burial. Eldest son acts as the chief mourner. They observe death pollution for three days but the mourning period extends up to 40 days. *Ziarat* is performed on the third day when *fatiha* is recited with the sprinkling of boiled rice, chicken curry and liquour on the roof of the house of the deceased for the crows to pacify the departed soul. *Fatiha* is recited on 10th, 20th, 30th at 40th days by the *kazi* and community dinner is given on the 40th day marking the culmination of the death rites.

The Siddi are a landless community. Domestic servant and fishing labour are their traditional occupation. They are also engaged in different government offices, private concerns, in labour and hawking. Domestic servants receive their remuneration in cash and kind. Children under fifteen are engaged as domestic servant. A few have been provided land by the government recently. Men, involved in hawking, make their transaction in cash.

The social control is governed by the *Siddi jamat* (caste council) at village level headed by Patel (head) and assisted by a *kotwar* (messenger) and *mehtaji* (accountant) and two members. Patel is elected by voice vote who nominates *kotwar* and *mehtaji*. The tenure of a Patel runs for five years. Social problems pertaining to adultery, marriage, inter-family disputes and religious matter are taken care of by the *jamat*. Excommunication is the form of punishment. Plan implent and welfare development activities are the role of modern statutory panchayat. The *jamat* is the postliberation orginasation when the cluster of *Kafira*, Landa and Gamtha assimilated into one as Siddi. Earlier they were governed by the norms and custormary laws of the different ethnic groups namely Kharwa, Vania and Muslims.

The Siddi profess Islam. But some of the Hindu religious practices are still prevailing among them. They are late converts. For example the name Ahmed Haridas Solanki denotes to the Muslim convert Ahmad's father was Haridas. They follow the Suni sect and have faith on *oliyas* and *pirs* is very widespread among them. Their chief object of devotion is Hazrat Baba Ghor, a *pir*, whose *majar* (mausoleum) is located at Ratnapur and Ankleshwar Nagasipur near Prachi in Gujarat which is the shrine of wider pantheon for the Siddi as a whole. Their religious belief also marks the existence of spiritual power. The interesting feature of their religion is that they also have faith on some of the Hindu deities specially the Sitlamata, the deity of small pox. Id-ul-Zuha and Id-ul-Fitr are their major festivals. Muharram and Urs-Sharif of Baba Ghor are the other festivals. They also celebrate the Hindu festivals namely Holi and *Janmashtami*. A few observe fast on Janmashtmi and prepare *pucca* food in the night. They also pay homage to the Hindu village deity during illness.

The Siddi do not have any materialistic art. Their non-materlialistic art is represented by *rasadas*, the folk songs, which describe the history of migration of their *pirs* and *dhamal* folk dance. The folk dances, have been borrowed from the Siddi of Gujarat. Both men and women participate in dance and use *mashido* and *dhamama*, percussion instruments, while dancing.

The traditional inter-community linkages existed with the Vania, Kharwa and Muslim at social and economic levels who brought up them and assisted in their economic activities. They accept water, *kachha* and *pucca* food, and *sidha* from all the comunities except the Hadi, Bhangi and Vankars. The Hadi plays the role of musician during the marriage ceremony. They have their own burial ground. They participate with the Hindus during Holi and Janmashtami festivals. They share the mosque with the Muslims. They have their own water resources. They receive the services of *maulavi*, *kazi* and *hajam* (barber) from the other Muslim communities in Diu and Gujarat. Employer-worker relationship exists with the Vania, Kharwa and Muslims. Political awareness have undergone change. Leadership has emerged out in the form of *agyawan*. They have teachers.

Though the development programmes under tribal sub-plan have been introduced by the government to uplift their condition, they are not fully aware of the facilities provided by the government. Formal education is favourable for both boys and girls but the boys study at secondary level while the girls at primary level. They drop out from studies because they are poor and have to earn to support their family. Their attitude towards modern medicare is positive and make full use of them. Though they favour the family planning scheme but prefer to have four or more children. They avail of the facilities of drinking water through well and piped water, IRDP, self-employment, viz. tailoring and vendoring, mid-day meal scheme for the children, ICDS, ration distribution. They use electricity and their fuel resources are firewood and kerosene oil. The net work of road is good which links all the villages of Diu and Gujarat for the transportation. They are exposed to other places by radio, television, cinema, extension agencies and post office. Though the banking facilities are there but their attitude is not favourable towards saving and they depend on money lenders and shopkeeper in their need.

N.K. Sinha

REFERENCES

Crooke, William, *The Tribes and Castes of North West Province & Oudh*, Vol. II, 1896, Calcutta, The Government Central Press; Reprint, *The Tribes and Castes of North West India*, Vol. II, p. 473, 1974, Cosmo Publications, Delhi.

Enthoven, R.E., *The Tribes and Castes of Bombay*, Vol. III, 1922, Bombay, The Government Central Press; Reprint, Vol. III, p 332, 1975, Cosmo Publications, Delhi.

Russell, R.V. and Hiralal. *The Tribes and Castes of the Central Provinces of India*, Vol. I, 1916, London, Macmillan and Company; Reprint, Vol. I, p. 409, 1975, Cosmo Publications, Delhi.

Trivedi, R.K., *Siddi, A Negroid Tribe of Gujarat*, Census of India 1961, Ethnographic Series, Gujarat, Delhi, Vol. V. Part V-B, No. 1,

VANIA

The Vania, a community of traders, are also called Gujarati Vania and Mahajan Vania. The Gujarati word Vania has been derived from the Sanskrit word 'vanij' meaning 'trader'. They are divided into three endogamous sub-divisions namely Modh Vania, Soni Vania and Saurathia Vania on the basis of their places of origin and occupation. Modh are from Modasa near Ahmedabad. Saurthia from Saurath (the south coast of Kathiawad) and Soni are the Vania having the occupation of goldsmith. Modhs and Saurathias have been residing in Diu since immemorial times and history of their migration is not available. The Soni migrated from Bagsara of Junagadh district and the first Soni to settle in Diu was Bhimji Visham about 60 years back. The Modh claims to be of Rajput origin and the Soni claim to be the descendant of Modh Brahman and Vania is the occupational term for them. Enthoven (1922:413) has divided the Gujarati Vania into 40 sub-divisions including the Modh and Sorathia. There is no stratification among the sub-divisions. They are distributed in all the villages and the town of Diu. Somehow, they are also distributed in Gujarat namely Modhs in Ahmedabad, Junagadh and Cutch; Sonis are in Cutch, Junaghadh, Amreli, Porbondar and Jafrabad; and Saurathias are in Porbandar, Mangrol, Verawal and Jafrabad. Gujarati is their spoken language as well as the script within the community. Besides Gujarati, they are also conversant in Cutchhis, Hindi and English. They dress like Gujarati.

They are fully vegetarian. Their staple food includes rice, wheat, pulses of *urad, tur* and *mag* (green gram) and jaggery. They take plenty of locally available fruits and vegetables. Only men take alcoholic drinks which they purchase from the local market. They use groundnut oil for the cooking purposes. *Puri* (fried bread), *dudh pag* (rice boiled in milk mixing sugar), *srikhand* (sweet preparation of curd) and *lapsee* (a paste like preparation of wheat flour, ghee and sugar) are their special food preparations which are made use of on the festive occasions. They enjoy smoking *bidi*, cigarette and chew loose tobacco and betel.

The Vania are divided into eighteen exogamous divisions based on *goter* (clan). The two endogamous divisions, viz. Modh and Saurathia Vania have five exogamous divisions namely Shah, Kachdia, Gardhi, Javeri and Longaria while the Soni have thirteen *goters* (clan) namely Dharoda, Dhakan, Luhar, Dhank, Sagar, Vaya, Satee-Kunwar, Patni, Jhagda, Ghaghda, Dhakka, Thadeshwar and Shudy. The basis of differentiation is social and teritorial. There is no stratification among the clans of the Modh and Saurathia but among the Soni Vania, Dharoda is considered the highest *goter* followed by Dhakan and others. They suffix their *goter* names to their names. The chief function of *goter* (clan) is to regulate marriage alliances, to trace the descent and to particiapte in the life cycle rituals. They consider the Brahman superior to them in regional social hierarchy and other the same. They are well aware of the *varna* system and recognise their position as Vaishya.

The Vania follow the norm of endogamy at community and sub-division levels and most of *goter* (clan) exogamy. Marriage is not permitted among the parallel cousins but is prmitted with the mother's sister's daughter or son. They practise adult marriage. Marriage is settled by negotiation and the form of marriage is monogamy. *Kentho* (vermilion mark on the hair parting), *kanku* (red mark on the forehead) and *bangdi* (bangles of turtle shell and ivory) are the marriage symbols for women. They have practice of *dej* (dowry) in kind, i.e., gold, which is fixed during the negotiation. Patrilocal is their rule of residence. Divorce is not permitted among them. *Natra* (remarriage) is allowed between widow and widower. Sororate is also prmitted. A widower marrying an unmarried girl is restored to the regular form of marriage. Marriage among the sister's children is a recent change which is an adjustment with the traditional norm during the Portuguese rule.

The institution of family consists of nuclear and mixed extended types. They have prescribed practice of kinship usages. Avoidance relationship is maintained with mother-in-law and son-in-law, with father-in-law and daughter-in-law, with younger brother's wife and with husband's elder brother. They have joking relationship with elder brother's wife and husband's younger brother, with wife's younger and elder sisters and with wife's elder and younger brothers. It is obligatory for the sister's husband to attend the role of *anvar* (accompanier) and for the maternal uncle to bring *maushala* (ceremonial gift of marriage dress) during his or her marriage. Conflict and confrontations in the family arise after father's death on financial matters. All sons get equal share in parental property and the eldest son succeeds the authority. In absence of son, the widow or widower can have their will to the daughter's son before his or her death. Inter-family linkages can be envisaged during the life-cycle rituals, economic and political activities. The Vania women have low status. Their roles are restricted to religious, social, ritual and domestic fields. They also contribute to the family income by doing service. They do not have right of inheritance. *Fui* (father's sister) has an important role during *bare-basia* (naming) and *balmovra* (tonsure) or *mundan* ceremonies as per their custormary obligation.

Srimant is the pre-birth ritual performed in the seventh month of a woman's first pregnancy for the safe delivery. The expectant mother leaves for her parent's house fifteen or twenty days after *srimant* is performed. She stays there till the new born child becomes three to four months of age. *Chhathi pujan* is performed on sixth day after birth where *gotrej* (clan deity) is worshipped. The mixture of *dhana* (corriender seeds), *gurh* (jaggery) and water is fed to the infant by the eldest male member of the family. *Bare-baria* (name giving) is performed on twelfth day after birth by the *fui* (father's sister) after procuring the *rashi nam* (zodiac name) from the Brahman. The mother takes purificatory bath on the tenth day but the pollution is extended for 30 days. She is forbidden to enter the kitchen and to visit the religious places. *Balmovra* (tonsure) is performed by the barber after the completion of one year with the help of *fui*. *Brahm-smaran* (sacred preaching) is performed to the boy by the Modh Brahman only among the Modh and Saurathia when the boy becomes seven to nine years old, as the adoption of Vaishnavism by putting *tulsi-kanthi* (basil chain). Among the Soni the thread ceremony is performed in ordinary way. *Sagai* (betrothal) takes place a few months or even one year prior to *lagan* (marriage) either at the residence of boy or girl. The marriage day is fixed and written on a roll of paper and is sent by the girl's family priest to the boy's father. Marriage rituals are performed for three days at both the places but is solemnized at the bride's residenc. The three days rituals start with the worship of Ganpati and installation of *manek-stambh* (*gotrej*) and *mandva* (marriage booth) is erected on first day. *Pithee* (mixture of turmeric and ground nut oil) is rubbed on the bodies of the both for three days at their respective houses. *Maushala* is brought by mother's brother at both the places on second day. *Jan* (marriage procession) leaves for the bride's village on third day where they are given *janiwas* (separate lodging) on their arrival. The bridegroom with the *jan* arrives at the bride's house where *pankhavan* (reception of the groom) is performed by the bride's mother. *Har-toda* (exchang of garland) is performed at *otah* (inner venendah) and the groom is led to the *chauri* (square of sacrificial fire) in the *mandava* by the *anvar* (accompanier) and his family priest and is seated on a *patli* (wooden plank). The bride also comes in the *mandva* and sits opposite to the groom. A piece of cloth is stretched between the two and *hast-milap* is performed when the right hands of the bride and groom are joined by the priest reciting the luck bringing verses and cloth is taken off to one side. *Kanyadan* is performed and groom is presented with a golden ring by the bride's mother. *Chauri-fera* is the last and principal ritual performed when the bride and the groom circumambulate four rounds of the *chauri* and after completion of fourth round, the bride sits to the left side of the groom and *knsar-khawa* (feeding of sweets to each other) is performed. The bride's brother plays an important role during *fera*. The clan deity is worshipped in the oratory and the game of odd and evens are played by both. *Dej* (dowry) in kind (gold and ornaments) is given by the bride's parents. The groom, with his bride, returns to his house next day and pay homage to his clan deity. Marriage feast is given by the bride's side while the community dinner is given by the groom's side after the return of *jan*. Consummation of marriage takes place at the groom's residence in the *suhag-ghar*. *Ana* (return of bride) takes place twenty days or three months after marriage. The Vania cremate their dead and *srevani* (death rites) is performed by the eldest son or youngest son, the chief mourner. The female members and the widow of the deceased accompany the funeral procession up to *gondra* (village boundary) and return back. Ashes and bones are collected in a cloth and disposed off in the sea. A *kalash* (earthen pot) full of water and a lamp is kept in the house of the deceased for ten days for the use of departed soul. The community members visit the house of the deceased to mourn the death. They are served with salty tea to mark the state of mourning. They observe death pollution for ten days and the chief mourner, male family members and clan members shave their heads and moustaches on the same day. *Kriya* is performed on eleventh, twelfth and thirteenth days and cooked food is thrown to the crows by the chief mourner on twelfth day. Bedsheets, bed cloths and some amount are donated to the Brahmans on thirteenth day and community dinner is given. In case of the death of an old man, the invitees are presented with steel/copper/brass utensils by the daughter of the deceased after the community dinner. *Darha* (calling of the departed soul) is performed in the night by the *bhua* (magico-religious specialist). At the end of each months for a year after death, *masiso* is performed. *Barsi* (memorial rite) is performed after the completion one year and community dinner is given.

Land is their major economic resource. Traditionally they were traders and jewellery-makers. In present situation, the Soni Vania are engaged in their traditional occupation of working on gold and silver for making of gold ornaments and precious stone setters. The Modh and Saurathia owned land during the Portuguese rule, given to them against their services but after the abolition of Properitership Act (1962) the land was acquired by the government. The Modh and Saurathia were in the habit of making voyages to Arabian countries, Zanzibar and Mozambique for trade, going in their youth and returning back to Diu after nine or ten years, when they generally marry. The present day primary occupation is trade and business. They are dependent on the markets of Gujarat and purchase wheat, *bajra* (millet), sugar, *sing tel* (groundnut oil) from there and sell in Diu. Service in different government offices is the other means of livelihood. Those who own land, engage the Khedut Koli as their tenants on contract and rent basis.

Their social control is regulated by the traditional council Vanik Mahajan Samaj comprising whole of the Diu district. The council is headed by a President who is elected by voice vote. He is assisted by a *mehta* (accountant) a *mukodam* (massenger) and four *sabhya* (member). They are nominated by the President. Cases pertaining to inter-community marriage, adultery, breach of traditional norms are delt with by the *samaj*. The election of the office bearers takes place after every three years. Inter-community marriage is considered as the biggest social offence and in such case an offender is excommunicated. Other form of punishment is fine in kind imposed by the *samaj* which includes one kg. of vegetables which is given to the *samaj* for the use of temple priest. The introduction of adult franchise and the periodical elections have caused differences among the community members at their association level with the political parties. The traditional rules, framed by the traditional council, has been liberalized after 1955 in case of inter-community marriage and taking of the alcoholic drinks. Plan implementation and welfare development activities are the role of modern statutory panchayat.

The Vania profess Hinduism. While the Modh and the Saurathia resort to Vaishnavism, the Soni resort to Jainism and Swaminarayan sect. Their religious practices recognize the Hindu deities namely Lord Vishnu, Laxmi and Shiva etc. The Soni's belief resort to Lord Mahavir who is their community deity. The Vania keep the Hindu fasts and feasts and visit the places of Hindu pilgrimages. Their *goter* deities are Hinglaj Mata, Modeshwari Mata and Randhal Mata who are worshipped daily and during the life cycle rituals. Gopal Ashtami and Diwali are their main festivals associated with the worship of Lord Krishna and Goddess Laxmi. They also celebrate the other Hindu festivals viz; Ramnavmi, Shivratree and Holi. Their new year starts next day after Diwali. Ujjani/Mome is celebrated in the month of Ashadh in the form of picnic. Mahibij is celebrated on Shukla Paksha Dwitiya of Magh month which is associated with the worship of sea-god, an adaptation to sea ecology. Modh and Saurathia consider Nathdwara in Rajasthan as their major sacred centre while the Soni consider Pawapuri in Bihar. A Vania is supposed to pay visit to Srinath at Nathdwara just after his marriage as a part of tradition. The Modh Brahman is their sacred specialist who officiates at their ritual performances and paying homages. Their art is represented by both the non-materialistic and materialistic elements. *Satiya* (floor design) which is designed in front of the entrance of the house to welcome the deity of prosperity and the oral traditions in the form of folk-songs in Brij Bhasha which are sung by the female members only. *Garba* and *ras* are the folk-dances enjoyed only by the women folk. Making of gold and silver ornaments and carving designs on them are their materialistic object of culture. Traditionally the use of coating sword handles was in the hands of the Soni.

The Vania are linked to all the communities in terms of their occupation of trade and business. They accept *pucca* and *kachha* food from the Brahman and Salat. Landlord-tenant relationship exist with the Khedut Koli. They also engage agricultural labour from the Khedut Koli on monthly contract basis and the wages are paid in cash and kind. During the Portuguese regime they used to pay the wages in *escude* (Portuguese currency). They have their own temples, though they allow the other Hindu communities except the Hadi, Vankar and Bhangi. They do not share the crematorium. Employer-worker relationship exists with the Koli, Khedut Koli and Vania. Modern linkages are sought during the economic activities and during the periodical elections.

The Vania have a positive attitude towards the different developmental programmes. Literacy has gone up. Boys study up to postgraduate level and some drop out from study as they have to earn to support their family. Girls study up to secondary level and drop out from studies due to social reasons. Majority of the Modh and Saurthia are employed in different government offices. They have businessmen, creative artists, teachers, engineers and doctors. They avail of the facilities of drinking water through piped water and tube well. They make use of both the traditional and modern medicine. They favour family-planning programme and prefer to have two or thre children. They make use of modern family planning methods. They use electricity and avail of the facilities of public distribution system, mid-day meal scheme for children undr Nutritional programme, ICDS and banking. Firewood, cowdung cakes, kerosene oil and L.P.G. connection are their fuel resources. The region has well set of metalled road which has linked Diu with the other parts of Gujarat to avail the transport facilities. They are exposed to outer world through by radio, television, cinema, post office, newspaper, extention agencies and the political parties.

N.K. Sinha

REFERENCES

Enthoven, R.E., *The Tribes and Castes of Bombay,* Vol. III, 1922, Bombay, The Government Central Press; Reprint, Vol. III, pp. 412-442, 1975, Cosmo Publications, Delhi.

Sinha, N.K., 'Study of Ethnography and Change in a Diu Village'. Unpublished report submitted to the Anthropological Survey of India, 1980.

VANJA

The Vanja claim to be Kshatriyas. Their Jati Puran asserts that when Parashurama started killing the Kshatriyas in Vindhyachal, some of them took asylum with Hingaraj Mata who promised to save them provided they started the occupation of weaving. In course of time they learned the art of weaving and the term 'Vanja', i.e. 'van' and 'ja' which means 'to go and weave' for their livelihood, was applied to them. Gradually they mixed with other communities and adopted their cultural traits. Enthoven (1920) has discussed the process. Jati Puran says that they migrated from different parts of Kathiawad and the first man to settle here was Amraji Vaghela in A.D. 1224. He was followed by the others Vanja sections namely the Khedu Yadav in 1270, the Jethwa in 1398, the Unewal in 1595 the Gohel in 1346. The Shamal, Padhia, Parmar, Makwana, Rathod and Kataria came after liberation. The Solanki migrated from Titapur (Rajasthan) in 17th century to Chorwad in Kathiawad and then to Diu. They perceive their distribution in the villages of Vanakwara, Ghogla and Diu municipal area. They are also distributed in the adjoining districts of Gujarat. Gujarati is the language as well as the script used by them. Besides Gujarati a few of them speak Portugese, Hindi and English

Originally they were vegetarian. Taking of non-vegetarian dishes is the recent development. Their staple food includes *bhat* (rice), *bajra* and pulses of *tur* and *urad* (pulses of red gram and Urad). *Bateta* (potato), *kanda* or *dungri* (onion), *ringna* (bringal), *dudhi* (pumpkin) and *tameta* (tomato) are the vegitables used by them. Fruits viz. *amrukh* (guava), *keri* (mango) and *kel* (banana) are taken occasionally. *Daru* (liquor) and *neera* (toddy) are commonly used by them daily which they purchase from the market. They also take beverages like tea, milk butter milk. The special food preparations are *puri* (fried bread), *lapsee* (paste like preparation of wheat flour), *pla* (viriyani of rice, fish, meat or begetables), *potaya* (prepared of flour, sugar, toddy after trying in ground nut oil) and *dudh pag* (porridge) are taken on the festive occasions. They smoke *bidi*, cigerattes and chew betel.

They are divided into fifteen exogamous sub-divisions on the basis of *goter*. Out of fifteen twelve, viz. Vaghela, Solanki, Yadav, Parmar, Rathod, Padhiya, Chudarma, Makwana, Shamal, Gohel, Kataria, and Unewal are found. The basis of differentiation is at social level through which they trace their descent. The main function of *goter* is to regulate the marriage, to trace the descent and to invite them during the life-cycle ceremonies. There is no stratification among the *gots*. They perceive their position inferior to the Brahman, Vania, Soni and Salat and equal to the Sangharia. They are well aware of *varna* system and recognize themselves as Kshatriyas. They practise community endogamy and *goter* exogamy. Their matrimonial relations are restricted to Diu district and Bombay only. The Vanja, settled in Bombay, are only from Diu. A marriage is allowed with the father's sister's and mother's brother's sons and daughters. They practise adult-marriage and the ages for boy and girl range from 22 to 25 years and 18 to 20 years respectively. Marriage is settled by negotiation only and the boy's father approaches the girl's parent with the help of his wife's brother. Monogamy is the common practice. Polygyny is permitted in case of any incurable disease of wife. *Kanku* (red vermilion) mark on the forehead) and *bangdi* (bangles of ivory) are the symbols of married women. They have practice of *dej* (bride price) in kind. *Far-gati* (divorce) is not permitted and *natra* (remarriage) takes place only between the widow and widower in the presence of *gnyat panch* (caste council). The rule of residence is patrilocal. Originally they were practising child marriage and the practice of adult marriage is a part of change.

Kutumb is the local term for the family. The most common system is that of the joint family. Respect is duly paid to the elders. Elders assist and look after the youngsters as a part of their duty and obligation. Avoidance in terms of talking with husband's elder brother and between son/daughter's parent-in-laws is maintained. Joking relation is maintained with the elder brother's wife and wife's younger sisters/brothers. It is the part obligation of mother's brother to play an important role during his sister's son/daughter's marriage. Sister's husband attends the role of *anvar* (accompanier) during the time of a boy's marriage. Family tension arises after son's marriage and after father's death. Male equigeniture is the rule of inheritance. In absence of son, it is the rule of female equigeniture. Eldest son succeeds the authority in the family. Inter-family linkages are sought during the life cycle ceremonies, economic activities, during the election of *gnyati* Patel (caste-chief). The significant change in the institution family is the formation of nuclear family due to conflict in the family after father's death. The Vanja women have low status in the society. They do not have decision making powers. In absence of son, daughters inherit the property. They contribute to family income by doing various services. They are mainly assigned to do the household jobs. They have role in social function, rituals and religious spheres. They do not have any role political spheres except to cast their vote in the periodical elections with the consultation of the head of the family.

Life-cycle rituals are common to all the Hindu communities of Diu which have been discussed in the Introduction. They do not perform some of the death rituals namely *tutko, neel* (ghost marriage) and *darha*.

The Vanja are a landless community and tailoring is their present primary occupation. Weaving was their traditional occupation and *saree* was their main product. The Kharwa bridal dress was specially woven by the community with a specific design. Clothing for *lugra* (skirt) and *ghaghra* (peticoat) are addition to this. Only one family is still doing the traditional occupation and the cost of *saree* ranges from Rs. 80/ to Rs. 159/-. Service in the different government offices are their other means of livelihood in changing situation. They have tailoring shops and the transaction is done in cash only. Some of them are settled in Mozambique and Lisbon and have been doing the job of tailoring, carpentry and services before liberation. A few shifted to Bombay after liberation.

The political organization of the Vanja consists of Vanjhak Gnyat Panch (Vanja traditional council) at village level only which functions at a fixed place called *gnyatighar*. The composition of council includes five *sabhya* (member), one *sikriwan* (accountant) and one *mukadam* (messenger) who elect a Patel (the chief) by voice vote. The age factor is an important point. The tenure of Patel changes after four years. Social problems pertaining to disputes in marriage and disputes with intra and inter-family are referred to it. A marriage takes place only after the permission is given by the Patel after going through the marriage registration certificate issued by the Marriage Registrar office, Diu. Other functions include the maintenance of the traditional norms and values of the community. Plan and implement welfare and development activities are the role of modern statutory councils after liberation. Excommunication and cash fine are the forms of punishment inflicted by the *panch*. The political organization has undergone change after liberation. Cash rewards have been introduced recently for the students studying from first to H.S. standards, and who secure first to third position in class as a part of encouragement. The periodical elections for panchayat, Pradesh Council and Parliament have given the passage of linkages betwen the *gnyat panch* and the political parties.

The Vanja belong to Hindu religion and are the follower of Kabir Panth (Kabir sect). Hinglaj Mata is their village deity. Apart from they worship all the leading Hindu deities. Their *goter* deities include Chamunda, Harshadh, Varnai, Chorwad, Kankai, Ganga Bhavani and Jagri who are worshipped during birth, marriage ceremonies and before doing any auspicious work. The offering of goat's blood with its ear is given to the caste deity during the time of marriage. On every Ashadh Shukla-Ashtami *lapsi* (wheat flour cookd into a thick paste and sweetned with molasses) is offered to Hingalj Mata, followed by the offering of *makshar* (head of rabbit) on Shukla Chaudas. These offerings are in the memory of her having protected the community from Parashuram. Their major festivals include Tusli-Vivah on Kartik Shukla Iggyaras and Kijrha on Shravan Krishna Chauth with the religious significance. Kijrha is associated with Kabir's worship which is celebrated through weaving and taking out of Kabir's portrait in procession. They also celebrate the festivals like Navratri and Holi. Somnath, Gupta Prayag and Chorwad are considered at their sacred centres. There is temple of Chamunda Devi at Chorwad which is visited once in a year by the community. Brahman officiates as sacred specialist and helps them in the religious offerings and homages during their visit. The major fairs are Poonam Mela and Shivratri Mela and these are common to all the Hindu communities.

Their art of weaving has been discussed earlier. The special design of saree is prepared by them for the Kharwa's only and which is still surviving. Smt. Lilawati Behan Harakchand Chudasma alone is maintaining the traditional art of weaving which is a single handloom industry in Diu. The Kharwa from the neighbouring districts of Gujarat used to purchase the bridal dress from them. Tattooing, folk songs and floor designs are common to all.

Traditional linkages of the Vanjas with the Kharwa community exist at economic level as they used to weave their special bridal dress. In social and religious spheres the services of Brahman is required during name giving, marriage and death rituals. The cordial relation is maintained with all the Hindu communities except the Hadi, Vankar and Bhangi, due to participation in common religious fair at Kalinki Mata temple at Patelwadi and Fudam. They accept water, *pucca* and *kacha* food from the Brahmin, Vania, Soni, Salat and Sangharia. They have their own crematorium. In changing situation they have linkages with all the communities in economic and political level. Tailoring is the changed occcupation for them where they have interaction with all the communities. The periodical elections for the statutory panchayats, Pradesh Council and Parliament have given the way of modern linkages of the Vanja with the other communities in political sphere. The feeling of untouchability has hardly any importance for the youngsters who visit the Hadi and Vankar during their marriage ceremonies. They have doctors, engineers, teachers and service in various government offices.

Their attitude is positive towards the development programmes. Litreacy level has gone up. Boys study up to college level while girls study up to school level. They avail of the facilities of modern medical care. They favour family welfare and planning but prefer to have not more than three children. Due to extension of the GIDC and other offices and establishment of educational institutions, the prospect of employment has widened. They avail of the facilities of ration distribution and banking. The construction of Thud bridge between Diu and Gujarat has provided them transport facilities for frequent visits to the markets of the adjoining areas of Gujarat. They are exposed to mass communication by radio, television, newspaper and cinema. Apart from their positive attitude regarding the development programmes they feel that they should be constitutionally classified as a backward class in the Bakshi Panch (a commission setup to identify backward classes in Gujarat) which will facilitate them more to uplift their economical conditions.

N.K. Sinha

REFERENCES

Enthoven, R.E., *The Tribes and Castes of Bombay*, Vol. III, 1922, Bombay, The Government Central Press; Reprint, Vol. III, p. 442, 1975, Cosmo Publications, Delhi.

VANKAR

The Vankar are a Scheduled Caste community. They call themselves as well as others call them Vankar. They trace their origin from the Rajputs. No information is available in existing literature regarding them except in Enthoven (1920: Vol I, page 322) who has described the Vankar as an endogamous division of the Dhed. The Vankars maintain matrimonial relations with the Dhed from the adjoining areas of Gujarat. They have been inhabiting the area long before the Portuguese established their rule in A.D. 1539. They are also found in Amreli and Junagadh districts of Gujarat. They perceive their distribution in the villages of Vanakwada, Pawti, Buchadwada, Fudam and Diu town with the population of 159 according to Census of India 1971. Gujarati is the language as well as script used by them. Besides Gujarati, a few of them also speak Portuguese and Hindi.

Food habits of the Vankars have been largely governed by the ecological condition. As Diu is situated on the seashore, the Vankar depend upon fish, rice and *bajra* (millet) which form the major contents of their food. The consumption of vegetables is low. Fruits are not included in staple food and are taken occasionally. Both the home-made as well as the alcoholic drinks, available in the market, are used by male members only, while toddy is used by both the male and female. The special food preparations, i.e. *puri* (fried bread), *lapsee* (paste like a sweet prepration), *pla* (biriyani or pulaw), *dudh pag, sew, potaya* (made of wheat flour, sugar, toddy after frying with ghee) are taken on the festive occasions. They smoke *bidi, cigar* (cigaratte) and chew betel.

The Vankar are divided into twenty *ataks* (clan) namely Wadhero, Jethwa, Makwana, Barat, Jhala, Parmar, Rathod, Kaitra, Wagheli, Sasa, Athiya, Solanki, Wada, Chawda, Bariya, Bamania, Bagda, Vaghda, Maru and Charaniya. These are exogamous sub-divisons which are suffixed to their names. There is no stratification among them. The main function of clan is to trace descent, to regulate marriage alliances and to participate in the rituals performed in every walks of life. They perceive their position superior to the Hadi, Siddi and Bhangi. They are well aware of the *varna* system and recognize their place as Shudra. They practice community endogamy. Marriage within the village is not encouraged. The rule of exogamy is applied to the *atak* level and up to the extent that both the boy and girl should not have relation for the last four ascending generations from both the father's and mother's sides. They practise adult-marriage and marriage age for a boy ranges from 22 to 28 years, and that for a girl from 18 to 20 years. One of the main reasons for the late marriage has been *dhej* (bride-price). The way of acquiring mates is through negotiation. They are overwhelmingly monogamous. There is, however, no restriction for a man taking more than one wife. But this is extremely rare due to high brideprice. The amount of brideprice ranges from Rs. 5,000/- to Rs. 10,000/- which is fixed during the course of negotiation and is paid during *nakee* (betrothal). Patrilocal is the common form of residence practised by them. The practice of matrilocal residence was also reported, but is not common and is practised only by those who have no male issue to help them in daily life. *Chhutta-chhedi* or *farwa-gati* are the local terms for divorce. The reasons for divorce are extramarital relation and in case of no issue. The right of divorce is granted to both man and woman by the *gnyat panch*, (traditional council), who so ever approaches for divorce, has to pay fine in cash as imposed by the *panch*. Being economically weak, this has been an discouraging factor for the practice of divorce. One third of the fine is paid to man or woman and two third to the *panch* which is used for the needy persons in any emergency. Children are th liability of mother in divorce cases. They allow *natra* (remarriage). This is allowed in case of divorce or death of either of the spouses. This is not the regular form of marriage and no rituals are performed. In case of marrying wife's younger unmarried sister, the regular form of marriage is resorted to in full. *Devar-batu* is the local term denotes to levirate and the form of junior levirate is practised. The consent of both should be ascertained for such union. They also allow junior sororate. No major change was reported in the institution of marriage except that they have increased the marriage age.

Kutumb is the local term for family. The institution of family has been studied under two types namely extended and nuclear. Eldest male is regarded as the *karta* (head) of the family. He dominates the domestic scene. A widow also becomes authoritarian when her sons are not grown up. In ideal terms the head of family commands respect and authority.

They maintain avoidance relationship with wife's elder sister, all the elderly members of the wife and the husband. Joking relationship is maintained, with elder brother's wife, wife's younger sister, wife's younger sister's husband, sister's husband's sister and brothers and younger brother's parent-in-laws. Eldest son succeeds the authority in the family. A man can have *dattak* (adoption) if he has no child. The property inheritance is governed by the Portuguese Code of Usages and Custom of 1854 when after the death of father the widow gets 50% and the remain 50% is distributed among the sons. Men and women are equal partners in day to day economic activities including certain aspects of agricultural works. The female members look after the household works. So far the status of women is concerned, they have low status. Though family is an independent domestic unit but the entire family linkages becomes the natural phenomenon for the Vankar in birth, marriage, religious and economic activities. Joint and extended families have lost their significance giving way to nuclear family under the impact of economical changes. Respect and obedience to the elders in the family have lessened.

Life-cycle rituals are common to all the Hindu communities of Diu which have been already discussed in the Introduction.

Land is the main economic resource of the Vankar. Their economy revolves round agriculture and allied activities. Traditionally, they were weavers. They used to purchase cotton threads from the Vania, prepare clothing and use to sell in the villages. There are two factors which affected their traditional occupation. One, in 1954 Portuguese came into conflict with India and as a result the area of Diu was blocked for all purposes and the Vania stopped the trade in cotton from Gujarat. Secondly, after liberation they could not compete with modern textile. The Vania, who were also the land-owning community, provided land to them for cultivation on rent basis which has now become their primary occupation. They do agriculture at subsistance level due to the ecological condition, salty water and sandy soil. The main produce is *bajra*. Their subsidiary occupations are agricultural labour in near by Gujarat villages, casual labour on road and building construction and in salt industry. The Vankar from Fudam village are engaged in the building construction at Bombay. There are two agricultural seasons for them namely *unadu* (summer) and *chaumasa* (rainy season). *Bajra* and the vegetables like brinjal, pumpkin, beans are grown and sold in the market in exchange with food grains. The land tenure system between them and the Vania was well defined. The tenant had to pay 100 *escude* (Portuguese currency) as the annual rent to the Vania which was finally passed to the then government, in the form of land revenue. Apart from this, half of the total produce went to the land owner. Change was reported in their economy after liberation. The whole land was acquired by the government. The tenants became the landowner under the Goa, Daman and Diu Mundakar Act which protected the rights of *mundakar* (tenants). The Act came into force in October, 1969 and was finally implemented in 1979.

Social control is better understood by the traditional council and their functions. *Gnyat panch* consists of five elderly members who elect the Patel (chief) by voice vote. The Patel is elected from the community on the basis of social standing. The age factor is also an important point. All the meetings of *gnyat panch* are called at a fixed place in the village called *baithale*. It imposes fine on persons breaking traditional norms and values such as inter-caste marriage, adultery and insult of the traditional council. Cases of divorce are refered to the *panch*. He also interferes in the religious matter and during marriage. Inter-community disputes are settled in consultation with the Patels. *Gnyat bar* (excommunication) and cash fine are the forms of punishments imposed by the Patel. An offender is accepted back in the community after he or she throws a community feast. After 1961, the whole set up of administration and political organization has undergone change. But the traditional council continues to be more powerful than the statutory village panchayat.

The Vankar affirm belief in Hinduism. Their religious belief, rituals and practices recognize the existence of two different supernatural powers. First, there is belief in deities, chiefly of Hindu origin. Ram Dev Pir is their village deity. Images of other Hindu deities, viz. Hanuman, Durga are kept in the house for worship. Clan deities are worshipped during birth and marriage. They have temples of their village deity. After the liberation under protection of Civil Right Act in 1955 the untouchables can enter the temples constructed by the higher communities. The change in the form of the observance of Ramnavami, Janmashtami and Hanuman Jayanti has also been reported followed by the daily and monthly worship of the Hindu deities. Foor designs, tattooings, folk songs used by them during festive occasions are parts of the common heritage in the territory. The type of design is common among all other communities living in the rural area. The tattoo marks used by the

Vankar are *choiful* (leaf shaped marks), *trishul* (trident), *marlo* (peacock) and name of husband and wife vice-versa. This is done with lamp black decoation of bea-wood bark and juice of green leaves of *val* (creeper) with the help of occacia thorn. *Dandia Ras* and *gher* are the folk dances used by them during marriage in the separate group of men and women.

Inter-community linkages are reflected through interaction and mutual participation in every sphere of life with the other communities. Traditional linkages with the other communities existed at economic level when land tenure system existed right upto liberation and to some extent in political level due to the existance of heterogeneous/traditional village panchayat. Brahman is called to perform life-cycle rituals. They accept water, *pucca* and *kachha* food from the communities except the Hadi, Siddi and Bhangi. In terms of modern linkages, the feeling of untouchability has lessened as they are invited during birth and marriage ceremonies. They do also invite the other communities but relationship is maintained only up to exchange of gifts. The periodical elections for the statutory panchayat, Pradesh Council and the Parliament seats have been important factors of interaction for them with other communities through their *gnyat panch.* Participation in the multicaste religious fair festivals and visits to the sacred centres like Somnath temple in Gujarat provide further opportunities for interaction with other communities. They have their own crematorium and water resources. They have members holding white collar jobs including teachers.

Their attitude is positive towards the development programmes initiated by the Government of Goa, Daman and Diu after its liberation in the field of economy and education. Boys study up to secondary level and drop out as they have to earn to support their family. Girls study up to primary level and drop out due to social reasons. They make use of both the indigenous and modern system of medicines. They avail of the facilities of health, drinking water through piped water, employment guarantee scheme under reservation policy, loan-cum-subsidy for agriculture, mother and child care under ICDS, ration distribution system. They make use of electricity, chemical fertilizer which they get from Agricultural Departement. Firewood, cowdung cakes and kerosene oil are fuel resources. They practise agriculture at subsistance level and have no saving. In this situation they have to depend on shopkeepers and moneylenders.

N.K. Sinha

REFERENCES

Census of India, *Goa, Daman & Diu,* Part X-A&B, Series 2, Registrar General, Panaji, 1971.

Enthoven, R.E., *The Tribes and Castes of Bombay,* Vol. I, 1920, Bombay, The Government Central Press; Reprint, Vol. I, p. 322, 1975, Cosmo Publications, Delhi.

Sinha, N.K., 'The Study of Ethnography and Change in a Diu Village', Unpublished report submitted to the An.S.I., 1980.

APPENDIX

TRANSLATION OF HISTORICAL MATERIALS FROM THE PORTUGUESE SOURCES

"Historical dates in respect of discovery, conquest and reconquest of Daman town", ***NOTICIAS E DOCUMENTOS PARA A HISTORIA DE DAMAO*** **(NEWS AND DOCUMENTS FOR THE HISTORY OF DAMAN) By J.F. Pereira**

YEAR 1523

The first Portuguese to discover Daman was Diogo de Malo, who was sailing towards Ormuz in a "Caravela" (ancient Portuguese sail boat), in 1523. On his way he had the misfortune to go through a violent storm in the Indian ocean, and when he thought his situation was hopeless, the "Caravela" was washed towards the shores of Daman.

YEAR 1529

Antonio de Silveira, under the orders from De Nuno da Cunha, left on 16th December 1529, to conquer 'Surrate' (Surat) and Reyner, the most remarkable and opulent cities from the Cambay Kingdom.

Antonio da Silveria landed in Daman and dividing his armed forces into two squadron he attacked the fort, countering the forward command to Manuel de Sousa de Sepulveda and keeping for himself that of the rear. This battle force attacked from the land while the ships going up the river helped with their artillery.

Great where the spoils and ruins caused by the Portuguese in the occasion. They burnt all the boats that existed in the port and others that were under construction. They put fire to the gates of the fort from where they took useful copper plates. They knocked down the walls and undid the turrets. They ruined the villages and abused its inhabitants. In the end after committing all sort of cruelties, victorious, they took shelter at Chaul.

YEAR 1531

In February 1531, D. Nuno da Cunha proceeded along with a sizable army of 3600 men to conquer the town and island of Diu.

First he come to Daman and in one day be ordered his whole army to land, being Sunday, he ordered Fr. Sebastiao Peres, General Vicar, to say mass on a platform - covered with tiles, that existed on the shore, belonging to the Muslims. It was a High mass with the accompaniment of flutes, charamelas (type of rustic flutes) trumpets and percussion (tablas)- During the elevation the army saluted with artillery, and when the Mass ended, the commissioner of the Order of St. Francis, preached and impressive sermon on the passion of the Redimer, giving in the end, general absclation to the army, present there.

This was the first Holy Mass to be celebrated on the Daman soil.

Next, D. Nuno da Cunha, a proclamation to the army, to be read by an individual known as Pobre, who had a Lieutenant holding the royal flat, on his right. In the proclamation, in the name of King Don Joan III (D. Joao III) of Portugal, he granted a prize of one thousand Cruzados to the one who first erected the standard (banner), on the walls of Diu, to the second - five hundred and to the third three hundred.

Don Nuno remained for six days in Daman, proceeding later to Diu.

YEAR 1533

Monoel de Albuquerque, Don Pedro de Menezes and Manoel de Vassconcolos were sent by Don Nuno da Cunha alongwith 12 ships and 300 men to conquer the town of Daman.

The first Captain Manoel de Albuquerque knowing that the town was well provided with artillery and well fortified, returned half way.

YEAR 1534

In this year, Martim Afonso de Souga arrived in India,with the designation of first Captain of the seas of India, taking along his brother, Diogo Lopes in the naval ships.

After taking charge of his high port, he received orders from Don Nuno da Cunha to attack Daman.

His armed forces comprised of 40 navel ships and 500 men. In Chaul, the fleet was reinforced with another of (pg. 17) Vasco Peres de Sampaio and Diogo da Silveira who came from Ormuz.

Martim Aponso de Sousa felt that in major part, the town of Daman was destroyed by its own Captain who was sheltered in the fort with 500 Turks and raspontes.

The first one to climb the fort walls was the intrepid (fearless) Francisco da Cunha, however, the ladder having broken as is was rotten, he and all others fell down.

Later on, the Muslims who were lacking the necessary courage, were getting ready to retreat having opened a door from the port, where a bloody struggle took place. The first one to enter through the gate was Diogo Alvares Tales A bloody battle was fought in a vast Square, where many enemies were killed and the Portuguese victory complete.

Martin Afonso de Susa ordered to raze down the fort of Damam or Daman and ruin the whole coast till Diu, fighting a great war against Cambay.

In consequence of this war the king of Cambay sent an ambassador, Haibez, shrewd and sensible man, to the Vice-roy Don Nuno da Cunha, and by a public peace Deed, the same king of Cambay granted to the King of Portugal the possession of Bassain (Vasai) town, in compensation for Daman town that went to the former Muslim Possessor.

YEAR 1556

For the safety of the soil of the Bacaim (vasai) town the governor of India Francisco Barreto,. thought that the possession of Daman town was necessary.

The Captains, whom he consulted on the matter, were of the opinion that to obtain "disderatim" it was convenient that "Modre Maluco", the ruling King of Cambay, minor in age, should be paid tax.

Tristao Paiva was deputed for this purpose in the mentioned year 1556 as ambassador, taking valuable gifts to the king of Cambay, with precise instruction that in case the gifts did not produce the needed effect, to offer, the half of the customs revenue of Diu from where Diogo-Noromla expelled Abix-Cao.

On reaching Cambaiete, capital city of the sovereign of Cambay, Tristao, accompanied by six horsemen and a big number of servants, he went, via land, to Amdabad (Ahmedabad). The gifts consisted in ten Arab ponies and tow dozen rabbits.

After one month, the King of Cambay, having gathered his court he decided the grant of Daman and its forts to the Portuguese Crown accepting the more profitable exchange of half of the revenue from the Customs of Diu. The grant of *tauadarias* of Daman were not included. In this situation, Tristao declared to the Council that he was authorized by his superiors to accept the conditions established by the same council and therefore he should depute an ambassador of his own.

The council decided to send on the return journey of Tristao de Paiva, along with him a Turkish, named Xeque Estabolim, who carried letters and gifts from the King of Cambay and from its ruler Madre Malueo, to the Vice-Roy.

The governor Francisco Barreto, having not accepted the proposal of the Council of the King of Cambay, Sent. Xeque Estabolim back along with Cristovao Couto who when he reached the Court of Cambay he found a new rules, Ithimitican, on the occurrence of death of Madre Maluco.

The truth is that the cunning governor Francisco Barreto, in this year or on the following one obtained from the King of Cambay that the fort of the Daman town was offered to him or to Portuguese Crown as a gift with the condition to expel from there a brave Abessinian named Sidi Bofeta who along with three thousand soldiers was resolute to defend it against all powers from the State of Cambay.

II

"Surto do imperio discombrimentis & conquistas" (Expansion of the empire discoveries and conquests) *PELA INDIA* (THROUGH INDIA)

By Jaime F. Pereira, page 137

VASCO DA GAMA

For some reason, Don Joao II was not able to send immediately another expedition to explore the way (route) announced by Bartolumen Dias after his journey in 1488. The result of Columbus' journey and the negotiations with Castelo (Spain) were at the bottom of further post-ponements up to 1494. Don Joao II died in 1495 after beginning the preparations for the decisive expedition which would reach India and also of having appointed its supreme commander, Vasco da Gama. Wisely (Cautiously) the new King did not introduce alterations to the set up plans, which were executed as soon as his authority was established in the Kingdom.

Vasco da Gama left Lisbon with three ships and one store ship in July 1497. He anchored at the island of Santiago in Cabo Verde, and from there he sailed straight to the south, what would be the farthest from land, till then sailed. He turned southwest to avoid the clamarias of the gulf of Guinie, later south-east to again reach the African Coast. After a span of ninety days without seeing land, he reached the bay of

Santo Helena, in today's south Africa (November 1497). He crossed the Cape of Good Hope (Cabo de Boa Esperanca) with certain difficulty caused by the weather. After having crossed the boundaries of the sailings (voyages) of Bartolumen Dias, the expeditions started its own discovere;Natal on 25th December, the river Zambeze one month later, the island of Mocambique (15's) in the beginnings of March. They were already in Muslim land and there were pilots available. The fleet reached Mombaca, in present Quenia (Kenia), next to Melinde, a little to the North (April 1498) where they could establish friendly relations and to obtain a famous Arab pilot (Ahmad Ibn Majid) who guided the ships up to India. Pushed by the south-west monsoon, the fleet sighted India on 18th May. The landing look place four days later. They had accomplished the great feat.

After three months of negotiations, alternate, velly friendly and opend hostile, Vasco da Gama bagan his return journey, bringing the ships loaded with spices and other valuable goods. Setting sail on 29th August 1498, reached Lisbon, with great difficulties and after having lost one ship, in the end of the summer of 1499. The journey on the whole, lasted more then two years, but the results were spectacular and promising.

GLOSSARY

aghora: a plant: *Achyrautter Aspera*
agyaree: purification of the home
agyawan: initiator
aja: mother-in-law
ajan: call of prayer
Akashi Mata: deity of evil eye
amabasya: moonless night
amb: mango, *Mangiera Indica*
anjuri: paying homage
annaprashan: first feeding of the cereal
anvario: accompanier
anguthi: ring
apta: a type of fruit
aqiqa: tonsorial ceremony
Ashadh poonam: a festival
Ashper dev: village deity
atak: surname
atham: eighth day
auna/ana: return of the bride
aunla: Phyllattus Emblica
avaldar: messenger

babul: Acacia Ambica
bajra: millet
bai: husband's sister
baithak: settlement and meeting place
baithale: meeting place

balmaudi: head-shaving or tonsure
Bamania bhoot: king of spirits
bangdi: bangles
barghori: ritual in marriage
barmal: exchange of garland
barnha: twelfth day celebration
barse/khirja: naming ceremony
barshi: annual death ritual
bateta: potato
batuque: percussion musical instrument
behavan: mother-in-law
bestman: companion to the groom among the Christians
bhabhi: elder brother's wife
bhagat/bhuva: magico-religious specialist
bhagidar: share-cropping
bhaibij: festival
bhat: rice
bhavad: sister's husband
bhen: sister
bhoot: ghost
bhu: magico-religious specialist
biriyani: fried rice with fish or meat
bichiro: pomfret, a fish
botan: Ist ceremonial feeding
Brahma dev: caste deity
brahman dev: priest
bumla: Bombay dock, a fish
buti: ear tops

chal: dance
chala: wife's younger brother
chali: wife's younger sister
chandla: red mark on the forehead
chhathee/chhathi: sixth day

chaudash: fourteenth day
chaula/badhauttarauni/mundan: tonsure
chaumasa: rainy season
chauri: celestial fire
chipiya: hair-pin
choful: leaf shape mark
chokha: rice
cholee: blouse
chore-na-anta-ferwa: round of celestial fire
choree-samharo: handing over of the bride
chundar/churdar: tattooing
chhutta-chedi/chhutta: divorce
comprary: church committee
coolie: porter

dan/bal utrawnu: head-shaving
dand: cash fine
dandia ras: folk dance
dantal: plough rake
darah: death ritual
daram: pomegranate
dargah: mausoleum
darha: calling of the departed soul
daru: liquor
datedu: sickel
datree: red snapper, a fish
dayan: local trained mid-wife
deedar: meeting ritual after birth
dej: dowry/ bride-price
deo puja: clan deity worship
dev: house deity
dev-santak: worship of house deity
devar-nata/devar-batu: junior levirate
deyar: husband's younger brother

deyar-baty: junior levirate
dhamal: a folk dance
dhani: landlord
dharam behan: putative kinship
dhokra: stuffed fried chapati
dhoti: loin-cloth
dhup: incense
dingla-dingli lagan: mock-marriage
divaso: associated with mock-marriage
doha: widower
dohi: widow
dohada: community dinner
dudhi: pumpkin
dudh-pak: rice boiled in milk

escude: Portuguese currency

falia: hamlet
faliya panch: hamlet council
faliya patel: hamlet chief
fargati: divorce
farsan: food preparation
fatiha: recitation from Koran
fera: circumambulation
fui: father's sister

gamthas: strains of Vania and Kharwa
gandra/gondra: village boundry
ganpati: elephant god
gaur matas: clan deities
ghagra: petticoat
ghanti: grinder
ghara: rice pounding
gharena/chandla: betrothal

gharghara: remarriage
gher: folk dance
gheriya: folk dance
gnyati panch: traditional council
goter or *got:* clan
gotrej: clan deity
gwar fali: beans

hakmore: mehr
hali: agricultural labour
hani: wife's sister
harvan: accompanier
hast-milap: joining of hands
hodi: small boat
Holi mata: a deity

jaimal: exchange of garlands in marriage
jamat: caste council
jamat-khana/khoja-khana: religious place of the Khoja
jaminis: witness
jamrukh: guava
jamtro: prawn
jan: marriage procession
janiwas: separate lodging
jawar: barley
jethu: husband's elder brother
jhar: net
jharee: small net
jhul: bridegroom dress
jumma: weekly Muslim holiday

kacha sidha: raw food
kachkeda: turtle-shell
kafira: strain of Muslims

Kakawalia: deity of smallpox
kalikanthi/kali canthi/kalganthi: marriage pendant
kalma: verses of nikah
kamdadia: accountant
kanhari: flower plant
kankotris: invitation
kanku: vermilion mark on forehead.
kansar: sweet
kansar-khao: feeding of bride and groom
Kansari Mata: deity of corn
kanti: Rajor edge, a fish
kanyadan: handing over of the bride to groom
kapad: blouse
karbhar: a ritual to ward-off spirit
karta: authority
Kartik: month as per Hindi calendar
karvali: accompanier to the bride
kazi: religious officiant
kel: banana
keri: a mango
khajanchi/karbhari: accountant
khalsashi: fishing labour
khara-pani: saline water
kharwa: sailor
khatla: wooden cot
khatra-dev: dead ancestor
khatrun: wooden image of the dead
kher-kurma: curry of meat
Khokholi Mata: deity of cough
kholobharna/khorobharnu/kholobharvo: guarding ceremony
khopra: coconut
khunti: hooks
kodali: hoe
kodari: yoke

korhi: robber
kosh: leather bucket
kotwal/kotwar: messenger
kriya: funeral rite
kuhadi: axe
kul: clan
kunda-ne-ful: pot with flower plant
kunj: Great Indian Bustard, a bird
kurma: meat/chicken curry
kutum/kutumb: family

lagan: marriage
lagna-no-kagaj: marriage bond
lapse/lapsee: pastelike preparation of wheat
Laxmi Mata: goddess of wealth
lodhiya: big boat
logas: a compulsory contribution in marriage among the Siddi
lunari: harbinger of auspicious omen
mag: green gram
magha: Jan.- Feb.
maha atam: religious festival
majar: mausoleum
Makkar dev: deity of corn
Malhwada Mata Mahabhu Mata: deity of pimples
malida: pastelike preparation of wheat flour, water and ghee
mama: mother's brother
mandav muhurta: erection of marriage booth
mandav-vidhi: installation of marriage booth
mando: a kind of tune
manek stambh: clan deity pole
mangal fera: making four rounds of sacred fire during marriage
mantras: verses
mantri: secretary
mardiya: sweet potato

Marki mata: deity of plague
mashan: cremation ground
matha charvu: shampoo
maushala/moshali: gift of marriage dress
mehta: accountant
mindhol: emetic nut
modaliya: chain
mode: rack
modhe jamanan: feeding of the departed soul
morla: peacock
mota awna: big return
mukadam: messenger
mukhi: chief

nai: barber
nake/nakee: finalization of marriage
namiya: a ritual of boat worship
namora: love
nampari: naming
nanai: wife's brother's wife
nani tadi: betrothal
nanu ana: brief return of wife
narial poonam: major festival
nath: nose ring
natra: remarriage
neel: ghost marriage
nikah: marriage
nyat bar: excommunication
nyat patel: chief
nyat panch/gnyat panch: traditional council

occasio: forest fruit
odhani: cloth covering the breast
okra/makambera: a tree, *hyphaene indica*
oliyas/pir: Muslim saints

otah: verandah

panchas: members
panchro: fifth day ceremony of delivery
panjani: anklet
parish: settlement
parjzri/parjon: clan feast
patel: chief
patla: wooden plank
patli/begetha: wooden plank
patra-farmanu: a death ritual
pavdo: shovel
pavitra-vandhana: holy rules
Pet-fori-mata: deity of evil
pheramoni/moti tadi: big feast
phool-padhraoni: disposal of bones and ashes
pirtan: religious saint
pithi: a paste of termeric, groundnut oil and *vano*, a scented herb
pla: fried rice
poonam: full moon
potaya: prepared of wheat-flour, sugar, toddy, after frying in groundnut oil
pramukh: chief
pucca: cooked food
puri: fried bread

ragi: a millet
rapeli: iron edge in plough
rakhadi: guarding
randel: widow
randela: widower
rasadas: folk songs
rashinam: zodiac name
ringna: brinjal

roho: daughter-in-law
rotli: wheat bread

sabhyas: members
sag: curry
sagai/vevisar: betrothal
saiid jamat: Siddi caste council
saityo/sathiu: mystic holy symbol designed on the floor
samaiya: mgico-religious specialist
samaj patel: chief of traditional council
samaj: traditional council
samast-koli-samaj: Koli caste council
Samya dev: deity of cholera
samya: reception of the groom
santek/dev shanti: worship of family deity
saptapadi: vedic marriage rite
sarangi: violin
sari lagna: junior sororate
shariyat: Muslim personal law
shravana: July-August
sharavni: broom
Shravani Poonam:: a festival
siara: winter
simant: a pre-birth ritual
sing: groundnut
sira: porridge
sitafal: custard apple
Sitla Mata: deity of measles
sitodi: girdle
sradhha: funeral ceremony
suhag-ghar: honeymoon room
sunnat sadi: circumcision
supudo: winnowing fan
suraj-puja: sun worship

sutak: ritual pollution
suva barth: Ist delivery

tadee: toddy
tahli: brass plate
tandel: captain
tapli: basket
tarjwana: tattoo mark
taweet: magico-religious thread
thamli: marriage booth
thur/tur: red gram
tika/tilak: red mark on forehead
titan: lobster, a fish
tok: evil eye
tora: perch fish
trishul: trident
tuniya: sponge fish
tutko: funeral rite

Ujjani: a festival
unadu: summer
urad: black gram

vadi: ear and nose piercing ceremony
vag baras: October-November
Vaghyo: tiger god
val: creeper
vevah: mother in law
vevai: father-in-law
vevisor: betrothal
vishama: village boundary
vishana: funeral boundary

wadee: hamlet

wal: a type of nut
yasthali: mediator, usmually mother's brother
yajnopavit: investure with sacred thread

zabla: frock
zanzeer: ankle chain
ziarat: Muslim ritual

SELECT BIBLIOGRAPHY

Bahadur, K.P., *Castes, Tribes and Culture of India*, Ess Ess Publication, Vol. VIII, Western Maharashtra and Gujarat, Delhi, 1981.

Bains, Strathestane, *Ethnography, Castes and Tribes*, Reprint, Concept Publication, Delhi, 1976.

Bhattacharjee, J.N., *Hindu Caste and Sects*, Edition India, Part X, A&B Series-2, Calcutta, 1968.

C.A.P., *The Gazetteers of Orissa and the Fudetory States*, Part I, Vol. XXII, 1910.

Census of India, *Final Population Totals*, paper 3 of 1991, India, Series-I, Controller of Publication, Delhi, 1993.

Census of India, *Goa, Daman and Diu*, Registrar General of India, Panaji, 1971.

Census of India, *District Census Hand Book*, Series 29, Goa, Daman and Diu, Vol XIII, part A&B, Panaji, 1981.

Chib, S.S., *The Beautiful India, Union Territories of India.* Light and Life Publications, Delhi, 1977.

Cottineau-de-Klequeen, D.H., *History of Goa*, Bombay, 1910.

Crooke, W., *Tribes and Castes of North Western Province and Oudh*, Vol I, II & IV, 1896, Calcutta, The Government Press; Reprint, *The Tribes and Castes of the North Western India*, Vol. I, II & III, 1975, Cosmo Publications, Delhi.

Das, A.K., Roychoudhary and M.K. Raha, *Handbook of SC and ST of West Bengal*, Director of Tribal Welfare Department, Calcutta, 1966.

Department of Planning and Statistics, *Indicators of Socio-Economic Development*, Daman, 1987.

Dessai, S.S., *States of Union; Goa, Daman and Diu, Dadra and Nagar Haveli*, Delhi, 1976.

Enthoven, R.E., *The Tribes and Castes of Bombay*, Vol. I to IV, 1920-1922, The Government Central Press; Reprint, Vol. I to IV, 1975, Cosmo Publications, Delhi.

Francisco, Antonio, *Noticas - E Documentas -Para, A Historia de of Damao*, Vol. I, II & III, Bastoria, (Goa), 1904-1928.

Gandhi, S.K., *Census of India 1971*, Series-28 part (X-A) & (X-B) page III, Directorate of Census Operation, Goa, Daman, Diu, Dadra & Nagar Havéli, 1972.

Gazetteer of Baroda State *General Information*, Times Press, Bombay, Vol. I, 1923.

Gazetteer of the Bombay Presidency, *Gujarat Population, Muslims and Parsees*, Govt. Central Press, Bombay, Vol IX, part II, 1899.

Gune, V.T., *Gazeetteer of Union Territory of Goa, Daman and Diu*, Part II & III, Daman and Diu, Panaji, Goa, 1979.

Hutton, J.H., *Castes of India*, Oxford University Press, Oxford, 1969.

Imperial Gazetteer of India, *Condapoor to Edwardesabad*, Clarendon Press, Vol. XI, Oxford, 1908

Menezes, Antonie De, "Daman and Diu, Union Territory", *Herald Magazine*, Panaji, Goa, 1987.

Pandey, Brij Mohan, 'Div Ne Parsi Avshesh', *Saptahik Hindustan*, May, Bombay, 1989.

Parmar, H.M., 'Ramnagerka Rajavi,' Typed unpublished material in Hindi, Collected by the administration of Dadra and Nagar Haveli.

Parmar, Y.A. *The Mahyavanshi: The Success Story of a Scheduled Caste*, Mittal Publications, Delhi, 1987.

Paul, J., 'Study of Ethnography and Change in a Daman Village', Unpublished report submitted to An.S.I., 1978.

Planning Department, *Tribal sub-plan for Daman: 1976 to 1979*, Secretariat, Panaji, Goa.

Raghavaiah, V., *Tribal Revolt*, Andhra Rashtra Adim Jati Sevak Sangh, Nellore, 1971.

Rajendran, S., *A Portrait of Population*, Census of India, 1981, Directorate of Census Population 600, Daman and Diu, Controller of Publication, Delhi, 1988.

Raval, Ramesh B., "Prachin Nagri Div" (Diu, the old city), *Navyug*, Junagadh. April, 1990.

Raval, Ramesh, B., "Prachin Jalandhar Kshetra-Na-Rajanu Div" (Diu in the Regime of Jalandhar King), *Sandes*, Junagadh, April, 1990.

Rose, H.A., *Glossary of the Tribe and Castes of the Punjab and North West Frontier Provinces*, Vol. II, 1919, Lahore, Punjab Government; Reprint, Vol. II, 1980, Amar Prakashan, Delhi.

Roy Shibani and S.H.M. Rizvi, *Dhodia Identity*. B.R. Publishing Co., Delhi, 1985.

Roy, Shibani, *Koli Culture*, Cosmo Publications, New Delhi, 1983.

Rubbeiso, Orlando, *Originali Da Expennao Portuguese* (Originality of Portuguese Aggrresion), Geographic Society, Lisbon (Portugal), 1956.

Russell, R.V. and Rai Bahadur Hiralal, *The Tribes and Castes of Central*

Provinces. Vol. I, III & IV, 1916, London, Macmillan and Company; Reprint, Vol. I, III & IV, 1975, Cosmo Publications, Delhi.

Sahay, K.N., *Christianity and Culture Change*, Inter-India Publication, New Delhi, 1986.

Shah, P.G., *The Dubla of Gujarat*, Bharatiya Adim Jati Sevak Samaj, Delhi, 1958.

Shah, P.G., *The Tribal life in Gujarat*, Gujarat Research Society, Bombay, 1964.

Sherring, M.A., *The Hindu Tribes and Castes*, Vol. I & II, 1872 & 1879, Calcutta, Thakar Spinks & Co.; Reprint, Vol. I & II, 1974, Cosmo Publications, Delhi.

Sinha, N.K. , 'The Study of Ethnography and Change in a Diu Village', Unpublished report submitted to An.S.I, 1980.

Sinha, N.K., "Funeral Rites among the Fishfolk of Diu", *Indian Anthropologist*, Vol. X, No. 9, Delhi, 1977.

Thurston, E., *Castes and Tribes of Southern India*, Vol. V, 1909, Madras, The Government Press; Reprint, Vol. V, 1975, Cosmo Publications, Delhi.

Trivedi, R.K., *Siddi: A Negroid Tribe of Gujarat*, Census of India 1961, Ethnographic Series, Gujarat, Vol. V., Part V-B. No. 1, Delhi.

MAP OF DAMAN

(SHOWING DISTRIBUTION OF THE COMMUNITIES)

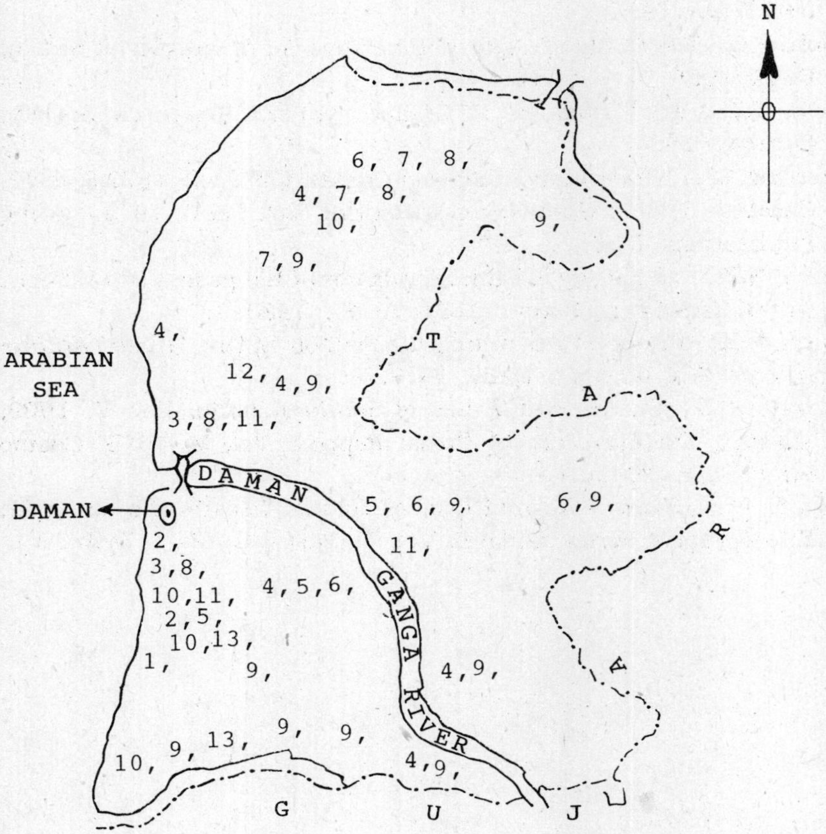

(NOT TO SCALE)

INDEX

1. BARIA
2. BHANDARI
3. CHRISTIAN
4. DHODIA
5. DUBLA
6. KAMLI
7. KOLIPATEL
8. MACHHI
9. MAHYAVANSHI
10. MANGELA
11. MITNA
12. MOMIN
13. SAGAR

MAP OF DIU

(SHOWING DISTRIBUTION OF THE COMMUNITIES)

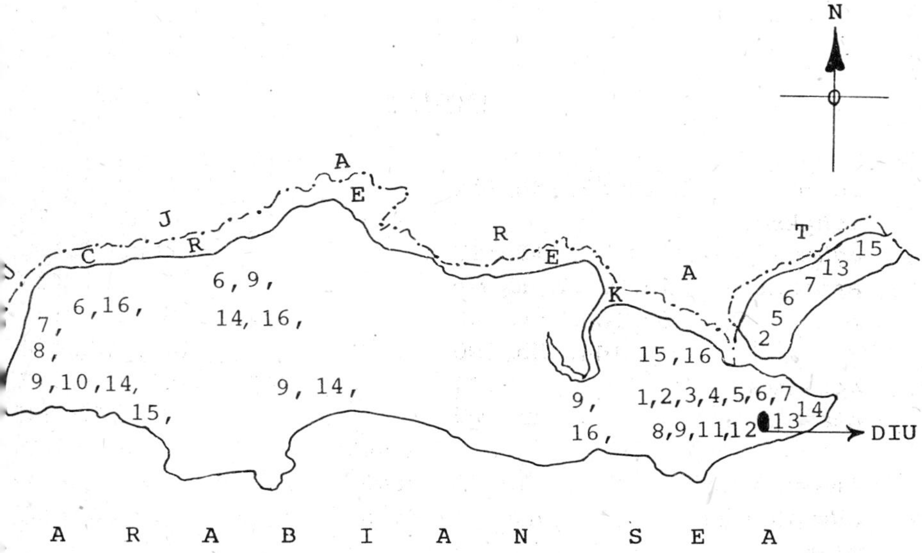

(NOT TO SCALE)

INDEX

1. BHANGI	9. KOLI
2. BHOI	10. KUMBHAR
3. BRAHMAN	11. SALAT
4. CHRISTIAN	12. SANGHARIA
5. DHOBI	13. SIDDI
6. HADI	14. VANIA
7. KHARWA	15. VANJA
8. KHOJA	16. VANKAR

INDEX

adarni 22, 82, 130, 154
adhyksha 23
aghora 115, 127
agriculture 13, 22, 28, 64, 70, 83, 105, 114, 133, 144, 155, 190
agyawan 174
aja 69

Akashi Mata 71
alho pimenta 51
amb 115, 127
ambat 89
amabashya 102, 123
ana 17, 28, 39, 59, 82, 132, 139, 144, 155, 160, 173, 179
anjuri 17
anvario or *anwar* 22, 58, 64, 70, 113, 165, 178, 185
aparanta 3
apta 116, 127
aqiqa 149, 172
ashirvad 22, 139, 155
Ashper dev 71
atak 31, 56, 68, 80, 87, 112, 118, 171, 188
atham 115, 151
aunla 212
avoidance relationship 21, 26, 32, 38, 45, 57, 64, 69, 75, 88, 96, 103, 113, 119, 124, 131, 137, 143, 148, 153, 158, 165, 171, 177, 184, 189, 345
avaldar 65, 71
avtara 48
azan 149, 172

babul 72
badha 78
badha-utravani 77, 133, 145
bafado 51
bahuteri 133
bai 69
baithale or *gnyat ghar* 33, 40, 76, 106, 166, 186, 191
bajra 56, 68, 74, 86, 95, 102, 137, 152, 164, 170, 183, 188
Balley 84
bal-maudi 17
bal movro 17
Bamania Bhut 71
banat 91
bangdi 45, 57, 88, 96, 103, 119, 158, 165, 177, 184

baptism 53
barakhi 166
bargam gnyat 91
bar-ghodi 139, 144, 155
barh 127, 162
Bari 20
Baria 20
bar-mal 17, 59, 97
barrada 51
barse 17, 22, 27, 82, 138, 143, 154
barshi 180
bateta 38, 86, 111, 183
batuque 54
bebinca 51
benhevi 132
bestman 53
bhabhi 58, 69
bhagat 28, 71
bhagidar 83, 114
Bhai-Bij 84, 108, 116, 127, 134, 140, 145
bhajya 142, 152
bhakti 134
bhandar 25
Bhandari 25
Bhangi 31
bhat 38, 118, 152, 164, 183
bhatt ji 27
bhawad 64
Bhoi Raj 37
bhongulee 29
bhua or *bhu* 34, 61, 66, 72, 78, 93, 108, 134, 181, 192
bhut 65
bhichiro 90
bidi 56, 158, 176, 183, 188
Bolley 29
bolo-de-sura 51
botan 17, 83, 138
Brahman 44
Brahman 158
Brahm Dev 65
Brahm Kshatree 164
brahm smaran 178
bride-price 21, 26, 31, 63, 69
broa 51
bumla 90, 106
buneli 72
business and trade 97
butti 167

cabidel 51
car 54
Carnival 54
chal 72
chala 69
chali 69
chalisee 150
Chamonda mata 60, 78, 121
chana 56
Chandala 31
chandla 39
chak 120
chhathi 17, 22, 27, 39, 46, 58, 82, 96, 132, 138, 143, 149, 154, 159, 172
chaturthi-karma 47, 160
chaudas 87, 102
chaula 17, 21, 27, 82, 138, 143, 154
chaumasa 65, 83, 106, 114, 191
chaura 133
chauri 46, 58, 132, 159, 179
chauri ferwa 17, 39, 59, 132
Chawda 34
child marriage 25, 45, 69, 124,

131, 138, 158
chitnish 23
choful 72, 78, 93, 108, 192
chokha 63, 74, 95
chola 64
Christian 50
chundar 29, 34, 66, 72, 78, 84, 93, 108, 127
chutta 38, 75, 96, 124, 131, 143, 153
chhutta-cheda 26, 63, 81, 88, 103, 113, 119, 138, 171, 189
cigar 188
Comparary 53
conflict and confrontation 22, 32, 39, 45, 64, 89, 96, 104, 113, 120, 125, 132, 138, 143, 148, 154, 159, 165, 178
consumption of alcoholic drink 25, 44, 68, 75, 87, 95, 112, 118, 130, 171, 176, 188
cowdung-cake 49, 61, 93, 110, 116, 162, 182
cross-cousin marriage 25, 51, 75, 96, 143, 147, 155, 171, 177, 184

dakhado 132
dam paca 51
Damao Grande 1
Damao Pequene 1
dand 51
dandia ras 97, 108, 162, 181, 192
dapu 242, 132
darah 125, 139
darha 3, 17, 28, 39, 59, 180
darham 89
daru 63, 102, 123, 137, 183
dathna 155
dattak 132, 154, 190
datree 90, 106
dayan 96, 159, 172
deedar 99
dej 20, 25, 45, 57, 113, 124, 143, 158, 165, 177
dev 71, 107
devak 28, 140, 155
devar - nata 63, 113
dev-santak 17, 47, 132
deyar 64, 69
dhamal 174
dhamama 174
dhana 178
dhani 70
dharma-behan 29, 84, 99, 116, 140
dharm-bhai 49
Dhed 129
dhej or *dej* 63, 69, 75, 88, 103, 119, 131, 138, 153, 171, 184, 189
Dhivar 137
Dhobi 56
Dhodi 63
Dhodia 63
dhokar 63
dhol 34
dhur 63
dingla-dingli lagan 66, 72

Divaso 65, 71
division 20, 26, 31, 38, 44, 56, 63, 68, 80, 87, 102, 111, 118, 123, 130, 137, 152, 158, 164, 171, 177, 184, 188
division, territorial 152, 176
Diwali 34, 41, 48, 61, 66, 72, 84, 93, 108, 116, 121, 127, 134, 140, 145, 156, 162, 167, 181
diyar - batu 21, 57, 69, 81, 88, 103, 119, 124, 131, 138, 153, 189
doce-de-grao 51
doha 89, 104
dohi 89, 104
dowry 81
Dubla 68
dudhi 87, 102, 112, 183
dudh-pag 20, 44, 56, 63, 87, 95, 102, 112, 118, 130, 152, 164, 176, 183, 188
Dulhendi 41, 93, 108, 167
Dussehra 66, 72

ear piercing 17
espetada-de-leitao 51

faliya 65, 71, 114
far-gati 57, 63, 69, 113, 184, 189
farsan 38, 63, 87, 102
father 54
fatiha 173
fishing 22, 70, 89, 105, 125, 139
folk song 41, 48, 61, 78, 99, 134, 151, 162, 186, 192
fui 22, 27, 32, 39, 45, 58, 64, 70, 81, 89, 96, 104, 113, 120, 125, 132, 138, 143, 154, 159, 165, 178
ful-padhrao 17, 39, 59, 139
gam panch 121
Gamtha 170
Ganesh Chaturthi 77, 134
garba 24, 48, 93, 108, 116, 162, 181
garoda 134
Gaur Mata 107
gayatri-mantra 159
ghaghra 185
gharena-ganthwanu 28, 138
ghee 25, 38, 44
Ghel Mata 77
gheria or *gher* 34, 66, 72, 192
ghod 120
ghod-ghode 32, 75
gnyat-bar 23, 28, 191
gnyat-no-bandhna 60
gnyat-panch 33, 40, 60, 65, 71, 76, 91, 106, 133, 155, 161, 166, 185, 191
gnyat-patel 28, 33, 40, 60, 65, 71, 76, 91, 106, 166, 185
Golie 34
Gomti mata 92 107, 121
gondra 59, 180
got 31, 38, 56, 75, 87, 102, 112, 118, 130, 152, 164, 177, 184
gotra 44, 137
gotrej 23, 28, 77, 83, 93, 115,

126, 133, 145, 173, 181
govt. service 55, 76, 97, 132, 139, 161, 173
grah-santik 17, 39
Gujarati Brahman 44
gurh 176
Guru poornima 48
gwar-fali 106

Hadi 74
hajjam 172
hakmore 171
hali 70, 114
Halpati 68
hani 64
hansadi 124
Harijan 31
Harshidh Mata 41, 92
hartoda 17, 47, 160, 179
harvan 45, 58, 81, 89, 104, 120, 138, 143, 159
hast-milap 17, 22, 28, 39, 47, 59, 82, 132, 139, 144, 155, 159, 179

hat 33, 120
Hingraj Mata 166, 181, 186
hodi 90, 125
Holi 24, 34, 41, 61, 66, 72, 78, 84, 108, 116, 121, 127, 134, 140, 145, 156, 162, 167, 174, 181
Holi Mata 28, 71, 115
hono 64
hunda 120

Id-Ul-Fitr 151
Idul-Zoha 151
ig yarras 126
ist devta 23
ivory and turtle shell works 165
jaimal 17, 22, 28, 82, 132, 139, 144, 155
jamat 98, 150, 173
jambo 90
jamrukh jamfal 63, 86, 152, 164, 183
jan 17, 28, 39, 47, 59, 82, 132, 144, 149, 160, 173, 179
janam - patri 46
janiwas 28, 47, 59, 82, 144, 160, 179
Janmasthmi 41, 48, 78, 84, 108, 116, 167, 174, 181, 192
jati puran 37, 157, 183, 337
jethu 57
jhar 90, 105
jhari 90, 105
joking relationship 21, 26, 32, 38, 51, 57, 75, 88, 96, 103, 113, 119, 124, 137, 143, 148, 153, 158, 165, 171, 177, 184, 189
jowar 20, 25, 63, 68, 80, 102, 111, 123, 142, 152
jumma 174

Kabir Panth 186
kachha 24, 29, 35, 42, 48, 54, 61, 66, 72, 78, 84, 90, 93, 109, 116, 109, 121, 127, 140, 151, 156, 162, 174, 181, 186, 192

Kachhapa-avtar 167
kachkaru 165
Kafira 170

Mahajan Vania 176
Kakawalia 65, 71
kalash 47, 160
kali-kanthi 21, 26, 64, 81, 113
Kaliinki Mata 34, 41, 60, 77, 93, 108, 162, 167, 186
kalma 150, 173
kamad 98
Kamaliya 80
Kamli 80
kanderu or *kuded* 96, 166
Kanhari 83, 115
kanku 21, 26, 31, 57, 75, 81, 88, 96, 103, 113, 119, 124, 131, 138, 143, 153, 158, 177, 184
kansar 47, 160
kansar-khao 59, 179
Kansari Mata 66, 72
kanthi 124, 131, 138, 143, 153
kanti 90, 106
kanyadan 16, 22, 27, 39, 47, 82, 132, 138, 144, 149, 159, 179
kar bhari 114, 126, 139, 150, 155
Kar-Bhar 92, 108
kari-ganthi 69
kariyawar 172
Karkimata 72
karobhari 23, 83
karta 27, 70, 113, 125, 138, 143, 154, 190
karvali 70
katch-korh-bangdi 26, 75
kayado 133
kazi 149, 172
kel 63, 86, 164, 183
kentho 58, 179
keri 63, 158, 183
khajanchi 23, 28, 60, 114, 133
khajura 20
khalashi 70, 70, 106, 126, 139
Kharwa 86
kher-khurma 131
Khijra 136, 152
Khodia 34, 60, 77, 107, 121
Khoja 95
khojakhana 99
Khokholi Mata 71
kholo bharva 17, 22, 58, 96, 132, 172
khopra 116
khunti 90, 105
Kijrha 184
kodi 105, 125
kodia 120
Koli 101
koli dance 84, 127, 140
Koli Patel 111
kotwal or *kotwar* 66, 133, 173
kriya 17, 47, 59, 160, 180
Kshatriya 26, 56, 63, 87, 112, 118, 123, 130, 142, 152, 164, 184
kul 20, 26, 63, 112, 137, 152
Kumbhar 118
Kumbhi 118
kunda-ne-ful 108
kurma 95
kurta 147
kutumb 26, 38, 45, 57, 64, 69, 75, 80, 88, 101, 111, 122

140, 141, 151, 163, 182, 187
Lagionnary of Mary 53
lagna-no-kagaj 17, 89
Lakxmi Mata 28, 115, 161
Landa 170
landlord-tenant relationship 73, 84, 116, 134, 181, 192
lapsee 20, 38, 44, 56, 63, 68, 75, 80, 87, 95, 102, 112, 118, 130, 137, 142, 152, 158, 164, 176, 183, 188
lata 3
lodhiya 90, 105
logas 172
lunari 171
Machhi 123
machhwa 90
madhe-jamawan 17, 59
Nag Panchami 116
Maha Atham 116
Mahi-Bij 162
Mahyavanshi 129
Makar Dev 83, 154
Makar Shankranti 41, 72, 108, 127, 145
makshar 186
male equigeniture 22, 32, 64, 70, 76, 89, 104, 113, 125, 138, 184, 190
male ultimogeniture 22, 32, 64, 70, 76, 113, 125, 138, 190
malida 171
mama 70, 132
mami 131
mandava 16, 27, 39, 47, 59, 82, 132, 138, 144, 149, 154, 159, 172, 179
mando 54
manek-stambh 17, 46, 58, 159
Mang 137
mangal fera 17, 22, 27, 82, 139, 144, 155
mangal sutra 38, 45, 119, 138, 153, 165
Mangela 137
Mani Nagar 4
mantri 28, 114, 161
mardiya 102
mashido 174
masiso 180
mass 54
matta 132
maushala 21, 27, 44, 58, 64, 70, 81, 89, 120, 132, 138, 143, 154, 159, 178
Mawli 116
majar or *pir dargah* 150, 174
mehar 148
mehta 60, 91, 106, 120, 173, 180, 185
Meman 147
migration 20, 37, 44, 56, 63, 80, 86, 95, 101, 118, 123, 147, 152, 157, 164, 170, 176, 183
mindhol 173
Mitna 142, 262
mogra 126
Momin 147
monogamy 21, 26, 38, 43, 51, 57, 65, 75, 81, 88, 96, 103, 113, 119,

124, 131, 138, 143, 148, 153, 171, 177, 189
moong or mag 20, 25, 38, 56, 63, 68, 80, 102, 111, 123, 137, 142, 147, 152, 162, 176
morla 72, 78, 93, 108, 192
Muharram 151, 174
mukadam 91, 106, 121, 180, 185
mukhi 98
mund 120
mundan 17, 46, 149, 159, 178

nagli 83
nampari 17, 39, 46, 58, 89, 96, 132, 159, 172
namaze janaza 150
namiya 92, 108
namore 51
nanai 64
nate panch 65, 71
natra 21, 26, 32, 57, 63, 69, 81, 88, 103, 113, 119, 124, 131, 138, 143, 153, 158, 165, 171, 177, 189
Navratri 34, 41, 72, 121, 124, 132, 143, 153, 159, 165
nayat-bar 65, 71
neel 17, 89, 155, 187
neera 38, 74, 183
neolocal rule of residence 70, 88
night soil carrier 33
nikah 149, 172
Nossa Senhora dos Remidios 127, 140

ojah 90
orhi-jhori 39
otah 47, 58, 159, 179
oliya 174

padarma 28
paijama 147
pakoda 38
palanquin carrier 39
pallu 57, 131
pana 166
panch 133, 191
pancha 40, 65, 71, 76
panchayat 48, 77, 107, 121, 133, 145, 150, 155, 166, 186, 191
pao-de-lo 51
parish 53
parallel cousin marriage 96, 147
patel 23, 33, 40 ,60, 65, 71, 76, 83, 98, 106, 114, 120, 133, 139, 145, 150, 155, 161, 166, 173, 185, 191
patli 59, 179
patrilocal rule of residence 32, 45, 57, 63, 69, 81, 131, 143, 158, 184, 189
pavitra bandhane 99
peedhee 38, 164
Pet-Fori-Mata 65, 71
pind-dan 47, 160
pipal 48
pirtan 95
pithee 16, 27, 39, 46, 58, 82,

96, 132, 138, 143, 154, 159, 172, 179
pitra-dan 47, 160
pla 56, 63, 75, 87, 102, 112, 118, 183, 188
polygyny 26, 88, 102, 148, 171
ponkhavan 46, 58, 159, 172, 179
Poonam-mela 34, 61, 93, 108, 121, 162, 186
pota 126
pottery 120
potya 20, 56, 68, 75, 87, 120, 118, 130, 137, 183, 188
Prajapat 118
pramukh 23, 28, 40, 60, 83, 114, 120, 133, 161
pre-material relation 65
prem lagna 81
priest hood 28
pacca 24, 29, 35, 42, 48, 53, 61, 66, 72, 78, 84, 93, 99, 109, 121, 127, 140, 151, 156, 162, 174, 181
pudim 51
punah-lagna 38
puri 20, 25, 38, 68, 75, 80, 87, 102, 112, 130, 137, 142, 152, 158, 164, 176, 183, 188
putative kinship 66, 99
Ravli 83, 115
ragi 65, 83, 106
Rajput Dhobi 56
rakhadi 17, 82, 143
Raksha Bandhan 61, 84, 155, 161
Ramnavmi 48, 186, 192
rasadas 174
rashi 17, 39, 159
Ramdev Pir 77, 191
ringna 86, 102, 111, 183
Rio Calern 1
Rio Sandalcalo 1
rishi 44, 74
Roman Catholic 50
rotla 74, 80, 111, 118, 152

sabha 23, 114
sabhya 28, 47, 91, 106, 114, 126, 133, 139, 150, 166, 180, 185
sagai 17, 22, 46, 58, 96, 143, 149, 159, 172, 179
Sagar 152
sagpan 39
sak 38, 68, 137, 152
Salat 157
salt making 114
samaiyu 172
samaj 23, 28, 40, 83, 114, 126, 139, 145, 180
samaj patel 23, 114, 139
Samra Dev 23, 114, 139
samri 131, 138
samuhik lagna 96, 124, 138
Sanatan Dharma 23, 134, 140
Sangharia 164
sanskar 46
sapt-padi 17, 28, 46, 159
sarangi 72
sarchitnish 23
saree-batu, saree-lagna or *sali vatu* 21, 69, 81, 88, 96, 103, 119, 124, 131, 138
sari 132, 147, 185

sarpetal 51
satiyo 24, 29, 48, 61, 84, 93, 108, 116, 127, 140, 181
sculpture 160
sea-man 89, 125
seco-seco 51
sehra 149
self arranged marriage 69, 138
seer 70
sew 188
Shab-E-Barat 150
shami 57
shawarni 34
shiksha 133
Shivratri 24, 41, 116, 121, 127, 134, 140, 145, 162, 167, 181
Shravani Poonam or Narial Poonam 83, 98, 108, 116, 126, 140, 145
siara 64, 83, 106, 114
Siddi 170
sidha 29, 35, 109, 116, 121, 140, 192
sing 106
sing-tel 176
sira 63, 80, 111, 142, 152
sita fal 87
Sitla Mata 66, 72
skin and hide work 76, 132
skude or *escude* 64, 106, 133, 180, 190
Sompura Brahman 157
Sonai Mata 77
sradh 17, 22, 28, 39, 82, 144, 155
sravani 180
srikhand 44, 176
srimant 17, 22, 27, 39, 46, 82, 138, 143, 154, 159, 178
Shudra 25, 75
suhag-ghar 46, 179
sunnat-sadi 96, 149, 172
supoddo 34
Suraj 46, 159
Swaminarayan 181
Swayadhaya Parivar 140
sayum 150

takbir 149
talak 148
tambaw 56
tameta 183
tandel 90, 105, 125, 139
tanki 121
tapli 34
tarjwana 116
tawdi 121
thali 66
thur 25, 63, 68, 111, 137, 152
tika 17, 27
titan 90
toddy 20, 25, 68, 80, 118, 123, 137, 188
toddy taping 28
tola 22, 155
tora 90, 105
toran 27, 46
totemism 63
trishul 78, 93, 108, 192
tulsi 34, 48, 162
tulsi-kanthi 181
Tulsi-Vivah 186
tur 66
tur or *tuar* 20, 38, 44, 50, 80, 86, 95, 102, 118, 123, 142, 147, 170, 176, 183

turiya 105
tutko 17, 89

Ujjani 23, 41, 92, 98, 108, 115, 126, 140, 145, 167, 181
unadu 64, 83, 114, 190
urad 44, 56, 86, 95, 102, 118, 170, 176, 183
uthama 17, 39

vad 48
Vagbaras 66
Vaghyo 83, 115
vaho 64
val 48, 72, 77, 161, 192
Vaishya 20, 38, 177, 323
val 70
Vania 176
Vanja 183
Vankar 188
varna 21, 26, 31, 38, 44, 56, 75, 87, 112, 118, 123, 130, 137, 142, 152, 158, 164, 177
vatana 38
vegetarian 20, 44, 157, 176
vevai 64
vevan 64
vevishar 17
vishama 17
vishaya 3
vivah 46, 132

wadee 91, 106
wal 54
weaving 150, 185, 190
well worship 28

yajno-pobit 46, 157

ziarat 170
zarda 145